The
Arab
Americans

**Other Titles in
The New Amercians Series**
Ronald H. Bayor, Series Editor

The
Arab
Americans

Randa A. Kayyali

THE NEW AMERICANS
Ronald H. Bayor, Series Editor

GREENWOOD PRESS
Westport, Connecticut • London

Library of Congress Cataloging-in-Publication Data

Kayyali, Randa.
   The Arab Americans / Randa A. Kayyali.
      p. cm.—(The New Americans, ISSN 1092–6364)
   Includes bibliographical references and index.
   ISBN 0–313–33219–3
     1. Arab Americans—History. 2. Arab Americans—Social conditions. 3. Arab Americans—Social
life and customs. 4. Immigrants—United States—History. 5. Arab countries—Emigration and
immigration. 6. United States—Emigration and immigration. I. Title. II. Series:
New Americans (Westport, Conn.)
   E184.A65K39 2006
   973′.0497—dc22   2005026182

British Library Cataloguing in Publication Data is available.

Copyright © 2006 by Randa A. Kayyali

All rights reserved. No portion of this book may be
reproduced, by any process or technique, without the
express written consent of the publisher.

Library of Congress Catalog Card Number: 2005026182
ISBN: 0–313–33219–3
ISSN: 1092–6364

First published in 2006

Greenwood Press, 88 Post Road West, Westport, CT 06881
An imprint of Greenwood Publishing Group, Inc.
www.greenwood.com

Printed in the United States of America

The paper used in this book complies with the
Permanent Paper Standard issued by the National
Information Standards Organization (Z39.48–1984).

10 9 8 7 6 5 4 3 2 1

To my father

Contents

Photo essay follows page 96.

Series Foreword

Oscar Handlin, a prominent historian, once wrote, "I thought to write a history of the immigrants in America. Then I discovered that the immigrants were American history." The United States has always been a nation of nations where people from every region of the world have come to begin a new life. Other countries such as Canada, Argentina, and Australia also have had substantial immigration, but the United States is still unique in the diversity of nationalities and the great numbers of migrating people who have come to its shores.

Who are these immigrants? Why did they decide to come? How well have they adjusted to this new land? What has been the reaction to them? These are some of the questions the books in this "New Americans" series seek to answer. There have been many studies about earlier waves of immigrants—e.g., the English, Irish, Germans, Jews, Italians, and Poles—but relatively little has been written about the newer groups—those arriving in the last thirty years, since the passage of a new immigration law in 1965. This series is designed to correct that situation and to introduce these groups to the rest of America.

Each book in the series discusses one of these groups, and each is written by an expert on those immigrants. The volumes cover the new migration from primarily Asia, Latin America, and the Caribbean, including: the Koreans, Cambodians, Filipinos, Vietnamese, South Asians such as Indians and Pakistanis, Chinese from both China and Taiwan, Haitians, Jamaicans, Cubans, Dominicans, Mexicans, Puerto Ricans (even though they are already U.S. citizens), and Jews from the former Soviet Union. Although some of these people, such as Jews, have been in America since colonial times, this series concentrates on their recent migrations, and thereby offers its unique contribution.

These volumes are designed for high school and general readers who want to learn more about their new neighbors. Each author has provided information about the land of origin, its history and culture, the reasons for migrating, and the ethnic culture as it began to adjust to American life. Readers will find fascinating details on religion, politics, foods, festivals, gender roles, employment trends, and general community life. They will learn how Vietnamese immigrants differ from Cuban immigrants and, yet, how they are also alike in many ways. Each book is arranged to offer an in-depth look at the particular immigrant group but also to enable readers to compare one group with the other. The volumes also contain brief biographical profiles of notable individuals, tables noting each group's immigration, and a short bibliography of readily available books and articles for further reading. Most contain a glossary of foreign words and phrases.

Students and others who read these volumes will secure a better understanding of the age-old questions of "who is an American" and "how does the assimilation process work?" Similar to their nineteenth- and early twentieth-century forebears, many Americans today doubt the value of immigration and fear the influx of individuals who look and sound different from those who had come earlier. If comparable books had been written one hundred years ago they would have done much to help dispel readers' unwarranted fears of newcomers. Nobody today would question, for example, the role of those of Irish or Italian ancestry as Americans; yet, this was a serious issue in our history and a source of great conflict. It is time to look at our recent arrivals, to understand their history and culture, their skills, their place in the United States, and their hopes and dreams as Americans.

The United States is a vastly different country than it was at the beginning of the twentieth century. The economy has shifted away from industrial jobs; the civil rights movement has changed minority-majority relations and, along with the women's movement, brought more people into the economic mainstream. Yet one aspect of American life remains strikingly similar—we are still the world's main immigrant receiving nation and as in every period of American history, we are still a nation of immigrants. It is essential that we attempt to learn about and understand this long-term process of migration and assimilation.

Ronald H. Bayor
Georgia Institute of Technology

Acknowledgments

While conducting the research for this book, I benefited from the assistance of many people without whom this would not have come to fruition. Although I have been influenced and helped by many people, in particular I would like to thank Jean-Paul Dumont, Paula Elsey, Sumaiya Hamdani, Alison Landsberg, Lisa Suhair Majaj, Deidre Murphy, Adam Sabra, Helen Samhan, and, above all, Janice Terry, for their insights and comments on various drafts. Their guidance helped make this book a better piece of work. I would also like to thank my editor, Wendi Schnaufer, and the series editor, Ron Bayor, for their helpful comments in crafting this volume. Working with them, and Greenwood Press, has been a very easy and rewarding process. Big thank-yous also go out to everyone who helped me find the photographs in this edition, including the Immigration History Research Center at the University of Minnesota, the Arab American Institute, the *Detroit News,* and *ARAMCO World* magazine. Abdul-Wahab Kayyali also generously shared his personal photographs for this book. My mother, Susanne Kayyali, my sister, Kinda Kayyali, and my friends, Carolina López and Vicki Watts, were also instrumental in reading drafts and providing insights into my work, especially in the last stages of this process. Finally, I must thank my husband, Ramzi, whose encouragement, input and cooking skills saw me through to the end. His seemingly boundless support, friendship, and love cannot be described with enough adjectives.

Introduction

Arab American is a popular, overarching identity for many Arab Americans, and it is a term widely used in the media and by community organizations today. Although Arab American is simply defined as "the immigrants to North America from the Arabic-speaking countries of the Middle East and their descendents," a great deal of controversy remains over the term *Arab*.[1] The generally accepted definition of an Arab is someone whose mother tongue is Arabic, but many question whether speaking Arabic is enough to make one an Arab. For Arab Americans, the link between language and identity is problematic because many of the second, third, or fourth generations do not speak Arabic. The term *Arab* also has a strong association with the Islamic conquests and religion, and so some Christians from the Arab world do not consider themselves Arabs. Despite these distinctions in the Arab world, many Arab Americans, particularly the youth, identify themselves as Arab or of Arabian heritage because they collectively trace their ancestry back to the Arabic-speaking countries of the Middle East and North Africa.

The origins imply historical and cultural commonalities, as well as shared experiences in the United States. Even some non-Arabs, such as Berbers, Kurds, and Armenians who have grown up in the Arab world and speak Arabic, group themselves with Arab Americans in the United States. The media has also contributed to a sense of communal identity as Arabs are grouped together, regardless of in-group distinctions. The ongoing challenge for the media, as well as for researchers, is to recognize and respect the different identities of Arab Americans without losing sight of the immense diversity of the community. In this book, I use the term *Arab American* for the sake of simplicity and will specify a particular group as the need arises.

The dilemma of labeling the community in the United States today can best be understood through learning about the social, political, and cultural history from which Arab Americans construct their individual histories, memories, and identities. Chapter 1 gives an understanding of the broader political and social history of the Arab world since the advent of Islam in 632 C.E. By providing an abbreviated primer on the histories, cultures, and religions present in the region, the uninitiated reader will have a better grasp of the complexities and backgrounds of the immigrants who came to the United States. Of particular interest to Arab Americans is the history of religious minorities, especially the Christians from Mount Lebanon, who formed the majority of the first immigrants. The country of Lebanon was named after Mount Lebanon, a mountain range that extends across it, and dominates the national landscape.

Like other immigrants in the United States, the so-called push factors for the move across the oceans profoundly impacted the development of the community. The Arab immigrants in the late nineteenth century left their homelands mainly for financial reasons, and the poor economic situation remains the largest factor in emigration today. Chapter 2 explores how the U.S. immigration laws and the imposition of quotas influenced the history of the Arab American community. Most of the first-wave immigrants between 1880 and 1925 were Christian men from the areas of Lebanon, Palestine, and Syria. They arrived by boat, coming into ports such New York City, taking up the peddling trade of selling goods door-to-door or working in the new factories and mills. As the idea of moving back to their towns and villages of origin faded, they began to send for family members or to marry, permanently settling down in areas across the United States. This settlement led to the second period of Arab American history, which was one of assimilation as the immigrant quotas from 1925 to 1965 restricted the number of new entrants into the community. With the changes in the immigration laws in 1965, the Arab American community entered a new phase. The Arab American community became more diverse in terms of religion—the number of Muslims increased—and in terms of country of origin as more Egyptians, Iraqis, and Jordanians immigrated.

The influx of immigrants from the Arab world and the multiculturalism ethos that has developed in the United States since the 1970s prompted Arab Americans to become politicized in mounting efforts of self-definition in an ethnic revival of sorts. As a result, Arab Americans became more aware of their racial and minority status in the United States. Whereas in the early 1900s, Arab Americans fought for the racial classification of "white" to secure U.S. citizenship, in the 1980s and 1990s, Arab Americans began to seek special community designations. Articles titled "White, but Not Quite" and "Not Quite White" reflected the ambivalence the community felt with the designation as "white" in the census and in the legally required forms.[2] Chapter 3 traces how U.S. official classifications of Arab Americans have evolved and impacted the community and why Arab Americans continue to be unrecognized as minorities.

Arab Americans, like other immigrant groups, have adapted more than their group identity in the United States and have conformed to a more American style of living in various ways. Chapter 4 focuses on the cultural adaptations that Arab Americans have made in various realms and discusses how these changes are negotiated and renegotiated according to circumstances and outlooks. Although socioeconomic situations impact the options available to cope with change, migration always disrupts family networks and social structures. Examination of family and women's issues, including issues of household size and parent-child relationships, sheds light on the complexities of generational, gender, and linguistic shifts. Such cultural adaptations often coincide with discourses and interpretations of women working, Islam, and feminism, and so these issues are also addressed.

Between 1990 and 2000, the U.S. Citizenship and Immigration Services estimated that 300,000 Arabs immigrated to the United States. This influx of immigrants has changed the composition of Arab Americans. Although Lebanese are still the largest national grouping of Arab Americans, Egyptians are now the second largest, closely followed by Syrians. The changing demographics of Arab Americans indicate that this is a dynamic community, impacted by the political and economic realities of the Middle East. The divisions prevalent in the Arab world have deepened some of the differences between Arab American communities. Intragroup issues persist in three main divisions: (1) pan-Arab identifications, (2) Christian and Muslim identities, and (3) generational differences. Networks and social clubs can emphasize these differences or bring Arab Americans together. Holidays and celebrations can also be a forum for collective identification. Chapter 5 considers some of the statistical information available on Arab Americans and discusses in depth how Arab Americans differentiate groupings within the community.

The final chapter examines the arts—music, literary, visual—produced by Arab Americans and gives an overview of the political organizations and relations with other ethnic groups today. In the last decade, Arab Americans have become more vocal and prolific as ethnic American artists. There have been numerous publications and exhibits since 2000, and there is a healthy audience for expressions of Arab Americanness. This culture revival culminated in the opening of the Arab American National Museum in Dearborn, Michigan in 2005. These positive developments are partially in reaction to the events of September 11, 2001, and the increased market-ability and visibility of Arab Americans. The terrorist incidents of 9/11 have had many negative repercussions on Arab Americans, including increased racial profiling on university campuses and by law enforcement officers. Arab American political organizations have reacted by networking with other ethnic American groups and by continuing to work with federal, state, and local government organizations.

The literature available on Arab Americans has either been for children or is geared toward academics and specialists. This book aims to reach an audience that falls somewhere between the two, seeking to give a basic overview of the community in its many aspects and vectors, while providing some in-depth points of analysis. It is my sincere hope that you will enjoy this account of the Arab American community and gain a greater understanding of the experiences of Arab Americans. Perhaps this volume will be used as a springboard to further studies on Arab Americans. I hope that I have provided a useful book here that is both readable and informative.

NOTES

1. Michael W. Suleiman, Introduction to *Arabs in America: Building a New Future,* ed. Michael W. Suleiman (Philadelphia: Temple University Press, 1999), 1.

2. Nadine Naber "White—But not quite? An Examination of Arab American In/Visibility" *AAUG Monitor,* December 1998.

Helen Samhan "Not Quite White: Race Classification and the Arab-American Experience" in *Arabs in America: Building a New Future,* ed. by Michael W. Sullivan (Philadelphia: Temple University Press, 1999).

Abbreviations

AAI   Arab American Institute
AAUG   Arab American University Graduates
ACCESS   Arab Community Center for Economic and Social Services
ADC   American-Arab Anti-Discrimination Committee
AMC   American Muslim Council
ANA   Arab Network of America
ART   Arab Radio and Television network
CAIR   Council on American Islamic Relations
LEP   Limited English Proficiency (previously known as English as a Second Language)
MSA   Muslim Student Association
NAAA   National Association of Arab-Americans
RAWI   Radius of Arab American Writers

1

The Arab World: The Geography, History, People, and Cultures

THE LANGUAGE AND THE LANDS

Arabs are people who inhabit the lands that stretch from Iraq in the east, across western Asia through northern Africa to Morocco in the west. Today, there are approximately 270 million Arabic-speaking people. The Middle East and North Africa comprise four main cultural groups—Persians, Turks, Jews, and Arabs. For the most part, each of these groups has its own language, Farsi, Turkish, Hebrew, and Arabic, and its own country, Iran, Turkey, Israel, and the many countries that make up the Arab world. Arabs speak Arabic, which has many dialects as well as a standard written form that is the language of the Quran (the Islamic holy book). Arabic is a Semitic language, and at one point in early history, all Semitic peoples including the Hebrews, Phoenicians, Assyrians, and Chaldeans lived in the Arabian Peninsula—in the area now known as Saudi Arabia, Yemen, and Oman. The Arabic language has two main forms. The classical, more formal written version is called Modern Standard Arabic or *fusha,* and this is articulated in the Quran and in the media. The less formal, spoken dialects of Arabic vary greatly from country to country, even within a country, and are used for everyday spoken communication. Despite a sense of a shared language and culture among Arabs, the diversity of cultural traditions makes it more accurate to refer to the Arab cultures rather than one "culture."

Arabs only constitute a small portion of the number of Muslims worldwide. Many Americans use the terms *Muslim* and *Arab* interchangeably, but this is erroneous. A Muslim is a follower of the religion of Islam and is therefore not defined through geographical or linguistic boundaries. There are 1.7 billion Muslims in the world and 44 countries with majority Muslim populations. Most Muslims live outside the Arab world, mostly in sub-Saharan Africa, Southeast Asia, and the Far East. Arabs number approximately 16 percent of Muslims worldwide.

Arabs can be of any religion. Although 90 percent of Arabs are Muslim, there are also a substantial number of Arab Christians living throughout the Middle East. Many of the Jews living in the Arab world immigrated to Israel after its founding in 1948, but there are still a number of Jews living in Morocco and Yemen. The major religions and religious sects that exist in the region are examined further at the end of this chapter.

SHORT HISTORY OF THE ARABS

The word *Arab* derives from the A'raab people who established trade routes and pastoral networks between the Arabian Peninsula and Syria from 900 to 800 B.C.E. The nomadic Arab merchants traveled over great distances on trade routes that extended throughout the region, and they often brought news from other areas to the settled merchants in cities and towns. The established trading networks promoted relationships between the Arabs and the Christian and Jewish tribes in the Arabian Peninsula and cemented cultural and financial ties with the Byzantine Empire. This empire lay to the north of the Arabian Peninsula and ruled over most of the region of the eastern Mediterranean. The Byzantine Empire was the successor to the Roman Empire, and the Byzantines were Christians (Greek Orthodox), so Christianity was the official state religion. The Persian Sassanid Empire stretched from Roman Anatolia in the west to Taxila (now in Pakistan) to the east. The religion of the Sassanid dynasty was Zoroastrianism—a monotheistic religion founded by Zoroaster, a prophet who lived in eastern Iran around 600 B.C.E. and worked as a priest. The Byzantines and Sassanids fought expensive and lengthy wars that exhausted state resources before the Arab conquests of the seventh century. Although there were Christian and Jewish tribes present at the time of the advent of Islam in 622 C.E., many of the A'raab people, especially the urban merchants, were animists and polytheists who worshipped many gods and objects from nature and made religious pilgrimages to shrines in the cities that were also centers for major trade.

Arrival and Establishment of Islam and the Islamic Empires

The religion of Islam developed in 610 C.E. in the western part of the Arabian Peninsula when the Prophet Muhammad received a message from God. Muhammad, an Arab merchant who lived in Mecca (now in Saudi Arabia), was a member of the prominent Quraysh tribe, guardians of one the most important polytheist shrines, the Kaaba. The Angel Gabriel charged Muhammad with telling the people of Mecca to stop worshipping idols and accept one God, *Allah*. The first converts were his wife, Khadija, his slave, Zaid (whom he freed and adopted as his son), and his ten-year-old cousin, Ali. There was a great deal of opposition to the message that Muhammad was delivering, notably among members of his own Quraysh tribe. Fearing persecution, the Prophet led his followers out of Mecca to the safety of another major town at the time, Medina. This departure in 622 marks the beginning of the lunar Muslim calendar.

The early followers of Islam, or Muslims, were Arabs who lived in the two major trading centers at the time—Mecca and Medina. *Muslim* is the Arabic word for the one who submits. In 629, Muhammad led more than one thousand of his followers back to Mecca: a victory that marked the beginning of many successful battles. By the time of his death, the Prophet Mohammed had fought and won over the western half of the Arabian Peninsula. This Muslim conquest of land was called the Arab expansion because the victors were all from the A'raab peoples. In pre-Islamic days, the people of the Arabian Peninsula had many identities, including Babylonian, Assyrian, Chaldean, Amorite, Aramaean, Phoenician, Hebrew, Arabian, and Abyssinian. The expansion of Islam brought the Arabic language to people who spoke other Semitic languages such as Aramaic and Syriac. Within 100 years of Muhammad's death in 632 C.E., Arab Muslims had conquered lands that stretched from Persia in the east to North Africa in the west and extended from Southern Europe (including the Al-Andalusia region in what is now Spain) in the north to the whole of the Arabian Peninsula in the south. The territorial and material gains of the Arab conquests made the establishment of an Islamic empire possible.

The Arab expansion was a military campaign, yet the focus remained on the spread of religion, and many of the conquered peoples became Muslims. Christian and Jewish tribesmen and women were not forced to convert to Islam and were respected as *Ahl al-Kitab*, People of the Book, as Islam, like Judaism and Christianity, is an Abrahamic faith. However, Jews and Christians had to pay protection taxes from which Muslims were exempt and so financial considerations often fuelled more conversions to Islam. Islam spread peacefully through word-of-mouth by traders, merchants, and missionaries into Africa, Asia, and the Balkan region of Southern Europe. Although Islam was first a religion, under early Islamic rule—the Umayyad and Abbasid Empires—it "became a state, and finally a culture."[1]

Under the rule of the Umayyads and later the Abbasid dynasties, Islam became entrenched as an imperial power. Muslims achieved greatness in the development of the arts and culture, reaching a zenith during the Golden Age (750–1258 C.E.). This period saw Arabic become the *lingua franca* for the whole empire and the language used to express philosophic and scientific thoughts and ideas. The authority of the empire over its subjects, combined with the influence of Islam, created more commonalities between the cultures contained within the empire, which in turn led to more universal cultural values and traditions. By the end of the Abbasid era, there was a Muslim culture that integrated elements from non-Arab Muslims, especially Persians.

Political and religious splits in the Abbasid Empire, led to the fragmentation of the empire. During the decline of Abbasid Caliphates, the European Crusaders were able to invade and capture Jerusalem in 1099. The slow fragmentation of the empire led to smaller, semiautonomous states and a weakness in military strength that allowed the Mongols to capture Baghdad in 1258 C.E. and execute the caliph and his family, thus completing the destruction of the Abbasid Empire. In the fifteenth and sixteenth centuries, Muslim *sultanates* (areas ruled by a sultan) extended from Africa to Southeast Asia. Islam penetrated deeply into sub-Saharan Africa and into Southeast Asia as well as Eastern Europe through missionaries, merchant traders, and *Sufi* (Muslim mystic) brotherhoods.

The Ottoman Empire

The Ottoman (Turkish) Empire ruled the Arab world as well as portions of Eastern Europe and Africa from its capital in Constantinople (now Istanbul) from the fifteenth century (Egypt and Syria from 1516–17) until World War I. Although Ottoman rule over much of the Arab lands spanned several centuries, the empire declined as an economic and political power in the eighteenth and nineteenth centuries, and by the advent of World War I, the Ottoman Empire was known as the "Sick Man of Europe." The fall of the empire's strength had negative effects on the Arab world that impacted the development of today's states in a myriad of ways. In the eighteenth century, European countries eclipsed the Ottomans in economic development and technology, and Western European transatlantic trade with the Americas made the Mediterranean a less important mercantile route.

European powers invaded and wrested parts of North Africa from Ottoman control. In 1830, France occupied Algeria. In 1798, Napoleon invaded Egypt, which led to the seizure of power by Muhammad Ali (1805–48), who became the unofficial governor in Egypt. In 1831, Muhammad Ali sent his son Ibrahim Pasha to invade Greater Syria to expand his authority and rule. The local inhabitants were unhappy with the Egyptian rulers because they increased taxation threefold on both Muslims and non-Muslims. Egyptians also conscripted young men and imposed forced labor. Political unrest and revolts against the Egyptians by the locals in Nablus, Palestine, Tripoli, Houwran, and northern Syria followed. With the help of the British, Ottomans, and Austrians, the people of Mount Lebanon (located in today's Lebanon) defeated the Egyptians, and Muhammad Ali agreed to withdraw his troops.

In the years immediately following the Egyptian retreat, the Ottomans imposed reforms and divided Mount Lebanon into two administrative regions—one for the Druze and one for the Maronites. The Ottoman divide and rule policies pitted people against each other, and in 1845, there was an open war between the Druze and the Maronites of Mount Lebanon. Until 1860, massacres, pillaging, and general mayhem ensued in the area now known as Lebanon as the two groups fought for dominance in the political and economic spheres. This violence and turmoil led many young Maronites and Druze men to leave Mount Lebanon, and those who chose to go to the United States composed the first wave of Arab immigrants.

By the turn of the nineteenth century, Arabs and other groups under Ottoman rule had become nationalistic and aspired to political independence. In 1907–8, there was a revolution in the Ottoman Empire, and the Young Turks seized power. The new leaders centralized control of the provinces and attempted to "Turk-ify" the educational system by emphasizing Turkish history, culture, and language in schools and imposing Turkish as the central teaching language and the language of the empire. These attempts fostered growing hostility to Turkish rule, which led to the creation of Arab, Kurdish, and Armenian national movements that sought to unify their people in one nation independent of Turkish or European control. In the years preceding World War I, the Turks brutally put down the Armenian and Kurdish aspirations for nationhood through massacres and persecution. The turmoil and discontent in the Ottoman Empire in the late nineteenth and early twentieth centuries led many of its non-Turkish subjects to immigrate to countries far away from the empire. Many of these Ottoman subjects crossed the Atlantic and came to the Americas.

Some Arab nationalists seized the opportunity of World War I to negotiate their own independent nationhood. Sharif Hussein of Mecca exchanged correspondence in 1915–16 with Sir Henry McMahon, the British representative in Cairo, in which he promised to declare the Arab Revolt (1916) against the Ottomans and vouched for Arab loyalty to the British side of the war in exchange for British support for the creation of an Arab kingdom in the Levant (the eastern Mediterranean region) and the Arabian Peninsula. However, the British also made deals with the Zionists and the French that would conflict with their promises to the Arabs. The Sykes-Picot Agreement between the British and the French in 1916 secretly divided the former Ottoman Empire between the two European powers. The Balfour Declaration (1917) stated that the British government viewed with favor "the establishment in Palestine of a national home for the Jewish people" and encouraged Zionist aspirations that directly conflicted with promises for Arab independence. Thus, despite the Arab Revolt and the ultimate victory of the European powers over the Ottoman Empire and its allies, Arab independence was not achieved at the close of the negotiations of World War I. Instead, the Treaty of Sèvres in 1920 gave the French a mandate over Syria and Lebanon and the British a mandate over Iraq and Palestine.

The Mandate Period

The years between World War I and II, known as the Mandate Period, were a time of great upheaval and political discontent in the region. At the beginning of the Mandate Period, most of the Middle East and North Africa was under the direct or indirect control of Britain and France while Libya was an Italian colony.

The British Mandate over Palestine proved to be very problematic because of conflicting promises to both Jews and Arabs. The British limited Jewish immigration to Palestine just at the time that Adolf Hitler was carrying out the Holocaust, causing the Zionists to form militant organizations that fought the British as well as the local Arab population. The British colonialist occupation of the land and the influx of Jews wishing to establish a Jewish homeland were seen by Palestinians as threats to their desired independence. In the Mandate Period, as conflict increased between Arabs and Jews, the physical battles over the ownership of the land of Palestine began.

The French Mandate over Lebanon and Syria was less violent but set the stage for future conflicts, just as the British Mandate over Palestine had done. In Lebanon, the French established a confessionalist system, in which each religious group or sect was supposedly given political representation based on the population census of 1932. The French favored the Maronites, fellow Christians, and chose to empower their allies by dividing Syria and

Lebanon strategically to allow Lebanon to have an economically viable state while keeping the Maronites as the majority religion in Lebanon in numerical terms. Although the sectarian proportions have changed since the 1930s, aspects of this confessionalist system still exist in Lebanon.

During the Mandate Period, both the French and the British created the map of the modern Middle East and set the stage for a legacy of political troubles and difficulties in border and nation building in the Middle East and North Africa.

Post–World War II

Arab nationalism, which began as a reaction against Ottoman control of Arab lands, gained even more popularity with the rise of opposition to European colonialism. The twentieth century was a period of decolonization, and most Arabs living at the time experienced the political transitions from European domination to independence in the years following the end of World War II. Most of these independent states were secular and based on European legal and political systems. Many Arabs believed that these separate nations, divided by borders drawn by colonial powers, would soon unite to become one Arab nation. These Arabs were referred to as pan-Arab nationalists. Many of the postcolonial governments present in the Middle East today synthesized the political philosophies that were widely popular in the latter half of the twentieth century and incorporated elements of Arab nationalist, anti-imperialist, and socialist ideologies.

Palestine, however, had a different history. After World War II, the British withdrew from Palestine and turned the issue of sovereignty over to the newly created United Nations. In 1947, the U.N. General Assembly voted to partition the country of Palestine into seven parts: three for the Jews, three for the Arabs, and one to be administered by the United Nations (Jerusalem/ Bethlehem area). The Palestinian Arabs, believing the whole country belonged to them, rejected the plan. The Jewish Agency accepted the plan and declared Israel an independent nation in 1948. The armies of Syria, Lebanon, Jordan, Egypt, and Iraq declared war and attacked Israel. Most of the fighting was in the areas assigned to Palestinians under the U.N. plan. The outcome of the war was a victory for the Israeli forces, which expanded the U.N.–assigned Jewish territory and incorporated it into the state of Israel. Arabs refer to the 1948 war as *al-Nakba,* the Disaster, because it led to the loss of an entity called "Palestine" and to the rule of Israelis over Palestinians within the state of Israel, as well as the establishment of Jordanian annexation of the West Bank and Egyptian rule over Palestinians in the Gaza Strip. Almost 1 million

Palestinian Arabs left their homes and villages and found themselves in refugee camps in the West Bank, Gaza Strip, Jordan, and Lebanon, where they set up temporary lodgings because they expected to return to their homes in Palestine when the fighting was over. Hundreds of thousands of Jews also left their homes in Arab countries and moved to Isreal. Whether Palestinian and Arab Jews left their homes forcefully or voluntarily remains a controversial historical issue. In 1949, all the Arab combatants except Iraq signed armistice agreements with Israel, but with no peace agreements, both sides prepared for the next confrontation. The refugees stayed in the camps, which exist to the present day.

In the Arab-Israeli Six-Day War in 1967, Israel expanded its borders by occupying the Sinai Peninsula of Egypt and wrested control over the Gaza Strip from the Egyptians, the Golan Heights from Syria, and the West Bank from Jordan. The coalition of Jordan, Egypt, and Syria, as well as forces from other Arab countries, was not able to win a victory against the smaller state of Israel. As more Palestinians fled the fighting, the numbers in the refugee camps swelled. Defeat in the 1967 war was a watershed event in the formation of an Arab consciousness and identity. The most important long-term consequence was to highlight the weakness of Arabs in the face of Israel. Particularly after the death of Egyptian President Gamal Abdel Nasser in 1970, many Arabs were despondent about the concept of one strong Arab nation. Palestinians believed that relying on Arab countries weakened their own defense, leading to the strengthening of the Palestinian Liberation Organization (PLO).

In the post-1967 period, there has been substantial political instability, including wars. Indeed, as the list below illustrates, almost every country in the Arab world has been affected substantially by conflict, and so a great number of Arabs have experienced political violence firsthand. The conflicts that have occurred since 1967 include:

- 1970. A brief civil war in Jordan.
- 1973. The Yom Kippur War between Israel and Egypt, Syria, and Jordan. The governments of Egypt (1979) and Jordan (1991) signed peace treaties with Israel, but Libya, Syria, and Lebanon are still officially at war with Israel.
- 1973. Clashes between the Lebanese Army and Palestinians in Lebanon.
- 1975–91. A 16-year civil war in Lebanon that affected almost every home in the country.
- 1981–88. The First Gulf War. Iraq and Iran fought a bitter war of attrition with neither side winning.

- 1983–present. Ongoing civil war in Sudan.
- 1987–present. The *Intifada,* the Palestinian uprising, began against Israeli occupation of the West Bank and Gaza Strip.
- 1992–present. Ongoing civil war in Algeria between the Islamists and the state security forces.
- 1990–91. Kuwait invaded by Iraq. The Second Gulf War ensued in which U.S. forces restored sovereignty to Kuwait and imposed no-fly zones. A U.N. economic embargo was imposed on Iraq.
- 2003–present. U.S. troops entered Iraq to "find and destroy weapons of mass destruction" and overthrow the regime of Saddam Hussein. U.S. forces occupy Iraq.

Violence and wars indicate a larger problem of political instability in the region. As most Arab countries have authoritarian regimes, there is a general absence of democratic institutions. Although there have been some movements toward economic liberalization, there has been little political liberalization and restrictions continue to exist on the media. The Gulf States (Saudi Arabia, Oman, United Arab Emirate, Qatar, Bahrain, and Kuwait) have placed emphasis on the legitimacy of the royal families and combined "a concept of a loyal citizenry, with notions of religion, kinship, proper behaviour [*sic*] and economic welfare [that is] taking precedence over the importance of political rights."[2] The lack of input or contribution from the citizenry to their leaders, coupled with a lack of human rights and economic stagnation, has created widespread frustration in the Arab world and has led many to emigrate from the region.

During the fight for independence from colonialism, Arab leaders sought to gain economic as well as political independence and nationalized many foreign-owned industries upon independence. Through increasing the size and scope of government, the leaders were able to hire more graduates of the national universities. However, in the last few decades, Arab governments made some moderate moves toward economic liberalization. On the insistence of external forces, such as the European Union, World Bank, and the International Monetary Fund, as well as international trade agreements, Arab governments were forced to privatize some industries. Markets opened up to foreign investment and local elites through their contact with the ruling powers. These foreigners and elites have been able to purchase some former state industries and/or secure contracts that serve as monopolies, such as owning the only cell phone company allowed to operate in the country. As unemployment increased, it became harder for college graduates to find jobs, and those without contacts with the government private companies or multi-national corporations, have become increasingly alienated. Believing that there is little possibility of upward mobility, many young, educated, and enterprising individuals have left their countries of birth. The frustration of many people in the economic sphere has been acerbated by the lack of political freedoms, leading to emigration from the most populous countries such as Egypt.

CULTURES

Many vibrant cultures exist in the Arab world, and traditions vary from region to region, even from city to city. However, there are shared traits in these cultures and some agreed-upon ideals for individuals and society in general. It is hard to determine whether these ideals are a result of any one religion or a combination of religious tenets; nevertheless, Arabs of all faiths share a similar moral code.

The words *honor* and *pride* are often used together to mean that dignity is for people who live life in accordance within the norms of the shared Arab culture. For an individual, it is honorable to respect the family and the authority of the elders and to be generous and kind to others, including strangers. A life of hard work, sobriety, and frugality is an ideal that gives an individual extra status within the class structure. A humble approach to success is considered socially acceptable, and modesty is an important social leveler.

Family, and kinship, is highly valued and the most important social unit. A man or woman can live an honorable life, but an individual is not considered an entity independent of his or her family. The Arab family includes the nuclear family, grandparents, aunts, uncles, and their children. Family support is considered to be essential to the health and well-being of all individuals because the family acts as a personal support group that shares experiences and helps the individual family member, often acting as a network for business opportunities and jobs. Members of a family usually take part in all aspects of an individual's life, including births, marriage, illness, financial decisions, and death. At times of crisis, all family members are expected to show support by being there and offering financial assistance. The elderly and disabled are cared for by family members within the home because life without family is thought to be not worth living. The welfare, honor, identity, and status of an individual are directly tied to the family's name and reputation.

Arab families are structured and defined by the male line and are therefore patrilineal. Children are members of their father's family first, and then part of their mother's family. Although usually women do not change their last names to their husbands' after marriage—one keeps the name one was born with—in most traditional Arab cultures, the bride leaves her home and becomes part of the groom's family upon marriage. In this manner, his kinship and extended family are conferred on his new bride and later to their children. Marriage therefore unites families and as a result, parental consent is considered to be an essential prerequisite. Arranged marriages are no longer commonplace in the Arab world, and preference for first-cousin marriages is losing popularity because of the health consequences for the children. Single men and women tend to meet their spouses at universities or in other public spaces. Families will also introduce their children to prospective spouses under their supervision in the hope that there will be a match by mutual consent.

There is an emphasis on the hierarchies of power within the family, which favors the elderly as well as men, so that the authority of a grandfather or a grandmother usually supersedes that of a father or uncle. The eldest son is considered to have the most authority and responsibility of all the children in the family. Although men hold a position of power within the Arab family, it is inaccurate to consider Arab families simply patriarchal in structure, as there are usually more complex hierarchies in action. Arab families are considered to be male dominated because it is shameful (or not honorable) for a man to appear weak outside his family. In reality, this means that many of the choices made by women and children are often masked as decisions made by the father. For the children in an Arab family, obedience is valued over independence, and if it appears to the outside world that the father has made the decision and the child is obeying her or his father, then all is well in the household. The power of the young and of women is often invisible to the outsider, who sees family decisions as stated by men as proof of patriarchal control.

Roles and expectations for men and women in Arab societies are gendered. Generally speaking, Arabs believe that men and women have different natures, and thus biology, rather than society, has determined their behavior and their roles in the family and, by extension, in society. Men are considered to be the providers and protectors of the family, while women are nurturers and caregivers. Men are in charge of external social and political affairs, and women are in control of the household issues, including the welfare and upbringing of their children. Both men and women have final authority for the decisions made in their realms. The stress on women's primary role in society as mothers and wives is seen to complement the role of men. Despite the outward appearance of the public-private dichotomy of these gendered roles, women play an active part in public life in the Arab world. Women work outside the home in almost all countries of the Middle East, often running their own businesses. Women also run for public office and are civil servants. Women are usually given some latitude in their job choices, but it is not socially acceptable for women to do manual labor because it is considered "men's work." However, if a woman works, she is expected to do double duty by prioritizing the family and taking care of the household affairs, including cooking, cleaning, laundry, and childcare. Men are expected to support the family financially and be the main income earners, and so, like women all over the world, women often receive lower wages than men.

One area in which men exert their power over women in public is by controlling their mobility and dress. The reason given for physical restrictions is related to women's sexuality and the maintenance of the family's good reputation in the Arab social structure. In many cultures in the Arab region, family honor rests on the sexuality of all the women in the family. The greatest insult to either a Christian or a Muslim man in much of the Arab world is to smear the reputation of his mother or sister. Women are expected to be chaste until marriage; if there is evidence that they are not virgins, they can be punished by their families, or even killed. These so-called honor killings can also occur if a husband suspects his wife of infidelity. In marriage, however, healthy sexual relations are encouraged between spouses. Not only do these social mores control women's sexuality, but they also ensure that a child is from a particular patriline.

Controlling women's sexuality often extends into debates over modesty and what is considered to be proper dress. Christians and many Muslim women do not wear any form of head covering, but there is much debate about what constitutes modest dress and what is so-called Islamic dress. The reasons cited for and against adopting Islamic dress are cultural as well as religious in nature and are different for men and women. Men cite the need to protect women from the male gaze, and women often adopt the veil out of personal conviction and as a form of female empowerment, as described later. There are three main types of Islamic dress: the *hijab,* a headscarf that covers the hair only; the *abaya,* a robe that covers the arms and legs; and the *niqab,* a headscarf, one-piece robe, and a veil that covers the face, and sometimes also the eyes. Women who wear the *niqab* may wear gloves to cover their hands in addition to their bodies and faces. Even if they chose to wear a form of covering, women still assert their independence and individuality through clothing and make-up choices. It is common on the streets of major Arab capitals to see women wearing brightly colored headscarves that match their outfit and high-heeled shoes. Some young Muslim women wear tight jeans, loose shirts, and headscarves on university campuses. The only Arab country that requires women to cover up by law is Saudi Arabia, where women assert their individuality by wearing expensive *abayas,* sometimes with risqué clothes underneath their covering.

ISLAM

Islam recognizes one God (*Allah* in Arabic) and previous biblical prophets as messengers of God. Muslims see Islam as a return to the pristine monotheism of Abraham, from which both the traditions of Judaism and Christianity flowed. The Quran (also spelled Koran) is the foundation of Islamic belief and practice, and as such, is the most important source of reference for Muslims. Muslims believe that the Quran contains the exact words revealed by God to the Prophet Muhammad.

Muhammad was illiterate, and he memorized the revelations that he received from the Angel Gabriel in Mecca and Medina (now in Saudi Arabia), which were written down during Muhammad's lifetime by his early followers and compiled into the Quran shortly after his death. The Quran includes 114 chapters called *suras* that are divided into *ayas,* or verses. The first chapter of the Quran is the *Fatiha,* which means the "Opening," and it includes eight verses that summarize the message of the Quran. After the *Fatiha,* the *suras* are organized according to length, with the longest coming first. Practicing Muslims recite the *Fatiha* five times a day at the beginning of their prayers. The translated version of the *Fatiha* reads:

> In the Name of Allah, most gracious, most merciful, praise be to Allah, the cherisher and sustainer of the worlds, most gracious, most merciful, master of the Day of Judgment, thee do we worship and thine aid do we seek. Show us the straight path, the way of those on whom thou hast bestowed thy grace, those whose "portion" is not wrath and who go not astray. (Quran 1: 1–8)[3]

The word *Quran* is Arabic for "recitations" or "readings"; because the Quran was transmitted to Muhammad in Classical Arabic, the recitation of the Quran to this day must be done in its original Arabic form. Although all Muslims recite prayers in Arabic, the Quran has been translated into many languages to facilitate the understanding of its contents by the many non-Arabic speakers of the Muslim community. Nevertheless, the central role of the Arabic language in Islam was characterized as "the sacred language of Islam, because, in a very real sense, it is the language of God."[4] In turn, the Quran influenced the development of Classical Arabic through the syntax, vocabulary, and grammar contained in the Quranic text. The formal Arabic language of today is therefore based on the importance given to Arabic in the Quran.

Muslims consider the Prophet Muhammad a model that should be emulated, and after his death, his companions recalled his daily life, sayings, deeds, and actions, which are collectively known as the *hadith*. In the ninth century, al-Bukhari, among others, collected the *hadith* of the Prophet and checked them for authenticity. The consensus of the Muslim community, or *ijmaa*, the multiple volumes of the *hadith*, and the Quran are the sources of Islamic law, or *sharia*. Different interpretations of *sharia* are carried out in varying degrees through modern bureaucratic systems in Muslim countries today, especially in the family courts that deal with matters of marriage, divorce, and inheritance. There is substantial debate in majority Muslim countries about what the *sharia* requires and what it means for contemporary society.

The Five Pillars of Islam are the guidelines from the Quran that outline the duties expected of every practicing Muslim. These are:

1. Belief in one God (*Allah*) and his Prophet Muhammad, recited as a testament of faith (*shahadah*)
2. Prayer five times a day (*salat*)
3. Making the Pilgrimage journey to Mecca (*hajj*)
4. Fasting during the month of Ramadan (*sawm*)
5. Giving to charity (*zakat*)

These pillars act to unify the diverse and extensive Muslim community throughout the world. Muslims can do their prayers in homes or at work, with the use of a prayer rug, but Muslim men are expected to attend Friday noon prayers at the mosque (*masjid* in Arabic), a Muslim place of worship. Muslim women can pray at home or in a separate section of the mosque.

Jihad, considered one of the primary duties of Muslims, is sometimes thought of as a Sixth Pillar because it was emphasized in the behavior of the early Muslims. Literally translated, *jihad* means "struggle" or "effort." There is some debate among scholars and Muslims alike as to whether *jihad* primarily refers to a war against unbelievers whose territory borders on Islamic lands or to a personal, internal struggle against evil, or both.

Authority in Islam is based on the Quran and the *sunna*. There are no intermediaries between God and a Muslim such as a sacramental priesthood. There are, however, leaders called *imams, shaykhs,* and *khatibs,* who lead prayer and deliver the Friday sermon; they are considered well-read in Islamic texts, and so are sources of information and answers on the tenets of Islam. Their titles are not ecclesiastical and can be used to refer people who wield other kinds of authority, such as a tribal *shaykh*. However, every Muslim is directly answerable to God and able to make his or her own assessments of situations based on the Quran and the *sunna*, with or without agreeing with the *imam*. Mosques are not consecrated ground, and Muslims are able to pray wherever they wish, as long as the location is clean, usually on a prayer rug. Muslims pray facing the direction of the Kaaba in Mecca. The movements are specified for each of the five prayers, which coincide with times in the day: sunrise, noon, afternoon, sunset, and evening.

The concept of a Muslim community, or *umma,* can be traced back to the very beginning of Islam when the early Muslims were persecuted for their beliefs and fled to Medina. The philosophy behind the concept of the *umma* is that the brotherhood of Islam transcended tribal loyalties. As the Islamic empire grew, the definition of the *umma* expanded to mean that the integrity of the Muslim community was more important than national and ethnic loyalties. All Muslims, whatever the social or economic differences, are equal before God who will ultimately judge them and send their souls either to heaven or to hell.

In the Quran, women and men are considered equal before God (Quran 33:35), yet the sexes are not necessarily equal before the law either in the Quran or in many Muslim countries where a woman's court testimony is worth half that of a man, and women do not have the same inheritance rights as men. The Quran refers to the concept of veiling for women only once,

> And say to the believing women that they should lower their gaze and guard their modesty; that they should not display their beauty and ornaments except what (must ordinarily) appear thereof; that they should draw their veils over their bosoms and not display their beauty. (Quran 24:31)

There is a great deal of debate in the Muslim community about whether women should wear a veil and how extensive their covering should be. Some Arab countries such as Saudi Arabia have legislated that women must wear an *abaya* (a full-length black veil that goes over regular clothing), while others have no such requirements, and women are free to wear whatever they like in public. In countries such as Egypt, most women wear only a scarf over their heads to show modesty or religious piety while remaining fashionable.

Marriage in Islam is a civil contract that is sanctioned by God. Although a Muslim man can marry up to four wives, he must treat them equally—a feat that many argue is impossible. A Muslim woman may not marry a non-Muslim, and some couples are forced to leave their country of origin if they wish to marry against religious law or against the wishes of their families. In some countries, women have the right to divorce if they claim that right in the marriage contract, which is drawn up at the beginning of the marriage.

The main branch of Islam is Sunni Islam and the followers are called Sunnis. Sunnis refer to Muslims who follow the *sunna,* the actions and sayings of the

Prophet Muhammad and his companions. Most Muslims worldwide and in the Arab world are Sunnis. Therefore, any person who does not identify himself or herself as a Sunni in the Arab world is from a minority group.

MINORITIES

In Muslim majority countries, there has been a growing dominance of Islam in all spheres of life since the 1970s, and minority groups generally have not fared well. However, many Sunni Muslims have also been mal-treated under the nondemocratic regimes prevalent in the Middle East. As in many other developing countries, access to the economic and political leadership allows for more opportunities and protection from persecution. Belonging to the same religious and ethnic group as those in power does not necessarily translate into opportunities and wealth, but it may help.

Under Ottoman rule, non-Muslim groups were allowed to administer their own affairs with their own religious laws and so remain in control of their own communities. Many of the Arab countries chose to leave this system in place upon independence from the Ottomans and European colonial powers, so many churches of Christian sects still exert jurisdiction over their own members. For example, in Egypt, a Coptic priest must marry a couple if they are to marry within the church. Similarly, the Maronite Church regulates the family laws, including divorce and inheritance, of the Maronite Christians living in Lebanon.

Despite these laws, minorities in the Arab world have emigrated in greater percentages than have the majority Sunni population. This phenomena at least reflects a wish to leave the country of their birth and perhaps also reflects a desire to live in another society altogether. Because of dispropor-tionate emigration of minorities and the differentiations between religions and sects made within the Arab American community, the complex back-ground of minorities will be explained in some depth here. The follow-ing section first addresses minorities affiliated with Islam (Shia Muslims, Druze, Alawites), followed by Christians (Maronites, Catholics, Chaldeans, Orthodox Christians, Copts, Protestants), and then Jews.

Shia Muslims

Shia Muslims are numerically the largest minority group of Muslims. Most Shia live outside the Arab world, notably in Iran and Pakistan. In the Arab world, the Shia mostly reside in southern Iraq and southern Lebanon. Shia refers to *Shiat Ali,* the Party of Ali, because they believe that Ali, Muhammad's cousin, who died in 661, should have ruled the Muslim community.

The rift between Sunni and Shia Muslims began directly after the Prophet's death in 632, when disagreements over the leadership of the Muslim community emerged. The Quran did not specify leadership, and the Prophet's experience was a unique precedent as ruler and religious leader in Medina, so the community disagreed over how to preserve his success at uniting the Muslim community. The people who became Sunni argued that his companions were best able to maintain his legacy; those who became Shia argued that his family was best suited to the task. As a result of their divergence on this crucial issue, Shia claimants to leadership were often persecuted, and in the case of the Prophet's grandson, Husayn, martyred, by Sunni rulers. The martyrdom of Husayn is commemorated by all Shia on *Ashura,* the tenth day of *Muharram,* which is the first month in the Islamic lunar calendar. This event has served as a rallying point for Shia to oppose unjust policies and actions against their community, often sparking conflicts between Sunnis and Shia.

Shia follow the same Five Pillars of Islam as the Sunnis, but they developed some different devotions and religious practices. Although the Shia all share beliefs in the proper leadership of the Muslim community, there are many branches of Shiism practiced in the world today, including Twelvers *(Ithna Asharis), Yazidis, Ismailis* (also called the Seveners), and *Zaydis.* The Twelvers, or *Imami Shia,* believe that the twelfth Imam disappeared in 874 c.e., thus ending the reign of the imamate as leader of the Islamic empire, and they await the return of the twelfth (and last) Imam at the end of time. The Bahai faith is also a nineteenth-century offshoot of Twelver Shia-ism. Some Arab countries have substantial percentages of Twelver Shia Muslims, such as in Saudi Arabia (15%) and Iraq (63%), and these people usually maintain overlapping identities as nationals of a country, Arabs, and Shia.[5]

Druze

The Druze people, who live in Lebanon, Syria, Jordan, and Israel, were among the first groups to emigrate from the Arab world to the United States. The Druze are an offshoot of the Ismailis, although they formed a distinct religious sect that centered around the Quran and their own interpretations of it, which remains secret to outsiders as well as to some of their own community. The Druze community is divided into the "wise" and the "ignorant." The so-called wise are the men and women who are told about the mystical teachings of the religion, and they "are expected to lead an exemplary life of regular prayer and abstention from wine, tobacco and other stimulants."[6]

Although the Druze do not have mosques, the wise read the Scriptures and are distinguishable by a white turban, a red-and-white fez, or special dress, as both men and women can be in the group of the wise. The so-called ignorant are not made privy to the deeper religious teachings and are expected to lead a mostly secular lifestyle but are part of the tight Druze community. It is known to the outside world that the Druze believe in one God but do not fast for Ramadan or make the *hajj*—two pillars of Islam. They also believe in the reincarnation of the soul from one being to another on death. Sunnis and Shia alike regard the Druze as heretics and usually do not consider them Muslims. The persecution of the Druze community over the years has created a strong sense of solidarity, shaping an ethic of the fearless, strong warrior for Druze men. They do not accept converts or marry outside their community and practice monogamy in marriage, discouraging divorce. The Druze in Lebanon mostly live on Mount Lebanon, and the Lebanese Druze remain the largest community of their faith despite substantial emigration. The Druze in Lebanon generally consider themselves Arabs.

Alawis

Alawis live in the highlands of northern Syria and northern Lebanon and form 12 percent of the overall Syrian population—almost 200,000 people.[7] Although the Alawis are a minority group, an Alawi family, the Assads, has ruled Syria since 1970. The Alawis branched off from the Twelver Shia, who share the belief that Ali was the Prophet Muhammad's rightful heir, but the Alawis go further in their adoration of Ali as to be "infused with divine essence."[8] Most Muslims do not consider the Alawis to be Muslim, but the Alawis contend that they are Twelver Shia Muslims. Like the Druze, Alawis do not have mosques, do not follow the Muslim prayer rituals, are protective of their religion, and do not reveal the tenets of their religion. In the thirteenth century, a Syrian Sunni theologian, Ibn Taymiya, condemned the early Alawis (then called Nusayris) as dangerous and urged Muslims to declare holy war on them because he believed the Alawis to be infidels. Alawis, who rarely marry outside of their religion, consider themselves to be Arabs.

Maronites

The Maronites are the only Middle Eastern Christian group to exercise substantial political power in the region. Emigration and the long civil war have reduced the Lebanese Christian population since the early 1970s, and the total number of Christians in Lebanon now rests between 30 and

40 percent of the population, or roughly just over 1 million people. The Maronites were named after a fifth-century saint called Maron and in the seventh century, the leaders adopted a doctrine relating to the nature of Jesus that was considered heretical by the Byzantines. The Maronites were then forced to flee into the mountains for their protection, and they continue to be concentrated in the valleys and on the slopes of Mount Lebanon. During the medieval period, the Maronites assisted the Crusaders. This collaboration began the Maronite alliance with the West and with the Roman Catholic Church. Today, the Maronite Church is one of the Uniate Churches that signify an Eastern Church in union with the Roman Catholic Church; it acknowledges the Pope in Rome as supreme in matters of faith but maintains its own liturgy, discipline, and rite. The Maronites use the Syriac (a close linguistic relative to Aramaic) liturgy, but the lessons and some prayers are in Arabic. While Arabic, or Lebanese, is the language of religion and of the community, French is the language of education for the Maronites. Indeed, since 1860, the Maronites and France have had a special relationship, and many Maronites feel a stronger affiliation with the French than with their own neighbors—the Syrians, Palestinians, and Jordanians. In the civil war, the Maronites often sided with the Israelis, causing their further alienation in the region. The Maronites, who trace their heritage back to the Phoenicians, often identify as Lebanese and Phoenician and do not usually consider themselves Arabs.

Catholics

A number of Catholic Churches exist in the Middle East that are Uniate Churches with varying degrees of communion with the Vatican and the Pope. The Greek Catholics, or Melkites, have a Uniate Church and major communities in Lebanon, Syria, Egypt, the West Bank, and the northern villages of the Galilee located inside Israel. The Syrian Catholics maintain a rite separate from Greek or Roman Catholics, despite their small numbers in Syria, Iraq, Beirut, and Cairo. Small numbers of Roman Catholics who follow the Latin Rite and the Church in Rome, as opposed to the Uniate Churches, also reside throughout the Middle East.

Chaldeans

The Chaldean Catholic Church, the second oldest Uniate Church, is affiliated with the Roman Catholic Church through the Eastern Rite. Followers of the Church are usually referred to as Chaldeans, and they use

Classical Aramaic or Syriac in their liturgy and services. The term *Chaldean* refers to Aramaic tribes who created the Second Babylonian Empire from 605 B.C.E. to 550 B.C.E., which later fell to the Persians. The Chaldeans built the Hanging Gardens on the rooftops of Babylon, which are considered one of the Seven Wonders of the Ancient World. The leader of the Church, the Patriarch of Babylon, lives in Mosul, Iraq; the church has dioceses in Iraq, Syria, Lebanon, as well as Iran. Like the Assyrians and some Syrians, Chaldeans speak Aramaic in their homes and daily life, although they also usually speak Arabic fluently. Worldwide, Chaldeans number approximately 195,000, including a substantial community in the United States, particularly in Detroit and Chicago. Chaldeans usually consider themselves Chaldeans, not Arabs.

Orthodox Christians

Numerous churches in the Middle East are not allied with the Holy See of Rome. The largest of the Eastern Churches is the Greek Orthodox Church; its followers call themselves Orthodox Christians or, more simply, Orthodox. The smaller churches that are not in communion with the Vatican are the Armenian (Gregorian) Church, the Eastern (or Assyrian) church of the Nestorians, and the Syrian Jacobite Church. The Coptic Church is also not in communion with Rome and will be discussed further. All of these churches do not believe in the universal primacy or the infallibility of the Pope and celebrate different rituals. The Greek Orthodox Archdiocese is under the care of the Patriarchate of Constantinople, one of the original Byzantine Patriarchates. Like other churches, the Orthodox Church is hierarchal with the Greek Patriarch at the top, followed by more local Arab archbishops, bishops, and priests. Although there is no official liturgical language, most services are held in Arabic. The Eastern Orthodox Church emphasizes the more mystical aspects of Christianity, especially the Resurrection of Christ and the deification of man. Several hundred thousand Orthodox Christians live in Lebanon, Syria, Jordan, and Egypt. Most of the Greek Orthodox in the Arab world consider themselves Arabs, but the smaller eastern churches have different ethnic affiliations, some dating back to medieval times.

Copts

Copts are the largest of the Christian groups in the Middle East and number approximately 6 million strong, forming 10 percent of Egypt's population. The word *Copt* derives from the Greek word for Egyptian, and the Copts consider themselves descendents of the ancient Egyptian pha-raohs. Most Copts are from the Coptic Orthodox Church, although there is also a Coptic Catholic Church as well as Coptic Protestants. Copts are mostly concentrated in Cairo and the fertile lands of upper Egypt, along southern reaches of the Nile Valley. Coptic monasticism dates back to the fourth century C.E., and Copts were among the earliest Christians. After the seventh-century Arab conquests of Egypt, the Copts did not convert to Islam, choosing to maintain their own strong identity. A Coptic Patriarch leads the Orthodox Church, and the church's liturgy and sacred texts are in the Coptic language, which descends from ancient Egyptian and Greek. The Copts tend to consider themselves Pharaonic, or specifically Egyptian, rather than Arab.

Protestants

British and American missionaries and educators of the late nineteenth and early twentieth centuries brought their religion to the Arab world and estab-lished churches and schools, including the American University of Beirut. As a result of their activities and contact with locals, some Christians (mostly from the Orthodox faith), as well as Druze, converted to Protestantism. Several thousand of their descendents live in Egypt, Jordan, Syria, Palestine, Iraq, and Lebanon in both rural and urban areas. The Protestants are mainly Presbyterians and Anglicans—Presbyterians living in Lebanon and Syria, and Anglicans in Palestine and Jordan, according to the national and related religious orientation of the missionaries. Both Egypt and Iraq have a combi-nation of the two sects. Protestants generally consider themselves Arabs.

Jews

The voices of Arab Jews have been muted in the Arab American com-munity, the Arab world, and in Israel, because their identity as Arabs and as Jews is considered so controversial that they are looked on with suspicion. However, the term *Arab* refers to a common language and shared cultures, even if there are religious distinctions among Arab Muslims, Christians, and Jews. Approximately 800,000 Arab Jews lived in the Middle East pre-1948 when most left for Israel on its establishment. There are now only vestiges of the once-vibrant Jewish communities that existed in the major capitals of the Arab world, including Baghdad, Tunis, Cairo, and in the countryside of Morocco and Yemen. It is estimated that about 8,000 Jews are scattered across the Arab world, with the largest number residing in Morocco and

Yemen. Arab Jews use Arabic as a language of communication in the home and in their community as well as in their religious services at the synagogue. Most Jews who live in Israel use Hebrew as their first and main language of communication. Immigration to Israel marked a shift in language as well as identity for many Arab Jews. Because of the great controversy over the perceived conflict in affiliations, many have abandoned the term *Arab* when referring to their community, preferring to use other terms such as Oriental Jews, Sephardim, or, in Israel, Mizrahi.

Non-Arab Minorities

Some other minorities who do not speak Arabic as a first language live in the Arab world, such as the Armenians, Kurds, and Berbers. Beyond the differences in language, there are few cultural differences between these minorities and the larger society. On the whole, the laws prevalent in the Arab world have not been enough to protect the rights of minorities. When these non-Arab minorities emigrate, their tensions and differences with Arabs, which may have seemed so important and insurmountable in the Arab world, can diminish.

NOTES

1. Philip K. Hitti, *The Arabs: A Short History.* 2d ed., rev. (Washington, D.C.: Regnery, 1970), 61.

2. Roger Owen, *State, Power and Politics in the Making of the Modern Middle East,* 2d ed. (New York: Routledge, 2000), 241.

3. All Quranic quotes included refer to the translation by Abdullah Yusuf Ali, trans., *The Meaning of the Holy Quran,* 5th ed., rev. (Brentwood, MD: Amana, 1989).

4. John L. Esposito, *Islam: The Straight Path,* 3d ed. (New York: Oxford University Press, 1998), 19.

5. Paul Lunde, *Islam: Faith, Culture, History* (New York: Dorling Kindersleely, 2002), 141, 143.

6. Esposito, 47.

7. Lunde, 137.

8. Patrick Seale, *Asad of Syria: The Struggle for the Middle East* (Berkeley: University of California Press, 1989), 8.

2

Coming to the United States

Developments in the Middle East and North Africa region as well as U.S. immigration laws have profoundly affected the creation and evolution of the Arab American community. The push and pull factors behind the choice to immigrate have created three historical phases that form layers in the Arab American community. Motivated by the lure of economic opportunity, sojourners and settlers, mostly from Lebanon and Syria, came to the United States between 1880 and 1924 and established trade networks, and residency across the country. In the second phase of Arab American history, 1925–65, relatively few newcomers arrived, and the residents and their children mostly assimilated into mainstream society. The topmost layer within the Arab American community consists of the newest immigrants who have arrived since 1965, and their children.

U.S. IMMIGRATION LAWS

Immigration laws have punctuated the two waves of Arab immigration into the United States. The early wave of Arab American immigration started in earnest in the 1880s and continued until the laws changed in the 1920s. From colonial times until the passage of the Quota Act of 1921 and the Johnson-Reed Immigration Act (1924), Arabs were able to emigrate unfettered by quotas. The Quota Act of 1921 sought to severely curb migration from countries outside Northern and Western Europe; it banned all immigrants from Asia and reduced the numbers permitted into the country from Southern and Eastern Europe as well as the Ottoman Empire. The U.S. government determined numerical limits for the latter group by allowing in 2 percent of the group's foreign-born population in the 1890 Census. Because the first wavers had only just started arriving in the United States in 1880, very few Arabic-speaking immigrants were admitted into the country for three to four decades thereafter, effectively ending the first wave of Arab American immigration. The drastic decline in the number of new immigrants into the community, combined with the pervasive fear and prejudice of the early 1920s, ushered in a period in which Arab Americans settled down and mainly focused on assimilating into mainstream society in the United States. This period stretched from 1925 until 1965.

The passage of the Immigration Act of 1965 marked a significant change in U.S. immigration policy from one that favored immigration from Europe to a more equal approach to people from non-European areas of the world. The act established an annual overall quota of 170,000 immigrants with a fixed cap of 120,000 from the Western Hemisphere (a first) and an annual country maximum of 20,000 immigrant visas. From 1965 until the present day, preferences for immigrant visas are given for family reunification, refugees, and highly skilled workers. As a direct result of the new immigration policies between 1965 and 1992, 400,000 Arabs immigrated to the United States. Other destinations of choice include Australia, Canada, South America, and Europe. However, the long lines of people seeking visas at the U.S. embassies throughout the Middle East continue to testify to the popularity of the United States as a destination.

Since 2001, immigration officials have made it harder for Arab nationals to immigrate to the United States. After the September 11, 2001, terrorist attacks, security officials looked at how the perpetrators had entered the United States and found that the hijackers were all male, Arab nationals who had entered the United States by land and air, many with visas in their real names. As a direct result, U.S. immigration authorities increasingly focused on nationality, specifically targeting Arab and Muslim men. Visa applications of students, tourists, and businesspeople from the Middle East and North Africa were more likely to be rejected after 9/11, reducing the number of new immigrants as well as cross-cultural exchanges. Those residing in the United States with expired visas or in the country illegally were detained, jailed, and sometimes deported. Because immigration laws were unevenly applied to Arabs and Muslims, many viewed this selective enforcement as tantamount to racial profiling.

Targeting a large noncitizen proportion, this enforcement weighed heavily on the community and organizations tasked with protecting Arab Americans against discriminatory treatment. According to the 2000 Census, there are substantial differentials between the total population and the population of those of Arab ancestry in terms of birth abroad, nativity, and citizenship.

As Table 2.1 shows, whereas 6.6 percent of the total population is noncitizens, slightly more than one-fourth of the people of Arab ancestry were not citizens in 2000. Taking under consideration the Census Bureau's population estimate of 850,000 in its definition of a person of Arab ancestry examined in the sample group, this means, then, that 215,050 Arabs in the United States have temporary and permanent green cards, student or work visas, or were out-of-status with immigration authorities. These statistics reflect the strong impact that the changes to the immigration laws and subsequent enforcement have had on the Arab American community.

In November 2002 the Homeland Security Act became law. This act transferred the Immigration and Naturalization Services (INS) functions to the newly created Department of Homeland Security (DHS). INS immigration services were transferred to a new bureau called U.S. Citizenship and Immigration Services (USCIS), while INS enforcement oversight was placed within the Directorate of Border and Transportation Security, Customs and Border Protection, or Immigration and Customs Enforcement.

In 2003, the DHS implemented a Special Registration program formally known as the National Security Entry/Exit Registration System. Under this program, males older than the age of 16 who had entered the United States

Table 2.1
Comparisons of Nativity and Citizenship Status in Census 2000

	Arab ancestry of non-mixed heritage (%)	General U.S. population (%)
Native (born in the United States)	46.4	88.9
Foreign-born, Naturalized Citizen	28.3	4.5
Foreign-born, Not a Citizen	25.3	6.6

Source: Angela Brittingham and G. Patricia de la Cruz, *We the People of Arab Ancestry in the United States, Census 2000 Special Reports* (Washington, DC: U.S. Census Bureau, 2005), 8; also available online at http://www.census.gov/population/www/cen2000/briefs.html#sr.

since October 2002 from certain countries were required to report to immigration offices to be photographed and fingerprinted on an annual basis. This included nationals from Afghanistan, Algeria, Bahrain, Bangladesh, Egypt, Eritrea, Indonesia, Iran, Iraq, Jordan, Kuwait, Lebanon, Libya, Morocco, North Korea, Oman, Pakistan, Qatar, Saudi Arabia, Somalia, Sudan, Syria, Tunisia, United Arab Emirates, and Yemen. Immigration enforcement, particularly this program, was focused on Arabs and Muslims: 19 of the 25 countries listed were Arab; with the exception of North Korea, all were either Arab or predominantly Muslim countries. According to the American Immigration Lawyers Association, those men who reported to the immigration offices were "subject to arbitrary arrest, detention, abuse and possible deportation" for being out-of-status with the immigration authorities.[1] Although the main features of this program were suspended in December 2003, the men that fall into the Special Registration categories still must report to the USCIS at specially designated ports of entry before departing the United States. Nonimmigrants who are citizens or nationals of Iraq, Iran, Syria, Libya, and Sudan continue to be subject to Special Registration upon entry to the United States, and "others can be designated for Special Registration on a case-by-case basis."

As a result of this and other initiatives, in the two-year period after 9/11, the number of deportation orders from the 24 predominantly Muslim nations increased 31.4 percent over the preceding two-year period. There was only a 3.4 percent rise in deportation orders from other countries in the comparable time period. These facts caused Arab American leaders to file formal complaints of racial profiling. One lawyer for the American-Arab Anti-Discrimination Committee (ADC) summarized the opinion of many leaders when he said, "We're not saying not to enforce the laws. But this is selective enforcement."[2] The rise in security concerns has caused widespread racial profiling of Arab Americans that continues today; at issue is finding a way to ensure national security without violating the inherent civil rights of Arab Americans.

CAUSES AND CHARACTERISTICS OF IMMIGRATION

Arabs in America, 1400–1880

Commercial ties rather than immigration first brought the United States and Arab world together before 1880. It is believed that the first Arabs came to what is now the United States with the Spanish explorers of the fifteenth century. Arabs also actively traded with the early colonies, and by the late

1700s, countries in North Africa formed economic and political alliances with the American revolutionaries. Algerians exported horses to replenish George Washington's cavalry, depleted by the War of Independence. In 1779 when an Algerian ship wrecked off the coast of the rebelling colonies, the mariners chose to settle down in North Carolina. The descendents of the Wahab family of North Carolina, therefore, can claim to be the first Arab settlers in the United States. Morocco was the first country to officially recognize the independence of the United States in the Treaty of Friendship between Mohammad III of Morocco and George Washington in 1787. Since that time, trade and commercial goods from the Middle East have had an important impact on U.S.–Arab relations.

Some celebrated cases of Arabs who moved to the new republic before 1876 are Jeremiah Mahomet in Frederick, Maryland; Antoun Bishallany in New York (1854); and Hadji Ali, a camel driver known as Hi Jolly, in Arizona (1856). These early immigrants came to the United States in search of adventure and out of curiosity, intending to return to the Middle East with interesting stories and perhaps some money in their pockets. Despite their initial intentions, most of the early adventurers never returned home and died, without children, of old age or of diseases, such as tuberculosis, in the United States.

To mark the one-hundredth anniversary of the United States, Philadelphia hosted the Centennial Exhibition in 1876. The Ottoman Sultan, Abdul Hamid II, accepted the invitation to exhibit wares on the fairground and encouraged his subjects to display goods that highlighted the glories of the Ottoman Empire. Arabs and Turks sent 1,600 individuals and firms, winning 129 awards—more than all the exhibitors except the United States and Britain. The Arab traders and artisans sold a range of goods from cotton to coffee and found that their goods, particularly olivewood rosaries and crosses that were carved in Jerusalem, were in demand. Other popular exhibits were the Tunisian café that served coffee, sweets, and water pipes; and the Moroccan kiosk that was imported intact to sell arts and crafts from North Africa. The tradesmen were so impressed with their sales and the technology in the exhibition that some stayed on and set up import businesses. Others returned home with American goods and tales of the riches to be had in America. The 1876 Exhibition, which showed Arabs that one could become prosperous in the United States, is thus credited with starting the first real wave of migration from the Arab world.

The First Wave, 1880–1924

During the Great Migration (1880–1924), more than 20 million immigrants came to the United States from all over the world. At its peak in

1905–7, more than 1 million people a year immigrated, mostly from Eastern Europe, Italy, and Greece. As part of that period in U.S. history, 95,000 Arabs came from the Levant, and smaller numbers came from Yemen, Iraq, Morocco, and Egypt. Many of the original newcomers stayed and had families in the United States. By 1924, it is estimated that there were approximately 200,000 Arabs living in the United States.[3]

Among the first wave of Arab immigrants, about 90 percent were Christian, with the remaining being Druze and Sunni Muslim. The Christians were mainly Maronites, although Melkites and Greek Orthodox were among the disproportionate numbers of Christians emigrating from the Levant. One historian estimates that 90 to 95 percent of the immigrants originated from Mount Lebanon, but another estimates that about 10 percent came from Palestine, then under Ottoman rule.[4] It is hard to estimate such numbers because of the conflation of all Arabs under the category of "Turkey in Asia" or "Syria." The immigrants arrived with some money in their pockets—between 1899 and 1903 the average amount per capita was $31.85 for Syrians—placing them in the median range of all immigrants showing money at ports of entry.[5] The immigrants were farmers and merchants by profession and most were landowners, even if they only owned a small plot of land. Few of the immigrants could both read and write Arabic, indicating that many did not have more than a basic education in the missionary schools prevalent in Mount Lebanon at the time.

Nineteenth-century missionary activity in the Levant unintentionally contributed to the attractiveness of the United States. Christian missionaries from the United States and Europe went to the Middle East to convert Muslims and Eastern Christians to Protestant Christianity. Although their efforts were largely unsuccessful in the religious sphere, they did have a substantial impact on the literacy and education in the region. Missionaries set up schools and colleges, many of which are thriving today. For example, in Lebanon, missionaries established the Syrian Protestant College in 1866, later renamed the American University of Beirut, and the Beirut College for Women, now called the Lebanese-American University. Americans devoted to education and service in the Middle East founded the American University in Cairo in 1919. These universities are considered first-rate in the region today.

The missionaries made a good impression on the local people, and many thought the American people kind and generous. The missionaries taught Arabs English and shared photos and political ideologies that may have led some people to consider immigrating.[6] They showed that the United States was friendly to Christians, and it must have been an easier decision for Christians to move to a land where they could be assured that they would not be persecuted for their religious beliefs. Perhaps this accounts for the disparity in the numbers of Christians versus Muslims emigrating from the Arab world. Muslims and Druze may have been discouraged from emigrating for fear that the society would be unfriendly and possibly hostile toward their religious beliefs. The few Muslims and Druze who did move to the United States tended to do so with Arab Christian friends and were less likely to bring their families with them.

The vanguard of the early period in the first wave, 1880–1910, were therefore single men between 14 and 40 years old.[7] Women were a small proportion of the immigrants from the Ottoman Empire until 1899; thereafter, the percentage of women increased steadily. According to available immigration figures, women were only 32 percent of the total immigration between 1899 and 1910; from 1919 to 1930, they were 47.5 percent.[8] Almost all of the first female immigrants were Christian.

Most immigrants knew very little of the country that they were immigrating to—only that it was a place full of financial opportunity. What they did know was gleaned from the idealized stories told by missionaries and returning migrants Despite the fact that the "average Syrian peasant was a landowner," the main pull factor for the early wave from Greater Syria was earning money quickly and returning home with wealth enough to bring them and their families social prestige and luxury.[9] Only one-fourth of the immigrants did in fact return to Lebanon, but many of them chose to re-emigrate to the United States. Whether or not they left for the second time, they brought back wealth and stories that fuelled the so-called American fever—a departure of scores of others across the Atlantic. Another attraction for these young men, and a few women, in the 1880s most likely was the excitement of going to a new land and having fascinating adventures. As more emigrated, networks were established so that an émigré would know exactly where he or she was moving in the country, whom he or she would be working for, and where he or she would be living. As time went on, the adventure became more of a calculated risk for financial betterment rather than a thrilling journey into the unknown.

However alluring the economic gains and adventure of the United States were, there would have been little immigration without some push factors. Although there has been much debate about the role of the Ottoman rulers, taxation, religious strife, and political turmoil, the period of 1861–1914 was relatively calm and prosperous for Mount Lebanon. In late nineteenth-century and early twentieth-century Lebanon, emigration was caused by the raised material expectations of villagers and farmers: "Emigration, which deprived Lebanon of at least a third of its population, was not the result of poverty or persecution. Men left the Mountain in search of a way to guarantee, and possibly improve on, a standard of living they had grown accustomed to during the good times of the 1860s."[10]

The most important crop on Mount Lebanon was silk, and by 1879, the majority of the income for peasants on Mount Lebanon was linked to the silk industry. The 1860s and 1870s were prosperous times, and silk prices were high. By the 1880s, the price of silk was declining, while the growing population was making increasing demands on the land. Many of the generation born after 1860 expected to improve on the living standards of their parents and were disappointed when they were unable to do so. This disappointment led many younger peasants to emigrate from their villages to the United States.

These young men and women had to first raise enough money to bribe the Ottoman officials, pay for the voyage, and have as a cushion until they could establish themselves in their new country. The cost of a travel permit was often more than it cost to bribe the police officers to get onto the boats heading for Marseilles, Barcelona, or Liverpool. On arrival in Europe, the émigré would wait in the port area for a second boat to South, Central, or North America. They traveled in the lowest level of accommodations on board called "steerage," which was packed to the maximum without adequate food, water, or sanitation. The journey was an opportunity to get to know other émigrés and make new friends from other villages. As was evidenced by the sinking of the *Titanic,* on which more than 100 Syrians died, this cross-Atlantic journey was often hazardous. Unscrupulous ship operators exploited the aspiring emigrants by overcharging them for the journey or taking them to other destinations. Many thought they were going to New York, and on arrival, they discovered that they were in fact in South America.

During the first decade of the twentieth century, the motivations of immigrants changed from one of financial amelioration to desperation. The conscription of young Christian and Druze men of the Mountain into the Ottoman Army from 1908 onward caused many young men to flee their villages to avoid death, because Arab troops were stationed on the front line of battle. In 1917 the British and French Allied fleet instituted a blockade of the coasts of Syria and Lebanon to prevent food from being exported from the Mountain to feed the Ottoman soldiers on the battlefront. The blockade achieved its aim and stopped imported foodstuffs and remittances from abroad from entering the region. The seizure of foodstuffs by Ottoman soldiers, a yellow fever epidemic, and a destructive earthquake in 1918 further compounded the deleterious effects of the Allied naval blockade. It is estimated that one-fourth of the population of Mount Lebanon died of starvation during World War I.[11]

As with European immigrants, desperation and food shortages were obvious push factors for emigration during the latter end of the decade.

The departure of many young men and a few women in the 1880s created new circumstances on Mount Lebanon by the 1890s. The traditional patriarchal structure relied on a gendered division of labor—men worked outside the home, and women had children and cared for the family. As the men left, women became the central focus of the family, dealing with the farming and family decisions. Although most left with the intention of sending money back to their family in the form of remittances, the emigrants sent little money back in the first few years, and "that which was sent was intended mainly for buying up property in the man's name."[12] This left some overburdened and angry women on the Mountain. Throughout the entire wave of migration (1880–1924), most women who emigrated were married and went to join their husbands and share the burdens of raising a family, or they went without their husbands to improve the family finances or to escape bad marriages, such as poet and artist Kahlil Gibran's mother did in 1895.[13] If these married women returned after three or four years, they reportedly brought with them $300 or $400, with which many purchased land to grow crops for sale and subsistence. In this period, a large percentage (38.6%) of female immigrants above the age of 18 years old were unmarried.[14] By the mid-1890s, single men rarely returned to their villages to find a bride. By the turn of the century, single women began to emigrate to find a husband or to escape the drudgery of village life and gain the freedom that comes with disposable income and a different society. The choice of single women in the Mount Lebanon villages to emigrate also showed that the villagers were aware that the men had permanently moved to the United States.

After 1899, significant numbers of women arrived in the United States, and many families moved their home base from Mount Lebanon permanently. The men-only boarding houses were obviously inappropriate for married couples, and so the husbands moved out and set up their own family homes. This move marked a social change, as the sojourners became settlers who realized that the United States was home.

The Second Wave, 1925–1965

The second phase of Arab American history (1925–65) was mainly one of assimilation and acculturation. Although wives and dependent children of U.S. citizens were not counted toward the quotas imposed in the 1920s, few nonrelative immigrants were permitted to enter the country. The lack of newcomers from back home until the 1950s created a vacuum of communication between the Arab world and the community in the United States. As the primordial ties with the village and family loosened, there was a corresponding tightening of the ties with United States. Many Arab Americans assimilated into the mainstream, de-emphasizing their ethnic backgrounds at home as well as in public. During this period, many Arab Americans blended into mainstream and became invisible as an ethnic minority.

After World War II, revolutions and wars dominated the political and economic realities in Arab world. Some Arab elites came as political exiles, especially from Iraq, Egypt, and Palestine. The first Palestinians in the second wave were those with relatives living in the United States or those who already had U.S. citizenship. In all, almost 6,000 Palestinians came as political refugees in the 1950s and 1960s. In 1953, the U.S. Congress passed the Refugee Relief Act to accommodate refugees, particularly Palestinian refugees, as a separate immigration category. Under this law, (extended in 1957), almost 3,000 Palestinians were admitted to the United States between 1953 and 1963.[15] Many arrived with little financial resources. After the Refugee Relief Act, approximately 3,000 additional Palestinians came to the United States. More came as students and stayed after they finished their educational programs, so they were not accounted for in the statistics. Among the immigrants during this period were two renowned Arab American intellectuals of Palestinian origin: the late Columbia University Professor Edward Said, who came from Cairo in 1951 to attend prep school in Connecticut, and the late Ibrahim Abu-Lughod, who came to the United States in 1950 as a graduate student. Others, such as Hisham Sharabi, were at U.S. graduate schools when the 1948 war broke out and had little choice but to stay.

In the 1950s, a different type of immigrant moved from the Arab world to the United States: the elites. Although some Palestinians, such as Said, were from the upper class, most Palestinian immigrants were not. Most of the other Arab immigrants between 1950 and 1965 were members of the leadership in Egypt, Syria, and Iraq who were fleeing popular revolutions and new regimes that were confiscating their lands and wealth in their home countries. The 1952 revolution in Egypt and the 1958 revolt against the Iraqi monarchy left those associated with the previous regimes out of favor. Diplomats posted outside the country at the time often stayed in the host country, including those posted to the United States. Coptic Christians and middle-class Muslims concerned about the economy and religious freedom after the revolution also left Egypt for the United States or Europe. These exiled elites arrived educated, with strong English-language skills, and with vast resources. They generally moved to cosmopolitan areas and had little in common with the earlier wave of Arab immigrants.

The Third Wave, 1965–present

Between 1965 and 1992, more than 400,000 Arab immigrants arrived in the United States because of the changes in the immigration law and quotas as well as further upheavals in the Arab world. This third wave was substantially larger than the second wave and three times the size of the first wave. Although the first and second wavers had had children and their numbers had increased, the third wavers would become another substantial layer in the community.

The rise of pan-Arabism, charismatic leaders, and visions of greater prosperity gave many Arabs high hopes for the future in the 1950s and early 1960s. The defeat in the 1967 Six-Day War humiliated Arabs as well as their armies, ending a period of relative optimism and shattering the myth of Arab strength and unity. As a result, many Arabs were disillusioned and pessimistic about the future of the Arab world and chose to move to the United States and other non-Arab countries. There was a peak in immigration after the defeat in the Six-Day War, and other miniwaves of immigration stemming from other political events.

Since 1967, economic policies and wars have encouraged a cross-section of Arabs to emigrate. Because of the civil war and strife, 90,000 people emigrated from Lebanon from 1965 to 1992, and thousands of Palestinians, Syrians, Jordanians, and Egyptians have left their birthplaces. In the last 40 years, each of these labor sending countries experienced major political upheavals that have acted as propelling mechanisms for emigration.

The war in Lebanon from 1975 to 1991 forced many Lebanese and Palestinians living in Lebanon to fear for their lives and come to the United States, whether or not they had relatives who were citizens. The 1991 Gulf War impacted many communities, causing substantial migrations of people within and outside the region. In the 1990s, ordinary Iraqis fled the country because of food shortages caused by the U.N. sanctions and the extreme measures of Saddam Hussein's regime. Saudi Arabia, Kuwait, and other Gulf countries expelled thousands of its Palestinian and Yemeni workers in the early 1990s because of their leaders' positions on the Gulf War. As they returned to Yemen, Jordan, Lebanon, Syria, and the Palestinian territories, these workers had to find alternative employment in countries with high unemployment rates. Many Palestinians and Yemenis were forced to leave the region entirely in search of jobs. Palestinians, who are often recorded as being from Jordan, Syria, Lebanon, or the Gulf countries, probably form the largest segment of the recent immigrants. Egyptians working in the Gulf were affected by the disruptions of the war. Governmental corruption, mismanagement, and autocratic regimes have spurred on emigration from the Arab world. These recent immigrants are from a wide variety of social and economic backgrounds and are approximately evenly divided between men and women. Although they treasure the safety of the United States, many did not see their immigration as permanent, particularly those who fled their country only because of war. Rather, they expected to return one day to their country when it is at peace and full of job opportunities.

A good number of these immigrants came to the United States for postgraduate education or for career reasons, never expecting to return. Between 1965 and 1976, 15 percent of the immigrants were educated professionals and highly skilled technical workers. The educational system in many Arab countries was substantially upgraded after independence, and by 1975, Arab countries such as Iraq, Egypt, and Lebanon could boast of excellent universities in their capitals. The number of university graduates increased in the late 1960s and 1970s, but the number of jobs available did not correspond with their skills level. With few job prospects, many saw immigration as their only option for career advancement, and so they left, contributing to the serious problem in the development of the Arab world that is called the "brain drain."

The graduate educational opportunities available in the United States provided one of the incentives for many young, bright Arabs to emigrate. Although Arab universities had good facilities, U.S. schools offered superior academic programs, equipped with the latest technology for medical and engineering schools. Therefore, wealthier parents sent their children to the United States for undergraduate or graduate schools. Arab governments and U.S. institutions such as AMIDEAST also helped to facilitate the training of professionals in the United States, believing that they would return to their home countries, skilled and ready to contribute to their society and economy. But the corruption, stagnated economies, flat job market, and poor financial prospects back home forced many to rethink the concept of returning after their schooling was completed. Although some did in fact return, many stayed in the United States where educational opportunities developed into career networks and employment options. These skilled laborers and educated professionals established permanent residency because the lifestyle was better, and income was significantly more substantial than that which would be possible back home.

Other pull factors were the political institutions, tolerance of differences, and the guarantees of individual rights in the United States. Most of the post-1965 immigrants are Muslims who value the freedom to worship and the ability to establish mosques. As versions of Islamic fundamentalism grew, they pushed moderate and secular Muslims to leave Muslim-majority countries, making the United States an attractive option. The right to worship was also important to many Christians who emigrated after 1965. The Iraqi Chaldeans and the Egyptian Copts in particular believed they were in a disadvantageous and discriminatory position in their respective countries. The right of individuals to take pride in and display their ethnicity has been a pull factor for immigrants from all over the world. The rise of multiculturalism as the dominant social philosophy since the 1970s increased tolerance for differences and allowed for expression of heritage, language, and customs.

SETTLEMENT PATTERNS

The main point of entry for Syrians before 1924 was New York Harbor— first through Castle Garden and then Ellis Island, which opened in 1892. Other popular ports of entry were New Orleans, Boston, Philadelphia, Providence, and Baltimore. After the long journey by boat with dreams of setting foot on *terra firma,* every immigrant had to pass a medical test and go through an interview process. Many were turned away because of trachoma, an eye inflammation, and were returned to their villages without their families. Others circumvented U.S. immigration officials by going through Mexico or the Caribbean. Some families chose to continue their journey and join relatives in South or Central America. Today, there are descendents of early Lebanese migrants in Peru, Brazil, Venezuela, and other South American countries.

U.S. border officials usually did not speak Arabic and, as with other immigrants, the Arab names were anglicized on entry into the country. The long Arabic names were shortened and then made pronounceable for English speakers. The new name was often a dramatic change from their inherited identity: for example, "Yaccoub" became "Jacobs" and "Qaseem" became "Kasem." This initial name change heralded in a series of dislocations of identity in the United States.

For aspiring and actual immigrants, New York City embodied and represented the United States. "Nayirk" was often used in conversation interchangeably with the United States, which was generalized to be America, which in turn was called "Merka." New York, known as the Mother Colony for the early settlers, had the most diverse and most concentrated population of Arabs before 1900. The area around Washington Street in Lower Manhattan became known as "Little Syria," an ethnic enclave with many Arab-owned businesses and residents. It was to serve as the intellectual center for Arab Americans between 1880 and 1910 and was the base for many Arab American social institutions. Washington Street was full of noise and activity with weaving factories, storefronts, and cafés serving bubbling water pipes and coffee. Almost all of the intellectuals resided in New York City, and they played important roles in leading the community, founding churches, organizations, newspapers, and Republican and Democratic Clubs in the 1890s.

Little Syria was the commercial center for Arab Americans in its heyday. The first Arab-owned bank (founded by the Faour brothers) was established to provide capital for the new businesses. Some stores in Little Syria were import houses that bought cutwork embroidery from Italy and laces and silk from France and had workers from China and the Philippines making inexpensive goods for them, long before it became an economic trend. The stores also fuelled demand for cottage industry items, such as cheaper laces sewn in Mount Lebanon. They imported food, kitchen utensils, water pipes, and cultural items, such as musical instruments, from back home for the comfort of their fellow villagers residing throughout the United States. Many of the stores were dry goods stores.

Trade in Little Syria revolved around the peddling profession. In the 1880s, the new immigrants made their way directly to contacts in Little Syria. Once there, the owner of a supply store provided the immigrant with a little training and goods to sell. Between 1880 and 1910, most newcomers from Mount Lebanon became peddlers, traveling from place to place, selling goods and wares to customers. In their first few days in the United States, new arrivals were tested selling goods on the streets of New York, returning to a basic boarding house at night. After they had honed their skills and found the peddling trade acceptable, the peddlers would move out of the city, seeking new customers, usually in less urban areas.

The most common trade was pack peddling. The resulting stereotyped image of the early Arab immigrant inspired the character of Hakim in the Broadway musical *Oklahoma!*—an olive-skinned young man who sold goods to farms from a cart. The stereotype sidelined the role of women; by 1903 more than one-third of Syrian pack peddlers were women. Some found the peddling trade repulsive, but both men and women found it grueling work. The peddler would obtain his or her supplies on credit from stores, manufacturers, or warehouses that were usually owned by fellow villagers. Sometimes the peddler would make items himself or herself or have relatives sew finished pieces. His or her *qashshah,* or pack, would be full of goods such as holy items (rosaries and crucifixes), toiletries, notions (buttons, thread, ribbons, needles, and laces), handkerchiefs, trinkets, cloth (including linens), jewelry, clothing, garters, and suspenders. The peddler would carry as much as possible, and the pack could weigh between 50 and 200 pounds. The peddler would then walk door-to-door, selling her or his wares and sleeping wherever a spot could be found, sometimes in the homes or barns of customers and sometimes out in the cold. His or her personality and charm would determine whether he or she would get a hot meal at night as well as how many items he or she would sell each day.

As more peddlers entered the trade, a network of settlements fanned out from New York City. Many of the first wavers chose to not stay in the port cities and traveled by boat or train to find a spot less inundated by commercial outlets to set up their base. Sailing up from New Orleans, first wavers started businesses in Vicksburg, Mississippi, and other points along the Mississippi, Missouri, and Ohio Rivers. Supply points were established in cities and towns in the Northeast, then in the Midwest, and on the West Coast by the 1880s. The networks were headed by a merchandise supplier who received shipments and refilled inventory sold via parcel post or express delivery from the stores in Little Syria or other ports such as New Orleans. New York stores supplied Utica and Buffalo; New Orleans stores supplied settlements in Mississippi, Louisiana, and Texas; and St. Louis stores supplied the Midwest, including Indiana, Iowa, and the Dakotas. These merchandise suppliers would set up receiving stations, often along rail lines, for peddlers to pick up more goods, as the peddlers often traveled for months at a time. The local merchandise suppliers played a central role in the lives of peddlers through managing their finances, organizing peddling routes to prevent overlap, and running boarding houses for them to stay in between trips. Although the favor of the head of the settlement could impact the amount of income earned, the peddler remained his or her own boss with the independence to move to another city or choose another supplier. Some peddlers, particularly women, chose not to do overnight trips and instead sold in a city or in the immediate rural area, returning home at night.

The early settlers must have looked very foreign to Americans. In addition to their large packs, the itinerant peddlers wore roomy white collarless shirts and baggy black pants that had multiple folds from the hip to the crotch and then tapered to the ankles. They might also wear a fringed headscarf, a black vest, and waist sash. If they were dressing up or in the city, they would don a *tarboosh*—a red felt hat in the shape of a truncated cone, with a black tassel—and a suit. The women wore loose-fitting cotton blouses, long skirts, and a light shawl or kerchief over their hair.

New immigrants became peddlers because the trade required little training or English-language skills. The goods were sold on credit and only a small amount of capital investment was necessary to start trading. Other peddlers were Eastern European Jews, Greeks, Armenians, and Italians, and their trade gave many immigrants a better personal understanding of entrepreneurship as well as the American way of life and its emphasis on self-reliance and individuality. There were different types of peddlers, described according to the way they carried their goods. Pushcart or road peddlers sold their goods from mobile stands, which were wheeled throughout cities. Pack or foot peddlers carried goods on their backs, walking their goods to their customers. Although some Syrians were also pushcart peddlers, the early Arab immigrants specialized in pack peddling in rural and remote areas, including mining towns and farms as well as in heavily ethnic non–English-speaking neighborhoods. Indeed, there is evidence that some peddlers learned both English and German, which was widely spoken in the United States at the turn of the century. Some peddlers who worked in areas such as Texas also spoke Spanish. Arabs seemed to pick up these languages easily, and some even worked as translators and interpreters with the U.S. Immigration Service. The peddlers' main customers were women confined to the home because of language differences or remoteness of location. Although the life of a peddler was lonesome and tough, it enabled him or her to become financially successful. It is estimated that by 1910, American rural women had bought $60 million worth of goods from Syrian peddlers.[16]

Depending on their skills and goods, peddlers could earn up to $2,000 a year. The average peddler's income was $1,000, while industrial laborers earned an average of $650 a year, and the average per capita income for an American was $382 in 1910. Immigrants entered the world of peddlers to avoid dull factory work and to be outside in the fresh air with a sense of freedom and independence. Peddling must have been especially attractive to those accustomed to farming and to physical work outdoors. Peddlers would often barter their goods for food or other items, and so helped customers when they were short on cash. Even in harsh economic times, such as before harvest or in the Depression, peddlers were able to sell goods and to provide a service for families. Through establishing national networks, peddlers expanded markets and boosted profitability for products manufactured in the United States as well as suppliers in Europe and, to a lesser extent, Syria.

Considering the conditions and risks of peddling, it is perhaps surprising that women were involved in peddling. In fact, between 75 and 80 percent of the Arab American women peddled during the period 1880–1910. These women were considered to be more profitable and adept at the trade than men because they could more easily establish a rapport with the female customers and so increase sales. There were some well-known women peddlers who enjoyed the independence of overnight peddling but were usually accompanied by a close male relative (father, brother, or husband). More often, women were day peddlers who returned home at night. After they married, women might retire from peddling to take care of the children at home, but they sewed and crocheted items (another popular item was the Japanese kimono) for their male relatives to sell. If the need for extra cash arose, however, women returned to peddling for quick income, and Arab American women were known to have been peddling into the 1940s. This testifies to the fact that Arab American families, like other Americans, struggled financially during and after the Depression Era.

In the 1890s, some of the peddlers put down their packs and either bought new forms of transportation from which to peddle or opened a retail business. A horse and cart allowed the peddler to travel farther from the supply point. By replacing the pack with a cart or automobile, the peddler could carry more goods and was able to offer more expensive items, such as linens from Europe and Oriental rugs. This move to different forms of transportation to sustain the peddling industry was eclipsed by the arrival of the mail-order business. When companies such as Sears, Roebuck began their catalog mail-order business, and local department stores became more common, the need for door-to-door sales lessened. Improvements in transportation—cars, buses, and trains—delivered goods to the customer, and the peddling industry faded by 1910. In 1915, a New York State census found that peddling was no longer in the top five areas of employment for employed Syrian heads of households.

By the early 1900s, more peddlers were beginning to make the commitment to permanent settlements, and they generally clustered in Arab neighborhoods at old supply points, known as a *hara*. The typical *hara* was small, usually not more than 20 families, and in a mixed white ethnic area that was within walking distance of the central business district of a town or city. Some of the families lived in three-generation households, as other family members joined their relatives in chain migration. Although there were exceptions, living in clusters was the norm for the early immigrants and their children. Some of the bigger cities and towns had larger *haras,* but there were no grand arches or other visible signs to declare to outsiders that they were now entering an ethnic enclave. The residents of the *hara* were usually from the same village and were often related and of the same religion. The residential arrangement fostered a sense of close relations and conversation as people sat out on their porches in the evening or congregated at neighborhood picnics. Itinerant preachers and non-Arab churches usually served the spiritual needs of the residents, but a few Eastern Rite churches and a few mosques were established. Other community institutions, such as social organizations and clubs, sometimes followed the building of churches, but the roots of these *haras* were shallow, and few institutions from this era have survived. However, before and during the Depression, these *haras* gave the first wavers and their families stability and a sense of security.

Many former peddlers used their marketing and entrepreneurial skills to become independent merchants in both the retail and wholesale trade. Arab Americans opened shops in the peddling settlements and at the supply points for peddlers. Dry goods stores in Cleveland, Ohio, and Cedar Rapids, Iowa, which stocked and refilled the peddlers' packs in the 1880s, sold the same goods to outside customers in the late 1890s. Ex-peddlers also opened up grocery stores, bakeries, clothing shops, and haberdasheries selling small wares and sewing supplies. Typically bearing the family name, these stores were a family endeavor. Children went to school by day and stocked the shelves and swept the floors by night. The men ran the stores and did the finances, while the women were in charge of the household and continued to make popular decorative items and clothing. Their home was often based above or behind the store, blurring the distinction between home and work. Some ex-peddlers catered to a more upscale clientele and sold more expensive goods in their new stores, including Oriental rugs, expensive fabrics, and embroidered linens, often provided by the import houses of Little Syria.

Not all Arab Americans were peddlers or storeowners. Muslims and Druze immigrants in particular were attracted to the farming opportunities available at the turn of the century. Arabs arrived after the Homestead Act of 1862, which gave land to anyone willing to farm it to encourage westward expansion. They moved out West and to the Midwest to farm, as they had in their villages. Druze set up colonies in Appalachia and farmed extensively in West Virginia. Yemenis traveled to California to farm and work in the San Joaquin Valley, leaving families back home and sending back half of their earnings.

Many Arab Americans worked in the factories of the Midwest and New England for a wage. In 1914, Ford Motor Company paid its workers the then-substantial amount of $5 for eight hours of work. In 1900, there were 50 men working at the plant in Detroit; by 1916, there were 555 Syrian men registered as employees. As a result, Detroit grew to be an important center for Arab Americans, especially for Muslims who were more likely to work in factories, lumber camps, and livery stables than were Christian immigrants. One possible explanation for this preference, when peddling could yield a higher income, is that peddling was harder for Muslims than for Christians, who could reach a comfort level with the farm wives by quoting from the

Bible and finding a religious commonality with their customers. Another explanation is that factory work was more stable, involving less risk and danger than peddling. The woolen mills of Woonsocket, Rhode Island, and the sardine canneries of East Maine, and textile factories of Fall River, Lowell, and Lawrence, Massachusetts, were popular places to work for Arabs who chose not to peddle. Others established their own manufacturing plants with their savings. Many of these businesses, such as Haggar slacks and the Jacobs Engineering Company, are still in business today.

By the eve of World War I in 1914, many Arab Americans were settled into their new land. When the United States entered the war, they were eager to serve their new country and fight their old enemies, the Ottoman Turks. Many did not wait for the draft and volunteered to go to war even if they had just fled their homeland to avoid conscription into the Ottoman Army. In all, 15,000 Syrians (or 7 percent of the Arab American community at the time) served as American infantrymen, or Doughboys, in World War I. Some were decorated for their valor. It is estimated that 64 percent of the New York Syrians bought $1.2 million worth of liberty war bonds to boost American efforts, and perhaps make a profit to boot.[17] From 1910 onward, Arab Americans founded Red Cross chapters and Boy Scout troops. World War I was a chance for the early settlers to oppose the Ottomans and be patriotic for their new country at the same time. Rising to the occasion, they found a stronger sense of belonging in the United States and social status as veterans in return.

After World War I, the pioneers strove to attain a better life for themselves and their families in the United States. The men moved from cramped, men-only boarding houses to their own homes and had families. Parents focused on their children's education as a way to improve the status of the next generation; they no longer went peddling for months at a stretch and instead enrolled their children in schools. Although Arabic was spoken in the *haras,* these children grew up to be bilingual, speaking Arabic at home and English at school. Many of the first settlers who were illiterate in both English and Arabic when they arrived had learned to read and write Arabic to communicate with family and friends back home. They also read Arabic newspapers published in New York to keep abreast of the news. However, by 1920, Arabs were writing fewer letters, and the only form of Arabic used frequently was colloquial, spoken Arabic at home. The efforts taken to learn how to read and write Arabic were lost on their children, who avoided speaking Arabic outside of their social community in the 1920s and 1930s.

The immigration laws and nativist attitudes of the 1920s and 1930s were constructed to protect the interests of Northern and Western European–descent immigrants against those of the other immigrants. This created an atmosphere in which assimilation was encouraged, and ethnic expression suppressed. The first English-language journal published for Arab Americans, *Syrian World,* stated that "race prejudice" was leading the second-generation Arab American to "look with contempt upon the language and queer customs of his parents."[18] The loss of language was one of the effects of the period of assimilation between the world wars.

The Roaring 1920s challenged the family values of many Arab Americans and pulled the second and third generations further from their parents' control and influence. Before 1920, marriage was considered very important and schooling for girls less practical. Most of the marriages were arranged by mothers, priests, or within the social networks that existed within the *hara,* or between communities in different towns. As the second generation attended school, they learned English and met friends outside the community and at church, if they attended a Roman Catholic Church. Romances blossomed, and mixed marriages became more commonplace.

The rising number of naturalized U.S. citizens in the community gave more Arab Americans the right to vote, and thus more political clout, as Arab Americans became more involved at the local level. A 1924 survey by the Syrian American Club found that only 50 percent of the Syrians eligible for citizenship were citizens. After a campaign to increase the numbers of voters, raise political awareness, and stress the greater importance of politics in the United States than in Lebanon, the percentage of citizens shot up to 75 percent relative to those eligible for citizenship.[19] Some Arab Americans won local office, proving that they could participate in mainstream politics.

The Depression of the 1930s challenged the wealth and ties of the Arab American community. As the Great Depression took its toll on all Americans, Arab Americans sold their farms and vineyards on Mount Lebanon to give money to their relatives, to establish a church or mosque in the United States, or to pay off a mortgage. The income from the sale of the land eased financial burdens in the short-term. As the Depression continued, however, some Arab Americans, particularly women, reverted to peddling to subsist. During the Depression, most of the wealthy suffered financially. The Faour brothers, the main lenders to the merchants of Little Syria, lost $1 million, and George Faour died alone in a boarding house. The smaller grocers and merchants weathered out the storm, and most managed to stay in business. In a situation of economic choices, most chose to keep their assets in the United States over those in Lebanon. They also chose to build churches and mosques as well as social organizations in the United States, emphasizing the permanence of their migration. However, some of the second and third generations maintained close ties to those left behind and established charities to help the needy in Lebanon. They also quietly continued to send back remittances.

World War II and the antiforeign sentiment in the United States spurred along the assimilation process for many Arab Americans. At least 30,000 GIs of Arab heritage joined the U.S. armed forces in World War II, a greater percentage than enlisted in World War I to fight the Ottoman Turks on behalf of the United States.[20] There were Arab Americans fighting in many of the major battles, including the Battle of the Bulge, a D-Day landing in southern France called Operation DRAGOON, and in combat missions over Berlin. As in World War I, a result of the war was further assimilation and acculturation. By the end of the war in 1945, many Arab American *haras* had disappeared with the exception of Dearborn, Michigan. From 1925 to 1965, Arab Americans were a part of the larger internal migration occurring at the time. Although a few families in rural areas remained as farmers or merchants, many moved to cities and towns. The smaller *haras* disintegrated as their residents moved to the suburbs or to bigger towns. Arab Americans in Little Syria moved their residences out of Manhattan. The construction of the Brooklyn Battery Tunnel in the 1940s forced most remaining Washington Street businesses to close and relocate, and many moved their businesses to Brooklyn. Little Syria was replaced with office buildings. Only two nondescript buildings, on the northwest corner of Greenwich and Rector Streets, are now left of the Mother Colony in New York City.

By World War II, the Arab American community had dispersed and assimilated into neighborhoods and industries that were not ethnically signified. One historian concluded that without the influx of new immigrants after 1965, the "Syrian-Americans might have assimilated themselves out of existence."[21] This is incorrect, however. Although many families no longer lived in *haras* or spoke Arabic, they actively participated in social networks, such as clubs and churches. Expressions of identity and community became limited to spheres less visible to non–Arab Americans but were nonetheless still present by 1965.

NOTES

1. American Immigration Lawyers Association, http://www.aila.org.

2. Kareem Shora and Timothy Edgar, "After 9/11, an Assault on Civil Liberties: Interview with Kareem Shora and Timothy Edgar," *TRIAL* 39, no. 10 (October 2003), 56–61.

3. Anan Ameri and Dawn Ramey, eds., *Arab American Encyclopedia* (Detroit: UXL, 2000), 36.

4. Alixia Naff, *Becoming American: The Early Arab Immigrant Experience* (Carbondale: Southern Illinois University Press, 1985), 112.

5. Ibid., 114.

6. Gregory Orfalea wrote that American missionaries played a "wooing and salubrious role" in encouraging emigration from Mount Lebanon in *Before the Flames: A Quest for the History of Arab-Americans* (Austin: University of Texas Press, 1988), 53.

7. Although most of the immigrants from Mount Lebanon were Maronite Christians, both Maronites and Druze inhabit Mount Lebanon, then as now. See Naff, 112.

8. Naff, 115–16.

9. Ibid., 113.

10. Akram Fouad Khater, *Inventing Home: Emigration, Gender, and the Middle Class in Lebanon 1870–1920* (Berkeley: University of California Press, 2001), 70.

11. Orfalea, 66–68.

12. Khater, 67.

13. See also Appendix B: Noted Arab Americans.

14. Khater, 66.

15. Ameri and Ramey, 43.

16. Orfalea, 81.

17. Ibid., 93.

18. Quoted in Mary Ann Haick DiNapoli, "The Syrian-Lebanese Community of South Ferry," in *A Community of Many Worlds: Arab Americans in New York City,* ed. Kathleen Benson and Philip Kayal (New York: Museum of the City of New York, 2002), 23.

19. Ibid., 19.

20. Orfalea, 85.

21. Naff, 330.

3

Race and Ethnic Classifications

The official classifications and social constructions of nationality, race, and ethnicity have complicated the collection of information on the Arab American population since their arrival in the United States. In the early twentieth century, legal cases were brought forward against the early Arab American settlers to challenge their claims to U.S. citizenship. The Arab American community rallied to avoid the stigma and possible immigration exclusion of being classified as "nonwhite" by arguing that they were Caucasians. These arguments were rebuffed on the basis of what was perceived to be popular opinion, called "common knowledge" by the courts. This opinion took into account various factors such as skin color and stereotypes of attitude toward democracy, the United States, and Islam. Racial classifications, whether official or social, affect all Americans, and these legal cases provide insights into how mainstream U.S. society viewed Arab Americans as between white and nonwhite.

Perhaps as a reaction to these cases and the anti-immigrant climate of the early twentieth century, Arab Americans assimilated into mainstream society, losing many of their distinctly ethnic traits and traditions in public before World War II. However, as a result of the civil rights movement and the ethnic revival of the 1970s and 1980s, as well as the impact of the media coverage and Arab defeat in the 1967 Six-Day War, Arab Americans experienced an ethnic revival. Many of the new arrivals, and second and third generations alike, adopted the broad label of Arab American and formed political and social organizations. As an ethnic group currently recognized as white, Arab Americans have found that official categories complicate a sense of community. Although many thousands of people identify themselves as Arab Americans, what that means in terms of race or ethnic minority status in the United States today remains murky.

AT PORTS OF ENTRY

The first hurdle that the early Arab Americans faced was being labeled Turks or Ottomans at their port of entry. In Chapter 2, it was noted that immigrants in the late nineteenth and early twentieth century were originally classified as being from Turkey in Asia at their port of entry, and that this classification was, more accurately, changed to Syria in 1899. Although they were from Mount Lebanon and Palestine—areas within the Syrian province of the Ottoman Empire—many more closely identified with their religion and village or town than as subjects of the Empire. After the founding of community institutions and *haras* (neighborhoods) in the United States, these immigrants' perceptions of identity shifted, and they referred to themselves as Syrian, Syro-Arab, or Arab and, after the creation of Lebanon in 1923, Syrian-Lebanese or Lebanese.

As the countries of the Middle East broke away from the Ottoman Empire, experienced European colonialism, and waged independence movements, individual nations formed. The U.S. immigration authorities accordingly changed their categorizations of immigrants to reflect these newly independent countries. Immigration records are almost always broken down by country, meaning the country from which travel documents were issued. Such statistics are problematic because they simplify identity issues, equating nationality with country of origin. For example, Palestinians have travel documents issued by refugee agencies and many countries in the Middle East. Therefore, instead of being identified as Palestinians, these immigrants are recorded as being from Lebanon, Jordan, and Israel. Recording country of origin also does not account for the non-Arab population within Arab countries, such as Kurds, Berbers, Chaldeans, Assyrians, Armenians, as well as the groups who may not self-identify as Arabs: Egyptian Copts and Lebanese Maronites. Immigration documents do not ask the individual to self-identify, so it is hard to determine who does or does not identify with an Arab affiliation. The far simpler solution, used by immigration authorities and census takers alike, is to group people by country.

SOCIAL CONSTRUCTS OF RACE BEFORE 1965

The first wave of immigrants arrived between 1880 and 1924 when American popular opinion was becoming increasingly concerned with the large numbers of new immigrants. Nativists were anti-immigrant and advocated native-born Americans because they feared that the influx of immigrants was causing a national crisis. They maintained that the United States was a White Anglo-Saxon Protestant (WASP) country and that the new immigrants caused a racial and moral degeneration of the country. When anti-Chinese sentiment increased in California after the end of the Civil War and the completion of the transcontinental railway, laws restricting immigration were introduced in Congress. The Chinese Exclusion Act of 1882 was the first piece of legislation restricting the admission of new Chinese immigrants into the country and denied the Chinese in the United States citizenship and the right to own land. This act ushered in a period of Asian exclusion from 1882 until 1943.

The racialist logic behind this act was based on the historic constructs of race in the United States from the late eighteenth century. Only a few months after the ratification of the Constitution, the Congress of 1790 restricted naturalization to "free white person[s]." The acceptance of the Fourteenth Amendment in 1868 expanded national citizenship: "All persons born or naturalized in the United States, and subject to the jurisdiction thereof, are citizens of the United States and the State wherein they reside." Former slaves born in the United States therefore became citizens, but naturalization (the process by which an immigrant became a U.S. citizen) remained limited to "free white persons" according to the 1790 law.

The Chinese Exclusion Act began a period in which the courts strove to determine who was eligible to become a U.S. citizen and who was excluded from the U.S. polity. Taking the 1790 law as a guide, judges tried to determine who was white. Between 1882 and 1943, Hawaiians, Japanese, Burmese, Filipinos, Native Americans, and those with a combination of any of those designations, were ruled to be nonwhite and so ineligible for U.S. citizenship. Armenians and Mexicans were ruled to be white. However, Syrians, Arabians, and Indians were borderline cases difficult to categorize in U.S. racial terms that recognized people as simply white or nonwhite.

The courts were used to determine who was white and who would be barred from naturalization. The legal decisions and public discussions in newspapers used explicitly racialist theories and linked the predicament of thousands of immigrants to the authority of the state. These debates were important because they expressed the national identity of the United States, and the outcomes of the cases defined who was a desirable citizen. The courts' decisions set the parameters of citizenship and the structure of political life by determining who had the right the vote and become a member of the nation.

Until 1909, Arab Americans assumed the privileges of whiteness. The first wavers were granted citizenship without much deliberation, held political office, and owned property, even in states where property ownership by aliens was prohibited. The community had avoided the wrath of the anti-immigrant nativists, perhaps because Arabs were numerically small and geographically dispersed and so were not as visible as some other communities, such as the Chinese in California.

One of the factors that prompted a reconsideration of the assumption that Syrians were whites by the courts was a change in the census and immigration categories between 1900 and 1910. In 1899, Syrians and Palestinians were classified as white by race; by 1910 these same groups were included as Asiatics by nativity. This reclassification was ostensibly because of the location of the Syrian province of the Ottoman Empire in Asia, but it was also part of a move to exclude more groups of immigrants.

The change in the census and immigration classifications caught the early Arab American immigrants by surprise. Many believed that as Christians in a Christian country, they belonged to the dominant social group and so were entitled to the official nomenclature of the majority. The reason for this assumption can be traced back to the early immigrants' upbringing in the Ottoman Empire where religion, and not race, formed the basis of social structure. History and experience had taught the Christians and Jews under the Ottomans that the majority religion was at the top of the social scale. As outlined in Chapter 1, the Ottoman Empire was overwhelmingly Muslim, recognizing Christians and Jews as distinct political-social communities who were in charge of their own religious laws and customs. Christians and Jews were aware that they were in the minority because of their religion, and many believed that they suffered under Ottoman persecution and discrimination as religious minorities. Influenced by missionaries to understand that the United States was a Christian country, most of the early Arab Christian immigrants arrived believing that, as Christians, they would now be in the majority bloc and thus, part of the dominant group.

The courts vacillated over the racial status of Arab and Indian Americans many times between 1909 and 1923. The early Arab Americans were a relatively small population in the United States, and yet they composed almost one-third of the racial prerequisite cases heard in the U.S. federal courts between 1909 and 1923.[1] The disproportionate number of Syrian cases compared with the population illustrates that the color line was unstable and unclear to people at the time. In these debates, the early Arab Americans returned to the same argument: they were Semites, Semites were Caucasian, Caucasians were white. This was considered to be a scientifically based argument, rooted in then popular racial development theories that examined biological origins. To prove that the Syrians, as they were then known, were nonwhite, the prosecutors used other nonscientific arguments based on "common knowledge," meaning how the average American perceived whiteness. For the Syrians, this included issues such as skin color, religion (or perceived religion), notions of a "democratic mind," and assimilability. Judges deliberated and weighed arguments over the differences between white and Caucasian. They heard defense arguments about religion and how these Christians from Mount Lebanon were from the birthplace of Jesus. Some judges considered skin color and the language skills of the defendant to cast light on his or her racial classification. Other judges looked at legal precedents, including congressional intent in 1790 and court rulings. On the basis of contradictory results and rationales, the courts found these Syrians to be "white persons" in 1909, 1910, and 1915, but not in 1913 and 1914. However, by 1924, Syrians were officially classified as white.

The first Syrian racial prerequisite case was in Georgia in 1909. In *re Najour,* the judge found that scientific evidence outweighed skin complexion as the determining factor.[2] For this evidence, he referred to a prominent anthropologist text of the time, A. H. Keane's *The World's People: A Popular Account of Their Bodily and Mental Characters, Beliefs, Traditions, Political and Social Institutions* (1908), which was "typical of contemporary raciology."[3] Using the anthropologist's findings and scientific logic, the judge concluded that Syrians were Caucasians, and that Caucasians were white. Costa George Najour was therefore found to be white.

As was the situation in the Shishim case in 1909, Arab Americans relied on references to Jesus and shared Christianity to show their commonalities with the judge and the population at-large. In this case, George Shishim, a policeman in Venice, California, arrested a young man for disturbing the peace. The young man's father, a prominent lawyer, challenged Shishim's right to arrest his son on the basis that Shishim was not, and could not be, a U.S. citizen. His argument was that Shishim was from Lebanon, a part of Asia, and therefore of Chinese-Mongolian ancestry and so barred from becoming a citizen. The Lebanese community pooled their resources and hired Byron Hanna, a fellow countryman, to defend Shishim. As part of their case, they wrote to academics in universities to inquire about the ethnological background of their ancestry and argued that Syrians were Caucasians. In the court hearings, Shishim said, "If I am a Mongolian, then so was Jesus, because we came from the same land."[4] Many of the legal arguments in the early cases regarding the race of Arab Americans centered on being from the Holy Land and a practicing Christian "of good morals, sober and industrious."

By indicating to the court that they were Christians, early Arab Americans were distancing themselves from Islam. This was a strategy based on the negative image of Islam in the eyes of immigration specialists, who were particularly concerned with polygamy and its associative immorality. However, the judge did not consider religion a salient argument on race, and he noted that state and federal courts had defined Syrians as members of the white race for more than 100 years and determined that Shishim was white and eligible for citizenship. After the decision was read, George Shishim took his oath of allegiance to the United States and became a U.S. citizen before he left the court.

Despite the white rulings of the 1909 cases, the U.S. Bureau of Immigration and Naturalization denied Arab Americans citizenship after 1911. These denials led to more racial prerequisite cases in 1913 and 1914, in which the courts found that Syrians were not white, thus reversing earlier decisions. The nature and location of the Ottoman Empire and the immigrant's position as a subject of the Ottoman sultan gained prominence in these rulings. Nativists and some judges considered all subjects of the Ottoman Empire to be inappropriate candidates for U.S. citizenship because of their assumed political inclinations.

First, the Ottoman Empire was not a democracy, and so the immigrants were subjects, and not citizens, bound to autocratic rulings. In some cases, the judges expressed their belief that subjects of the Ottoman Empire did not possess the experience and intellectual capacity to vote and fully participate in the U.S. political system.

Second, the Ottoman Empire fought on the side of the Germans in World War I and so was considered an enemy of the United States. This position brought into question where the loyalty of the Ottoman subjects lay: to the United States or to the Sultan? Although the Declaration of Intention to become a U.S. citizen was originally intended to test the loyalty of new U.S. citizens to the British Empire, Ottoman subjects were also asked to sign the form. To make the form appropriate to an Ottoman subject, the court clerk crossed out the reference to Queen Victoria and the renunciation of allegiance to the crown of Great Britain and Ireland and filled in the name of the Ottoman Sultan. Clearly, there were questions about the loyalty of Ottoman subjects to their new country, and as the United States entered World War I, these questions became more urgent. Even after the Ottoman Empire lost its Arab provinces in 1918, this practice continued. As late as 1923, Arabs had to declare their renouncement of allegiance to the "present government of Turkey" when applying for U.S. citizenship.

Third, there was a close association between the Ottoman Empire and Islam, and although all the cases known involved Christians, their origins in

Ottoman lands implicated them as Muslims. Regardless of the complexities of the issue in Islam, in the early twentieth century, Muslims were considered to be polygamists and thus ineligible for U.S. citizenship. The link between polygamy and disqualification for citizenship developed as a result of the anti-Mormon campaign of the late nineteenth century, in which polygamists were explicitly excluded from entry into the United States. Unaware that there were small numbers of Muslims living in the United States at the time, the Chairman of the House Committee on Immigration and Naturalization said in 1922, "The laws of the United States prevent the admission of those who preach and practice polygamy, and most true Mohammedans are unable to deny that when they are asked . . . [and that] Mohammedans can not very well come in unless they deny the faith to which they adhere."[5]

Considering that the legislators in charge of immigration clearly did not believe that Muslims had a place within the parameters of the American polity, it is not surprising that the early Arab Americans brought before the courts to test their whiteness emphasized that they were Christians.

In the 1913 and 1914 cases, common-knowledge arguments swayed the courts' decisions in rulings that Syrians were not white. In a 1913 case, ex parte *Shahid*, the judge ruled that the defendant, a Christian from Zahle (now in Lebanon) was not white. He mentioned that Shahid's skin color was "about that of walnut," but he also protested "the uncertainties of color" and the futility of drawing "the dividing line between white and colored."[6] Although the judge's rationale is unclear, he considered skin color in his determination to reject Shahid's application.

After the lower courts in South Carolina twice rejected George Dow's application for naturalization in 1914, leaders in the Arab American community began to worry about their future in the United States. They formed the Syrian Society for National Defense (SSND) to "defend our historic, civil and social rights."[7] The SSND hired lawyers, who focused on avoiding another ruling that Syrians were nonwhite. Naoum Mokarzel, the editor and owner of *al-Hoda*, a popular newspaper based in New York City, and the president of the Syrian American Association, stood behind the campaign. *al-Hoda* kept its readers up to date on the latest developments in the case. The SSND collected donations for the defense of George Dow and notified the editors of *al-Hoda* of the names of donors with the size of their contributions. The campaign raised nearly $1,000, a substantial sum for a legal case at the time. Arab Americans composed letters to the editor of mainstream papers as well as to politicians arguing that they should be classified as whites. As part of this whiteness campaign, they wrote and published articles and books in English on the scientifically based racial classification of Syrians.

Defending the whiteness of George Dow was clearly seen as something urgent and important for the community.

In *Dow v. United States,* the judge commented on the deep feelings expressed by the lawyers and their claims that the community had suffered "humiliation" and "mortification" at the thought of being classified as Asian and not white. In the final appeal of Dow's case, the judge accepted the Dillingham Report of the Immigration Commission, which found that Syrians belonged to the Semitic branch of the Caucasian race and were of mixed Syrian, Arabian, and Jewish blood, and not the same Mongolian race of their Turkish rulers. He concluded that Syrians were "white persons" and the court granted George Dow his citizenship.[8] The issue of race for the early Arab Americans was officially settled by this case, and then again by the Immigration Act of 1917, in which Syrians and Palestinians were declared to be Caucasians and that their place of nativity, the Ottoman Empire, had no bearing on their race. Thus, the early Arab Americans successfully fought for classification as whites through the courts.

The immediate reaction within the community was not a sense of relief—many Arab Americans continued to believe that the whole race crisis derived from a series of misappellations in which they were confused with Turks and Asians. The racial prerequisite cases impressed upon them the importance of naturalization, and in the mid-1920s, there was a push for residents to become U.S. citizens. The early Arab American community continued to keep an eye on their legal and racial status as whites. One Arab American was quoted as telling a story frequently between 1931 and 1947:

> They [the government] were going to classify us, the Arab people, as Asian, but Mr. Maykel [a local leader and businessman in Worcester, Massachusetts] visited Congressman Pehr G. Holmes and asked him to fight this thing and make sure we are classified as white and not Asian. I'm as white as anybody who claims to be white is! Our people were going to be considered not of the white race but the senator made sure that we were classified correctly. He was behind the movement to classify us once again as Caucasian.[9]

From this quotation, it is clear that, even after the reversal of the Dow ruling in 1915, Arab Americans were insecure about their status as whites until the late 1940s.

In 1942, a new racial perquisite case was brought before the court when an Arabian—a Yemeni man—applied for naturalization in Detroit. The judge rejected his application on the basis of the geographical and cultural distance between Yemen and Europe and between his religion, Islam, and the Christian peoples of Europe.[10] The judge noted the he was "undisputedly dark brown in color," relaying that skin color was a relevant factor in determining race.[11] Following that decision, the immigration authorities issued a statement that a person of "the Arabian race" was eligible for naturalization thus reversing the 1942 case in 1944, and Yemeni Muslims were naturalized and became U.S. citizens thereafter.

The long-term effects of these legal cases were that the early Arab Americans reacted to the strong assimilationist pressure of the early twentieth century by adopting the mainstream's social traits and behavior without attempting to integrate many of the elements of their cultural background into their children's lives. Between 1920 and 1945, many Syrian-Lebanese American families abandoned the occupation of trading and shopkeeping, educated their children to become upwardly mobile professionals, and moved out of the *haras* (neighborhoods) into the suburbs, intermarrying and scattering the local community. The majority Arab Christian population attended non-Eastern churches, usually the local Roman Catholic Church. Muslims and Christians alike changed their names from Arabic names to more common names found in the United States to avoid possible problems with immigration restrictions and to achieve financial success. The preference for assimilation over ethnic pride showed an outward reorientation toward the culture of the United States, but a few new Arab American regional associations were formed and some families maintained uniquely ethnic aspects in the privacy of the home and within community networks.

The repression of language, culture, and Eastern religions did not directly translate into acceptance into the mainstream society, and the assertion of being white through the legal system remained an incomplete process in social terms. The stereotype of the Syrian before 1920 was of a pack peddler with olive skin, dark eyes, a large mustache, and solid frame. To some Americans, this image rendered the Syrians foreign-looking and therefore nonwhite. This assumption of race was used in the legal decisions that rejected applications for naturalization based on common knowledge. Arab Americans were called "wetbacks," "dago," and "sheeny," reflecting that many confused the darker coloring of Arabs with other ethnicities.[12] By the 1920s and 1930s, the ethnic slurs hit closer to home, and terms such as "camel jockey," "dirty Syrian," "blackie," and "Turk" were used. These comments, though, were inaccurate; the Syrians were not Turks, and there are not many camels in the Levantine area, and none in Mount Lebanon. These terms were meant to be personal insults, reflecting the fact that that many did not view Syrians as white, although the exact nature of what they *were* was confused and unclear.

Religion played a role in social acceptance or rejection in certain communities. Most of the early Syrian settlers were Catholics and Orthodox Christians who faced religious as well as racial discrimination in some areas of the country. For example, in Birmingham, Alabama, in the 1920s, the Syrians were grouped with the Greeks and became the target of political pamphlets in which a politician said that he did not want their votes, reasoning, "If I can't be elected by white men, then I don't want the office."[13] In the segregated city, Arab Americans were barred from entering "whites-only" restaurants and public facilities. Although skin color and national origin played a role, Catholicism, which "made the Lebanese more suspect," was a source for discrimination.[14] In Birmingham, the reaction of the community to "the stress of economic change and social ostracism" of the 1930s was to establish and maintain "strong, stable community institutions," such as the Maronite Church and the Cedar Club.[15] Faith was more than a focal point for the community because it also acted as a buffer against the prevailing strict classification of color lines. As practicing Catholics, the wealthier Arab American children attended Latin Rite parochial schools and established a separate burial site in Birmingham—two major issues in a segregated society. However, even in Catholic school, the Arab American children reported being teased for their dark, curly hair and the food in their lunch boxes that identified them as different from their classmates.[16]

After World War II, Japanese Americans, who had been interned in camps and then drafted into the U.S. Army during the war, lobbied for a new law that would eliminate the category of "aliens ineligible to citizenship." Japanese Americans fought for the 1952 Immigration and Naturalization Act (widely known as the McCarran Walter Act), which eliminated that category and affected a policy of color-blind naturalization. This act negated any further need for racial prerequisite cases, although the legal ramifications of the 1912–44 court rulings remained. The legacy of these cases is seen today as Arabs continue to fall under the "White" race category in the census, on official forms, and on applications meeting federal standards.

AS MINORITIES

As whites, Arab Americans are often not disaggregated statistically, although since the 1980s, they have the right to claim discrimination against their ethnic heritage or religion in a court of law. In a 1987 appeal, the U.S. Supreme Court found that Arab Americans and Jewish Americans had demonstrated discriminatory behavior against them, and the Supreme Court expanded the definition of protected classes of people to include national origin and religious groups under federal law. In this case, and in other examples, Jews and Arabs have been able to move beyond the official race classifications by demonstrating discrimination and bias against "ethnic whites." In other cases, lawyers used national origin and/or religion to vilify the defendant or to highlight the nature of discriminatory behavior in the workplace. In the mid-1990s, the Michigan Supreme Court found that references to the defendant as an Arab during the 1990–91 Gulf War was permitted because that did not jeopardize his right to a fair trial. However, the fact that the issue of racial and ethnic references at trial reached the state supreme court testifies that the defense had a basis for their allegations of prosecutorial misconduct through racial references to the Arab defendant.

In the business environment, Arab Americans are officially considered as minorities only in a few isolated cases. In the early 1990s, the Small Business Administration (SBA) recognized one Palestinian American federal contractor as eligible for minority-owned business status after he documented his experience of economic disadvantage based on national origin. The SBA's special status, however, did not transfer to other Arab American–owned businesses. The one exception is San Francisco, which expanded its human rights ordinance to qualify Arab Americans under the rubric of businesses owners who qualify for minority contracts. Minority-owned business status increases the chances of securing public contracts because many government contracts are laid aside specifically for minority-owned businesses. When competing with the large contractors that monopolize the process, being a minority has a strong benefit.

Racial categorization still permeates both private and public bureaucracies through the enforcement of the civil rights laws in education, the workplace, and other arenas. As a result, racial and ethnic classifications impact an individual in a number of life stages from grade school reports, medical forms, college applications, and unemployment insurance forms to many other documents. Inclusion in the generic "White" racial category blurs Arab American ethnic identity and distinctiveness. It diminishes opportunities for community outreach and the right to participate in multicultural structures and the racialized discourses of ethnic studies and scholarship.

At the local level, some Arab Americans fill informal minority positions of public service, but only if the Arab American population is demographically strong and visible. Arab Americans have been active in the Republican and Democratic political parties and have served in political offices at the federal, state, county, and municipal levels. As a result of the strong Palestinian presence in San Francisco, Arab Americans are considered to be minorities within municipal structures. Although the process is informal, Arab Americans are being represented in politics and at the policy level, notably in San Francisco and Fairfax County, Virginia. The only state where Arab American representation is formalized is Michigan, which has a large and visible presence of Arabs and Chaldeans in Detroit and its suburbs. As a result, Michigan classifies Arabs and Chaldeans (in one category) in statistical research and agency evaluations. Arabs are therefore included in the state's goals and statistics that monitor service delivery and minority achievements programs.

IN THE CENSUS

Census categories do not necessarily mirror immigration or legal racial categories. In the censuses in the first half of the twentieth century, the early Arab Americans were referred to as Ottomans, Turks, Asians, or Syrians by national origin, and sometimes race. In addition to the race checkoffs for White, Negro, and Indian (Native American), these censuses included other race categories, such as Mexican, Hindu, Jew, Chinese, Japanese, Italian, and Syrian. To the U.S. Census Bureau, ethnicities, as well as religions, sometimes had their own racial grouping regardless of the scientific and biological theories.

Before 1960, an onsite census worker administered the census, observed the race of the participant, usually the woman of the household, and checked off the category that he or she thought was correct. The census administrators observed the skin color and appearance of the participant in his or her home as the census administrator noted down race and national origin. Although the census worker did sometimes ask the participant where he or she was from, the superficial inspection of the participant was crucial to the final classification of an individual and, by extension his or her family, in the census. Arabs differ in skin color and hair texture and so resisted some of the simplistic Black/White/Native American racial boxes formulated by visual inspection. The net results were a mass of confusing statistics on the numbers of Arab Americans in the United States before 1960, all caused by not being able to define a social construct—race.

The switch to mail-in census forms in 1960 allowed the participant to check off his or her own race and marked a movement to the validity of the self-identification of race. The 1965 Voting Rights Act required the protection of civil rights, creating a need for better and more detailed data collection on race. As a result, the Office of Management and Budget put forward standards for delineating and defining race in *Directive 15: Race and Ethnic Standards for Federal Statistics and Administrative Reporting* in May 1977. The definitions of race have changed over the years and are sometimes reflected in updated versions of *Directive 15,* which still forms the standards used for public- and private-sector legal compliance with civil rights legislation and data collection at the state and federal level. In 2005, *Directive 15*'s racial categories are:

American Indian or Alaska Native
Asian
Black or African American
Native Hawaiian or Other Pacific Islander
White

The ethnic categories of "Hispanic or Latino" or "Not Hispanic or Latino" are also used. "White" is officially defined as, "A person having origins in any of the original peoples of Europe, the Middle East, or North Africa."

The Census of 2000 embraced *Directive 15*'s racial categories but included an additional category of "Other." As a default, many Arab Americans who did not choose the "White" category chose to identify with the "Other" category, but "Other" was not structured to be a catch-all race identifier. A person who marked his or her race as "Other" and identified himself or herself as a person from the Middle East or North Africa on the blank space next to the "Other" category was reclassified as "White" by the data collectors. Therefore, there are no data on Arab Americans from the short form of the 2000 Census.

The short census form was sent to most households, and the additional long or ancestry form was given to one-sixth, or 17 percent, of U.S. households. In the long form of the 2000 Census, the respondent was asked to answer, "What is this person's ancestry or ethnic origin?" People were free to answer according to their conscience in the blank space beside the question; their answers ranged from religions to ethnic groupings to countries of origins. Some of these answers were later tabulated by the Census Bureau and compiled into reports about groups or communities within the United States.

Two such reports were issued based on the results from the long form of the 2000 Census. The census brief, *The Arab Population: 2000,* and the more detailed special report, *We the People of Arab Ancestry in the United States,* were issued in 2003 and 2005, respectively. To compose these reports, the U.S. Census Bureau had to first define who was included under the grouping of "Arab," and it used country of origin classifications. For the purposes of these reports, the Census Bureau thus defined *Arab* as "most people with ancestries originating from Arabic-speaking countries or areas of the world are categorized as Arab."[17] Therefore, those self-identifying with the broader label of "Arab" and those primarily choosing a specific country were considered as part of the "Arab population" by the census.

The 2003 report did not distinguish between the population of Arab Americans, but the larger 2005 report focused on a smaller portion of Arab Americans. The 2005 report called this group "people of Arab ancestry," in which "ancestry refers to ethnic origin, descent, roots, heritage or place of birth of the person or the person's ancestors." The report focused on the "approximately 850,000 [who] reported Arab ancestries and no others."[18] Although the report acknowledged the additional 340,000 people who reported an Arab and a non-Arab ancestry (e.g., Irish and Lebanese), the bulk of the findings omitted Arab Americans of mixed heritage. The assumption underlying this report was that there are significant differences between those of mixed heritage and those of only Arab heritage, regardless of how long their families have resided in the United States. The goals behind this choice are unclear, but it seems that the Census Bureau is trying to locate loyalty to Arab heritage. It has been noted that "The ancestry question was not intended to measure the respondent's degree of attachment to a particular group, but simply to establish that the respondent had a connection to and self-identified with a particular ethnic group."[19]

In light of the tense security post-9/11 environment, this 2005 report on people of non-mixed Arab ancestry is particularly curious, especially as the Census 2000 did not ask any information on religious affiliation, so there is no information on Muslims in the United States. Although it is valuable to have statistics on the Arab American community, the question remains about why this distinction was made.

In the two Census 2000 reports, there were breakdowns according to "detailed group": Lebanese, Egyptian, Syrian, Palestinian, Jordanian, Moroccan, Iraqi, "Arab" or "Arabic," and "Other Arab." In the *Census 2000 Brief,* the Census Bureau identified the population of "Arab" or "Arabic" as those who self-identified as Arab, Arabic, Middle Eastern, or North African. The "Other Arab" category reported identifications that included Yemeni, Kurdish, Algerian, Saudi Arabian, Tunisian, Kuwaiti, Libyan, Berber, and "Other specific Arab ancestry." This latter category, a subset of a subset on a special report, included groups with populations of fewer than 1,000 in the year 2000, including Emirati (from the United Arab Emirates), Omani, Qatari, Bahraini, Alhuceman, Bedouin, and Rio de Oro. One problem with the census reports is that all nationals of Arab-majority countries, including non-Arab groups such as Berbers and Kurds, were included as "of Arab ancestry." Even if individuals specifically wrote down a non-Arab ethnic affiliation that is located in the Middle East, such as Chaldeans, they were still classified as "of Arab ancestry" in the census reports. In addition, other people who may identify as Arabs were excluded, as the 2003 Brief explains: "Some groups such as Mauritanian, Somalian, Djiboutian, Sudanese and Comoros Islander who may consider themselves Arab were not included, again for consistency [with the 1990 Census and Census 2000 data products]."[20]

Similarly, if these Mauritanian, Somalian, Djiboutian, Sudanese, and Comoros Islanders consider themselves Arabs but note that they are from a country that the Census Bureau does not count as Arab, they are not noted as Arab.

Even if the official population calculations are problematic, the number of people identified as of Arab ancestry in projections made from the long form responses grew by 40 percent between the 1990 and 2000 Censuses.[21] Among this number, there was a 62 percent increase in the population who identified as part of a general term such as Arab, North African, or Middle Eastern. This substantial increase indicates that Arab Americans are a growing minority who identify as such in the United States today, despite official classifications.

Arab American organizations contend that the census undercounts the Arab American population. Leaders generally consider the census numbers to be one-third of the actual Arab American population because of the effect of the sample methodology of the long form on a small, unevenly distributed population. In addition, community leaders argue that the breakdowns of the population are distorted because of the high levels of out-marriage (marriage to non-Arabs) and general distrust and misunderstanding of government surveys. Indeed, it is difficult to determine the accuracy of the population numbers because of the fluctuating nature of self-identifications and data collection problems. Arab American leaders thus believe the Arab American population to be 1.2 percent of the U.S. population or 3.5 million. To reach this number, the Arab American Institute Foundation triples the census numbers. Given that this is a flawed methodology, Arab American leaders have a solid rationale for their objections. See Table 3.1.

The government recognizes that racial and ethnic categories "are sociopolitical constructs and should not be interpreted as being scientific or anthropological in nature."[22] Indeed, the experience of the early Arab Americans as borderline Asians and whites testifies to the debatable nature of "race" and its ambiguous classification system. Confusion and debate still exist as to which race Arabs belong on federal forms and in society in general. A 1988 study of eighth-graders found that 15 percent of students from the Middle East were classified as being in the Asian/Pacific Islander category.[23] Although the first wavers fought to be designated as white, there is contentious debate among

Table 3.1
Conflicting Arab American Population Numbers

	2000 Census	Arab American Institute Foundation
Total Population	1,189,731	3,500,000
% U.S. Population	0.42	1.2

Sources: U.S. Census Bureau, *Census 2000* (Washington, DC, 2000); also available online at http://www.census.gov/prod/2005pubs/censr_21.pdf; Angela Brittingham and G. Patricia de la Cruz, *We the People of Arab Ancestry in the United States, Census 2000 Special Reports* (Washington, DC: U.S. Census Bureau, 2005), 1; also available online at http://www.census.gov/prod/2005pubs/censr_21.pdf; and Arab American Institute Foundation, "Arab American Demographics," 2004, http://www.aaiusa.org/demographics.htm.

contemporary Arab American leaders, academics, and activists whether today's Arab Americans, many of who cannot pass as white and are treated as people of color, should be officially classified as "White."

Since the 1980s, the race issue has been brought to the fore by Arab Americans leaders and organizations, as well as by a handful of lawsuits. In 1980, a former senator, Senator James Abourezk, established the American-Arab Anti-Discrimination Committee (ADC), and the issue of discrimination led to an open and ongoing debate about the racial classification of Arabs. In the 1990s, the two largest national Arab Americans organizations—ADC and Arab American Institute (AAI)—disagreed on how to classify their own constituency. The ADC wanted a separate race classification for Arab Americans, and AAI wanted a subclassification of Middle Eastern origin within the White race category. This Middle Eastern classification would include Arabs, Israelis, Turks, Persians, as well as other ethnic groups within the region, with an additional component to indicate the country of origin. Essentially, ADC was for an ethnolinguistic-based definition, and AAI favored a geographic-based identification. The two groups could not come to an agreement. Both the *Census 2000 Brief* and the special report acknowledged this tension and the Census Bureau cited two reasons for their decision not to add either category suggestion to the 2000 Census short form: lack of consensus among Arab American groups and the relatively small size of the population.

Although discussions on the content and categorizations in the next census are ongoing, the U.S. Census Bureau has decided that there will be no long or ancestry forms in 2010. On the short form, Arabs will continue to be counted in the White category. The 2010 Census will therefore have less accurate information on Arab Americans than the 2000 Census, leaving community activists and academics with further concerns about the quality of statistical data on the community in the future.[24]

The post-9/11 atmosphere has raised Arab Americans' fears that the census information is used to profile the community. In a 2004 response to a request by the Electronic Privacy Information Center, a civil liberties group, the Census Bureau reported that it had provided population data to the U.S. Department of Homeland Security in cities with more than 1,000 Arab Americans. The data included tabulated statistics broken down by postal zip codes and country of origin, including the categories of Arab/Arabic, Syrian, Palestinian, Moroccan, Lebanese, Jordanian, Iraqi, Egyptian, and "Other Arab."[25] In a letter to the director of the Census Bureau, a coalition of civil liberties organizations, civil rights groups, and ethnic advocacy groups questioned the Census Bureau's "judgment and discretion" at providing the data that eroded public trust in the agency. The letter stated that: "The harm done to Arab American confidence is immeasurable. Already victims of government policies that promote collective suspicion and feed backlash against them, our community sees this episode, regardless of facts at hand, as one more reason to feel unprotected and unfairly targeted."[26]

After the leak of this news to the media, the U.S. Customs and Border Protection agency stated in a press release that the census figures were "to assist in an outreach campaign to educate international travelers on the monetary reporting requirements when traveling abroad."[27] Purportedly, the data was needed to verify which airports would be most heavily used by Arab Americans and therefore where Arabic signage was needed. Many community activists believed that this request was part of the racial profiling that equated Arabs with terrorism. In the post–9/11 atmosphere, Arab American organizations have assumed that people from their community will be more reluctant to self-identify in future censuses and so are not pushing for inclusion as an ethnic or racial group in the 2010 Census.

IDENTITY

The civil rights movement and multiculturalism ethos that developed in the United States in the 1960s and 1970s prompted Arab Americans to become politicized in mounting efforts of self-definition. Although the first use of the term *Arab* in the United States was in Worcester, Massachusetts, in four publications in the early 1890s, Syrian or Lebanese were the most popular community identities until the 1960s. In the wake of the civil rights movement and the increasing politicization of ethnicity, some of those who had identified as Americans of Syrians and/or Lebanese descent began to identify as Arab Americans. This process began after the defeat of Arab armies in the Six-Day War in 1967, when the U.S. media coverage portrayed Arabs as inherently evil and opposed to the United States. For Arab Americans, adopting the Arab identity was a way of reclaiming the term and redefining how Arabs were perceived in the United States. The switch to an Arab American identity also showed a sense of shared ethnicity, heritage, and political consciousness with Arabs living in the Middle East.

The development of political and social organizations is examined in more depth in Chapter 6, but the role of these organizations in crystallizing a communal identity is acknowledged here. In 1968 an organization, the Association of Arab American University Graduates (AAUG), was formed and the choice of name marked an important public use of the term Arab American. In the 1970s and 1980s, more organizations incorporated under the label "Arab-American" or "American-Arab."

The creation and ongoing activities of these organizations have emphasized the collective identity of Arab Americans as one united community, although each Arab American organization tends to work on issues that appeal to its core constituency. Emphasis on the collective identity has not really translated into a unified or strong community voice in one all-powerful advocacy group or a coalition of organizations. The 2000 Census indicated that 85 percent of Arab Americans still identify first by country of origin, although this does not mean that Arab is not a secondary or tertiary identifier, or even the first choice in another setting.

Arab Americans, like all other Americans, have multifaceted identities that reflect their race, ethnicity, religion, gender, sexual orientation, political party affiliation, or other factors. Within the race/ethnicity identity, an Arab American may identify himself or herself by country of origin or by religion. In recent years, an increasingly Islamic consciousness rivals for primary identification as an Arab among Muslims. Therefore, many are choosing to call themselves American Muslims over labeling themselves as Arab Americans. The ascendancy of Muslim versus Arab identity as a source of change and tension is examined in depth in Chapter 5. Christians can also use religion as an ethnic signifier, especially among the non-Arab minority groups of Armenians, Assyrians, or Chaldeans. Some Lebanese Maronites and Egyptian Copts point to their pre-Islamic cultural and religious traditions and maintain ethnonationalist identities, even after immigration to the United States. In these cases, they may not identify in any way as an Arab and expressly do not wish to be classified as Arabs or as Arab Americans.

The original classification of Arab Americans as white has had an impact on today's racial classifications because it set up a status quo and caused a distancing between Arab Americans and people of color in the United States. Whereas in the early twentieth century, it was beneficial to identify as white to secure the rights of U.S. citizenship, today Arab Americans argue that they are not treated as white and identify more closely to people of color. Arab Americans have a range of skin tones, so it is hard to generalize how an Arab American's color is assessed and perceived without further studies. However, the race issue has somewhat divided the community, as the negotiations with the Office of Management and Budget over *Directive 15* and the Census Bureau indicate.

Arab Americans have written about their feelings of exclusion from political movements, especially the feminist movement. They believe that they are excluded from political discussions because of their support for Islam and the plight of the Palestinians and that these political alignments have created an atmosphere of political racism against Arab Americans. As these feelings have been shared and understood by some African Americans, alliances have been formed between the two communities, particularly in the political realm.

As a result of the lack of group consensus on the race or ethnicity of Arab Americans as a group, many Arab American activists and artists have replaced the racial debate with personal definitions of self. In her 1996 book, *Born Palestinian, Born Black,* Suheir Hammad wrote: "We gotta be for real. We need to own our definitions and live by them. We need not be afraid to adapt or change them when necessary. Borders are manmade, and I refuse to respect them unless I have a say in their formation. Besides, call Spirit what you want, essence is one and eternal."[28] Although individual identifications recognize essence and the complexities of personal affiliations, it is important to understand how and where these personal identifications become collective.

NOTES

1. Sarah Gualitieri, "Becoming 'White': Race, Religion and the Foundations of Syrian/Lebanese Ethnicity in the United States," *Journal of American Ethnic History* 20, no. 4 (Summer 2001): 31.

2. *Re Najour,* 174 F, 735 (N.D. GA 1909).

3. Ian F. Haney López, *White by Law: The Legal Construction of Race* (New York: New York University Press, 1996), 70.

4. Joseph R. Haiek, ed., *The Arab-American Almanac,* 5th ed. (Glendale, CA: New Circle, 2003), 24–26.

5. Quoted in Kathleen M. Moore, *Al-Mughtaribun: American Law and the Transformation of Muslim Life in the United States* (Albany: State University of New York Press, 1995), 40.

6. López, 213; Moore, 51–52.

7. Gualitieri, 44.

8. *Dow vs. United States et al.,* no. 1345 (4th Cir 1915).

9. Elizabeth Boosahda, *Arab-American Faces and Voices: The Origins of an Immigrant Community* (Austin: University of Texas Press, 2003), 135.

10. *Re Ahmad Hassan,* 48 F, Supp 843 (1942).

11. Gualitieri, 48.

12. Gregory Orfalea, *Before the Flames: A Quest for the History of Arab-Americans* (Austin: University of Texas Press, 1988), 80.

13. Nancy Faires Conklin, "'Colored' and 'Catholic,'" in *Crossing the Waters, Arabic-Speaking Immigrants to the United States before 1940,* ed. Eric J. Hooglund (Washington, DC: Smithsonian Institution Press, 1987), 77.

14. Ibid., 80.

15. Ibid., 70.

16. Evelyn Shakir, *Bint Arab: Arab and Arab American Women in the United States* (Westport, CT: Praeger, 1997), 113.

17. Angela Brittingham and G. Patricia de la Cruz, *The Arab Population: 2000, Census 2000 Brief* (Washington, DC: U.S. Census Bureau, 2003), 1; also available online at http://www.census.gov/prod/2003pubs/c2kbr-23.pdf.

18. Angela Brittingham and G. Patricia de la Cruz, *We the People of Arab Ancestry in the United States, Census 2000 Special Reports* (Washington, DC: U.S. Census Bureau, 2005), 2, 1; also available online at http://www.census.gov/population/www/cen2000/briefs.html#sr.

19. Ibid., 2.

20. Brittingham and de la Cruz, *The Arab Population,* 1.

21. Ibid., 2.

22. U.S. Department of the Interior, "Standards for Maintaining, Collecting, and Presenting Federal Data on Race and Ethnicity," Excerpt from Federal Register, October 30, 1997. http://www.doi.gov/diversity/doc/racedata (accessed August 22, 2005).

23. Helen Hatab Samhan, "Not Quite White: Race Classification and the Arab-American Experience," in *Arabs in America: Building a New Future,* ed. Michael W. Suleiman (Philadelphia: Temple University Press, 1999), 219.

24. Helen Samhan, Executive Director of the Arab American Institute Foundation, personal communication with author, 30 June 2004.

25. Electronic Privacy Information Center, "Freedom of Information Documents on the Census: Department of Homeland Security Obtained Data on Arab Americans from Census Bureau" July 23, 2004, http://www.epic.org/privacy/census/foia/; New York Times, "Homeland Security Given Data on Arab Americans," 30 July 2004, www.nytimes.com/2004/07/30/politics/30census.html.

26. Arab American Institute, "Letter to Census Director Re: Data Sent to Homeland Security," 2004, http://www.aaiusa.org/census_letter.htm.

27. Electronic Privacy Information Center, "Statement of U.S. Customs and Border Protection Commissioner Robert C. Bonner on Census Data," July 30, 2004. http://www.epic.org/privacy/census/foia/census_emails.pdf.

28. Suheir Hammad, *Born Palestinian, Born Black* (New York: Harlem River, 1996), x.

4

Cultural Adaptation

The diversity of the contemporary Arab American community makes the discussion of family issues, gender, and religion challenging. The process of "Americanization," or cultural adaptation to U.S. society, is nonlinear: identity and behaviors are not predicated by the years or generations spent in the United States. Socioeconomic status, education, religion, and personal experiences are factored into the strategies used by Arab Americans to cope with life in the United States. Shifts in individual economic, political, and social situations after arrival can shape how people negotiate life choices. Each person, whatever generation, chooses different combinations of behaviors that reflect his or her own grounded reality and reactions to experiences and situations. Most Arab Americans modified their cultural traditions and outlooks on various social institutions and made some changes in their lives accordingly. This chapter focuses on the adaptations that have taken place through examining the family and women's issues, including issues of household size, parent-children relationships, work, interpretations of Islam, and feminism.

FAMILY ISSUES

Throughout the years, Arab Americans have often transferred the importance of family, marriage, and children to their new country. In the Middle East, it is common to live with relatives or in-laws in the same household. According to the U.S. Census and the Arab American Institute Foundation (AAIF), Arab Americans live in larger households than the average American does, likely indicating that some of the traditions of family cohabitation continued beyond migration. Larger household size may indicate a larger number of children (under 18 or adult), or the presence of many generations within a household. Migration can disrupt the extended family and friends networks, so, more than 90 percent of Arab Americans report that they have family or close friends in the Middle East, and many travel back to the Arab world often and for long periods of time to see their relatives and friends.

Family issues are usually a significant factor in the choice to migrate—often single young Arabs make the choice to migrate to support family members who remain in the Middle East, and some parents make the choice to leave their countries for the safety of the family or for economic opportunities that would benefit their children. Despite the family-centered intentions behind the choice to migrate, the act of migration can separate migrating adult children from their parents, aunts, uncles, grandparents, nephews, and nieces. Although eventually there may be reunification of the family or one nuclear family may join their relatives in a chain-migration pattern, family members are often separated by continents.

Arab Americans have tried to maintain the interconnectedness of the Arab family in their lives in the United States. New immigrants tend to move to certain neighborhoods or suburbs to be close to people from their families, villages, or cities of origin. Traditional networks may be expanded to further include other Arabs not from their family or neighborhood to maintain a familiar social life. Physical proximity with co-ethnics not only means that the newcomers have security in numbers, but also that they can more easily maintain their traditions with people who understand their customs. Another reason immigrants chose to be near family and friends is to have networks that enable them to find jobs or clients. Many of the new immigrants, particularly those fleeing war or harsh economic situations, arrive in the United States with little money and no insurance. Networks can help the newcomers with places to stay, loans, and assistance in renting apartments, finding jobs, and enrolling in schools or universities. Arab American small business owners sometimes hire family members and friends, making it easier on immigrants to find their first jobs in the United States, particularly if they are unskilled and have poor English-language skills. Some Arab American–owned businesses catering to a predominantly Arab American clientele have concentrated in areas with Arabic grocery stores, bakeries, restaurants, and Arabic-language bookshops and video stores. There are only a few of these Arab American enclaves—such as the south end of Dearborn,

Michigan, and Patterson, New Jersey—but they can give an immigrant a sense of familiarity and security when all else seems foreign.

Some communities were able to establish networks that form an "ethnic safety net," allowing for the "cohesion, safety, security, and prosperity of Arab families through interaction, assistance and intervention."[1] Leaders in the Dearborn community established the Arab Community Center for Economic and Social Services (ACCESS) to provide social services to the surrounding residents that would augment assistance from relatives and neighbors. In the south end of Dearborn, a low-income urban area and home to 18,000 Arab Americans, ACCESS helped to mitigate the negative consequences that resulted from the economic downturns and influx of impoverished new immigrants in the 1990s. ACCESS ran a Family Support Center in which only 10 percent of cases cited alcohol and drug abuse as a cause of marital and family problems.[2] During this period, Dearborn was able to keep crime rates low, while communities in nearby Detroit suffered from much higher crime rates.[3]

In the Chicago area, the mostly informal ethnic safety net deteriorated in the 1990s with dire consequences for individuals and families. The Arab American community in the southwest side of Chicago is home to the largest concentration of Arabs in the greater Chicago area and a major reception area for new immigrants from Arab countries. Although more than 70 years old, the Arab American (specifically Palestinian American) southwest side of Chicago became insular, strong, and resilient in the 1970s and 1980s. By the late 1990s, the "ethnic safety net" was deteriorating. In 1997, economic hardship, underemployment, or unemployment characterized more than 60 percent of the Arab American households, with American-born children being most of those living at or below the poverty level.[4] The surrounding neighborhood problems with crime and drugs spread into the Arab community, particularly affecting the youth, who joined Arab street gangs. The increase in juvenile detentions and danger in the neighborhood caused great tensions within families. Sixty percent of Arab Americans surveyed in Chicago reported having ongoing domestic problems that required outside help. Alcoholism, drug abuse, domestic violence, and broken families were common, interrelated problems.[5] These statistics stand in direct contrast to the cases seen by ACCESS in Dearborn and insinuate that the maintenance of ethnic safety nets was crucial to the ability of the community to survive and repel serious problems within the family.

Arab immigrants since 1965 have had three main types of reaction to their move to the United States: (1) resisting assimilation and/or believing that migration was temporary, (2) fully integrating Arab cultures and customs into their lives in the United States, and (3) creating a dividing line between public and private spheres, organizing the home and family in a manner similar to their way of life in the Middle East.

As with every ethnic group in the United States, it is easier to maintain traditions and customs by living and working in concentrated neighborhoods. Major U.S. cities, including New York, Chicago, Washington D.C., Los Angeles, and Houston may not have visible sections of Arab-signified businesses, yet they have large numbers of Arab American residents. In these cases, it may be possible to exclusively socialize with Arabs and set up majority Arab institutions such as schools, day care, and health clinics. This situation may enable individuals to isolate themselves from some U.S. cultural influences and thus better resist assimilation in both the public and private realms.

Arab Americans have adapted to life in the United States by integrating Arab cultures and customs with the prevailing U.S. norms and trends. As with other immigrants, usually the first generation is more eager to retain the Old World traditions, and subsequent generations tend to become more Americanized. It is hard to gauge or even to generalize about how and what traditions have been maintained because the definition of traditions is rooted in the family's socioeconomic realities and customs in the home country. Just as each Arab family has its own customs, including food, dress, language, religious practice, and moral values, so do Arab Americans.

As the home is frequently considered a refuge for family and heritage, some Arab Americans have drawn a line between the public and private, between American and Arab. In this scenario, outside the house, Arab American men and women interact easily and extensively with coworkers, clients, or customers who are not predominantly Arab. At home, the relations between family members as well as the food and décor reflect influences from the Middle East. They might attend a church or a mosque and socialize with other Arab Americans on the weekends. This scenario is somewhat common among middle- and upper-middle-class Arab Americans who live in the suburbs.

As in many American families, mothers tend to spend more time with the children than do fathers. As a result of this reality and the gendered family roles, women are traditionally held responsible for their children's behavior and so bear a disproportionate amount of the stress when a child acts up or rebels. The mother, who is expected to be with the children more than the father teaches the children the accepted norms of family life and is expected to discipline the children if there are minor infractions of the rules. The father's role is to reinforce the lessons taught by the mother and to intervene if there are major or repeated breaches. When there are cases of drug abuse or alcoholism, the parents are often blamed, as the individual's behavior is considered to reflect badly on the family. The social interconnectedness of the community establishes gossip grapevines that serve to monitor children (as well as adults) and to inform the family of misbehavior. Although in theory this interconnectedness is supportive, it may be counterproductive, as additional peer commentary and judgments can add pressure to an existing problem. Children are expected to be deferential to their parents, their families, and the social norms. Although the norms and rules may differ from family to family, alcohol and drug abuse are clearly not acceptable. The high rates of alcoholism, drug abuse, and domestic violence in the Chicagoan case indicated that the family structure has been weakened. The Arab American immigrant parents reported that they did not know how to reharness their children in the U.S. urban neighborhood context. One of the recommendations of the Chicago Needs Assessment Project was that a stronger safety net was needed that "involves collaborative efforts on the part of all members of the geographic community ... a multiethnic, multiracial safety net."[6]

Arab American parents tend to teach their children how to behave by example and discipline, especially in response to situations in which their children are putting their own physical safety and health at risk. In Islam, alcoholic consumption is a sin, and many observant Muslim families discourage their children from socializing at a party where alcohol may be served. When first-generation parents see and experience the high crime rates in the United States, they tend to turn to disciplinary measures that may seem harsh to an American parent. Enforcing early curfews and hitting the child or young adult (but not to the extent of beating) are considered appropriate ways to handle discipline within the family. Because of the concept of teaching by example and the strong social reliance on family, babysitters are not the norm for social situations as children, even toddlers, are integral to the family and should learn how to behave in social settings as well as in the home. Young children and teenagers therefore usually accompany their parents to dinner or to friends' houses in the evenings or on weekends. The hierarchical nature of the Arab family structure and the expectation of obedience by parents have proved to be issues of contention for their children, whether, from the first, second, or third generation.

The communal, interconnectedness of more unassimilated communities runs counter to the widespread U.S. social system that values individualism, independence, and egalitarian relationships. For second- and third-generation Arab Americans, the family interconnectedness and hierarchy can sometimes be suffocating. When faced with the rebellion of their children, Arab American parents have a choice: either to adapt to the mainstream American culture, giving their children more freedom by loosening the traditional Arab family structure, or to discipline their children more within the family context. If unsuccessfully negotiated, the family members clash and do not resolve their differing viewpoints. If successfully negotiated, the younger generation remains close to their parents' ideals, in which family members are part of a larger social unit that communicates daily and shares emotions, experiences, and decisions with each other. In most Arab American families, there is a middle ground in which each family member brings her or his own conflicting or congruent views and experiences to discussions and interactions.

The Arab American population is younger than the national average; the average age is 30.8 years old—almost five years younger than the U.S. average of 35.4 years of age.[7] Arab Americans therefore face more youth issues than does the average U.S. family. Although discipline is considered important, education is seen as a means of upward mobility and a precursor for professional achievement that is highly valued in the Arab American community. Members of the early Arab American community did not attend segregated public schools with African Americans, Asian Americans, Native Americans, and Latinos. As is the case today, some children went to parochial schools, but most attended public schools—a factor that contributed to their fast assimilation. In education, the first and later generations have different needs. Some foreign-born children need extra help with English and adjustment to the U.S. schools. Children without sufficient fluency in English are placed in Limited English Proficiency (LEP) classes until they can be put into regular classes. The influx of new immigrants into some areas has increased the demand for LEP classes and teachers. One such example exists in New York State, where the public schools introduced the first bilingual Arabic class in the early 1990s, and children of Arab descent now make up one-sixth of the student population and 40 percent of the total number of LEP students.[8] The results and success of these programs are mixed. On one hand, some Arab American parents recognize that schools and teachers have a strong influence on their children and think that the public school system tries to eradicate immigrant culture through homogenization. These disgruntled parents are choosing to home school their children or send them to Islamic schools as alternatives to the public school system. On the other hand, some Arab Americans argue that a public school education teaches the children how to integrate into U.S. society and so is positive for their long-term success in the United States. Regardless of the choice of school, most Arab American teenagers are encouraged to finish high school and at least 85 percent of Arab Americans have a high-school diploma.[9]

Most Arab Americans chose to continue their educations beyond high school. More than 40 percent of Arab Americans have a B.A. degree or higher and 17 percent hold a postgraduate degree, twice the national average.[10] Many more traditional parents prefer to send their older children to nearby public colleges or universities so that they can live at home or visit on the weekends. The cost of tuition and housing are major factors in the choice of a college, but parents often want to feel close to their children and able to help them if the need arises. On U.S. campuses, there are students who come from the Arab world but have chosen to attend a U.S. university instead of a less-expensive local college or an elite regional school such as the American University of Beirut or the American University in Cairo. Arab students may choose to socialize together and form associations to speak out on political issues or, more commonly, concentrate on social activities—hosting *haflas* (parties), serving Arabic food, bringing in live Arabic music or a D.J. and inviting non-Arab members of the college community. Some Muslims join the Muslim Student Association, a national group with chapters at universities and colleges across the United States.

Depending on the ethnic composition of the school or community and personal disposition, Arab Americans often socialize together. Arab American peers can give culturally appropriate advice and look out for one another in a way that creates a communal bond. For young adults in particular, shared heritage and values allow for a better understanding of their parents' gender expectations and boundaries. Peer solidarity can give an Arab American teenager a feeling of security at a time when being different is not considered acceptable.

Within Arab American communities, peer groups and family members can overlap. The sibling relationship is one of the most important for Arab Americans; brothers, sisters, and cousins can be an individual's closest confidantes from youth until old age. In youth, the brother often protects his sister's reputation by acting as a chaperone among peers, while a sister may offer advice and pamper her younger brothers and sisters in a motherly way. As siblings age, they usually continue to be involved in each other's lives and decisions, even after marrying and having their own children. In this way, the interconnectivity and strong sense of family are passed down from generation to generation, regardless of the family's length of time in the United States.

Arab family members also show solidarity and familial loyalty by taking care of elderly parents. In the Arab world, age is respected, and elderly parents live with their children, usually with the eldest son and his family. As the U.S. immigration laws currently allow for family reunification of parents and children, some first-generation Arab Americans are housing and accommodating their parents. Elderly immigrants from all origins usually have a harder time adjusting to a new country than do their younger counterparts. First-generation Arab Americans generally look at the U.S. tendency to put the elderly in retirement homes or assisted living accommodations with "annoyance, skepticism and even anger."[11] However, upholding the family responsibility of taking care of elderly parents can be challenging. In homes where both husband and wife work and return home to care for the children and cook dinner, the added onus of tending to the needs and socializing with parents is substantial. If the parents' language skills are poor and they have no transportation, they may be unable to leave the house during the day, relying on their adult children to take them places after returning from work. The daily activities for these housebound parents are watching television, reading, and cleaning the house while waiting for their children and grandchildren to come home. As a result, many elderly immigrants feel lonely and yearn for the time when they were self-sufficient and mobile back in the Arab world. The need to find alternatives that would benefit the elderly and maintain family respect and closeness has become apparent to some families. To that end, the Bay Ridge section of the St. Nicholas Home for the elderly, now in Brooklyn, was established in 1978, housing 75 residents of different ethnicities and religions while serving Arabic food and teaching Arabic classes. A few of the larger Islamic centers have recently built or bought housing for older Muslims within walking distance of the mosque so that the elderly can retain some independence and self-sufficiency.

Issues of aging and death are not at the forefront of community priorities but are growing in importance as more people chose not to be buried in the Middle East. Civic-minded Arab American individuals and organizations have established cemeteries and burial grounds for community and family members. Early Arab Americans bought cemetery lots and placed the Muslim cemetery adjacent to the Christian Arab one. There is a growing demand for Muslim cemeteries as the immigrants who arrived in the 1960s and 1970s pass on. Traditionally, a Muslim corpse is wrapped in a cloth and laid directly in the ground but American Muslims have had to adapt to U.S. laws that require a casket in all burials. Another Islamic requirement more easily achieved by a Muslim cemetery than in a non-Muslim lot is that the body should face Mecca.

Gender Divisions within the Family

Women and girls usually are the ones who oppose the gendered roles within the family hierarchy. Although each family maintains its own norms and rules, boys are usually given more latitude and playtime, whereas girls are often required to help their mothers in daily household chores. As children become teenagers, girls are closely watched and often not allowed to date, whereas boys are usually allowed to have non-Arab girlfriends. A researcher of the Shia community in Dearborn concluded that the polarization created by their families treating boys and girls differently has caused boys to "take on more of the social characteristics of the dominant American society, whereas anti-assimilationist pressure is exerted on the girls through careful monitoring of social activities."[12] Especially in areas with high Arab concentrations (and therefore gossip networks), parents worry about "what people will say" about their daughters' behavior, in the same way that they did in the Middle East. However, in the United States, boys and girls both have non-Arab friends. The girls find that as puberty approaches, their freedom is curtailed as their non-Arab friends continue to go to the movies and parties. This double standard is the cause of many a complaint from Arab American girls. When parents justify their restrictions on the girls with their Arab and/or Muslim identity, the girls are more resentful of their backgrounds than are boys.[13]

Recent immigrant parents in the United States can be stricter with their girls than parents in the Middle East. With the media portrayal of U.S. women (in both the Middle East and in the United States), the higher crime rates, and the dominant social acceptance of dating and premarital sex in U.S. society, immigrant parents can be ultrasensitive to the activities of their unwed daughters. Afraid of "what's out there," they fear for their daughters' reputations and place restrictions on their movements. As Arab Americans become more comfortable in the U.S. society and open to the notion of assimilation, limitations on girls' participation in after-school activities, sports teams, or dating may be relaxed. Strict rules can set teenage daughters apart from their peers and cause ostracism, as one Arab American young woman recounted:

> In high school, my parents were stricter than other people's parents . . . people would say, "Your parents are so weird. . . ." They knew I wasn't allowed to have guys come over, but these guys come by our house and throw rolls of toilet paper into the balcony. . . . They were trying to make him [my dad] mad, to see what he was capable of . . . by the end of high school, I didn't tell people that I was Arab.[14]

Although some girls accept their parents' concerns about dating, some bring the issue to the attention of their parents, negotiating a middle ground in which they are allowed to date if they introduce their dates to their parents first. Others rebel and date behind their parents' backs, and if their parents discover them, the situation could become violent, and stricter rules would likely be imposed. Arab American girls who ignore the social taboos and are sexually active avoid going to Arab American community health clinics and centers because they are worried that gossip will get back to their parents.[15] For many Arab American families, the worst-case scenario is the pregnancy of an unwed daughter because abortions or out-of-wedlock births are completely unacceptable and a serious blemish on the family name in the community.

Marriage

Many, if not most families, however, counteract this possibility through educating their children on moral values. Marriage is considered so imperative that the concept of "marriageability" is sometimes used to curb behavior. In these cases, parents threaten their children who engage in taboo behaviors (such as drinking, dating, or doing drugs) with jeopardizing their reputations and so limiting their prospects of finding a spouse. With the double standard for girls and boys, these threats are mostly leveled at girls. Conservative and liberal parents alike generally accept boys dating and having non-Arab girlfriends until marriage, when they should marry an Arab or an Arab American girl of the same religion. There are instances of first-generation Arab American parents forcing or encouraging their daughters to marry early, while still in their teens. Arranged marriages still exist, particularly in low-income Yemeni and Lebanese Shia American families. Depending on the family circumstances, girls facing early or arranged marriages argue with their parents that they should postpone matrimony until they have completed their education and have a job.

Arab American youth, who are influenced by the dominant cultural emphasis on independence and romance as precursors to marriage, are demanding marriage more on their own terms. Although they want to appease their families, they want to choose their own spouses and to be in love before the wedding. Girls and boys alike increasingly want to wait until they are financially independent from their families before making the decision to marry. A smaller number of Arab Americans marry and then inform their parents. Most Arab Americans seek their families' approval or acquiescence before getting engaged in order to maintain peace within the families. The balancing act between finding an appropriate spouse and securing family approval can be challenging.

There has been some success in marriages in the United States: Arab Americans have a higher percentage of persons now married and a lower percentage of those currently divorced than the U.S. population as a whole. Even though the average age of Arab Americans is lower than the national average, the percent of Arab Americans who are married is 57 percent in comparison with 54 percent of the general U.S. population. The higher male/female ratio may be related to this outcome, or it may indicate that there are many single, younger men in the population, and the females tend to marry at a higher rate than the men. The statistics in Table 4.1 only tell part of the story.

Usually parents want their children to marry "someone like them"—of a similar socioeconomic status, ethnic background (village, city, country, or pan-Arab), and religion. If they are forced to prioritize their choices, Arab American parents often prefer their children to marry someone from the same religious and ethnic background. Historically, Arab Americans were flexible in their choices and judgments of marriage partners. The first wavers deemed those in the same religion or ethnicity to be acceptable marriage partners. For example, if the family was Catholic, possible spouses could be Arab Christians from a Greek Orthodox family or could be from Polish or Italian Catholic backgrounds. Although the couple shared religious affiliations, such pairings would be considered out-marriage because the spouses were not both of Arab backgrounds. As the Arab Christian community became more established in the United States, they built local churches that served to bring the geographically separate community together on Sundays and holy days. From these churches, they created social networks

Table 4.1
Comparisons of Age, Gender, and Marital Status of the Arab American Population to the General U.S. Population

	Arab American Population	General U.S. Population
Median Age (in years)	30.8	35.4
Male to Female Ratio	1.12/1	0.96/1
% Married	57	54

Sources: U.S. Census Bureau, *Census 2000* (Washington, DC, 2000); also available online at http://www.census.gov/main/www/cen2000.html; Arab American Institute Foundation, "Arab American Demographics," 2004, http://www.aaiusa.org/demographics.htm.

and complex social infrastructures, including regional associations that have a mainly social role and consider matchmaking an important component of this role. Some of these pre-1965 Arab Christian organizations are discussed in Chapter 5. Despite these organizations, many Muslims and Christians alike had high out-marriage rates until 1965.

Nowadays, many Arab American parents encourage their older children to attend community events, such as weddings and conventions, so that they can meet potential spouses. After 1965, the numbers of immigrants and thus potential partners increased, and the parameters of acceptability shrank. Although some groups within the Arab American community may be more accepting of non-Arabs, there is still a strong in-group preference. Generally speaking, there is a correlation between higher levels of education, income, and occupation with a more liberal attitude toward out-group and cross-religion marriages.

Both Christian and Muslim Arab Americans are more likely to approve of marriages to co-religionists over co-ethnics. Therefore, Roman Catholic or Eastern Rite Churches such as the Maronites increasingly married Catholics who were originally from Italy, Ireland, or other countries. In 1910, only 6 percent of children were from a "mixed" marriage (i.e., a Syrian marrying a non-Syrian); 10 years later, the number had risen to 8 percent and climbed throughout the 1920s and onward.[16] As a result, some married non-Arabs and tried to become more independent of the Arab influence and culture. The ideal of in-group marriage remains a major motivator for communities to keep in touch and form networks. For Christian families, the wedding itself takes place in a church with a ceremony presided over by the priest.

In the Islamic tradition, marriage is a contract, and the legally binding part of the ceremony is usually a small family affair with the *imam* presenting the marriage contract to the couple. (The illegality of polygamy in the United States is not much of an issue to American Muslims because polygamy is not widely practiced in the Arab world.) Among Muslims, interfaith marriage is discouraged, and a potential non-Muslim spouse is often expected to convert to Islam before the wedding so that their future children will not be confused about their religious identity. There is a gendered aspect to the acceptability of a marriage partner. Arab American parents may tolerate their son marrying a non-Arab but not a daughter; she would probably pay a higher price for breaking their expectations, even being cut off from all family communications in extreme circumstances. The Quran supports this gendered approval of a marriage partner by permitting a Muslim man to marry a non-Muslim woman but not vice-versa. In many Arab countries, this Islamic edict is law, but in the United States, it is not legally binding.

According to one researcher, 10 to 15 percent of American Muslim women are marrying outside of the Islamic faith today.[17] In religious terms, this pairing (Muslim man and non-Muslim woman) is acceptable, but the man's parents may worry that the Muslim faith will not be passed onto the next generation. Interfaith and interethnic marriage is one of the ways that the second and third generations are making choices that differentiate them from their immigrant parents.

WOMEN'S ISSUES

Some early Arab American women found that the United States was a place where they could earn more than men in the same occupations—peddling, sewing garments, and millwork. These working women gained economic independence from their male family members and became more active in the political and social realms, making friends outside kinship circles. With the demise of peddling as a trade, women continued to peddle or went into business with their husbands, sometimes as a partner in a grocery store or in a similar small enterprise. In the mid-twentieth century, women who worked in the textile mills of New England joined the unions and reluctantly helped to hold the picket lines in strikes and to feed the strikers.

Some of the biggest critics of women's new independence were women. Afifa Karam (1883–1925), the well-known Arab American woman journalist, wrote extensively for *al-Hoda,* the most successful Arabic newspaper in the United States. She, like many middle-class Americans at the time, thought that peddling was a morally suspect activity and that women living and working without their husbands would be tempted to succumb to temptation with other men. Karam also thought that husbands were exploiting their wives by sending them out to peddle and bring back money, and that working ultimately did not serve the interests of women, but of men. In 1908 she wrote:

> If the Syrian woman were cultivated and educated, the man would not have been able to twirl his mustache and hop from tavern to tavern and from house to house, after sending his wife to roam in the wasteland, exposing herself and her reputation to shame, that she might bring him back gold, and on her return not ask "Where have you been?" but instead, "What have you brought?"[18]

Women from the first and second waves were active in charity organizations, a socially acceptable activity for women that also played a crucial role in the Arab American social scene. In 1896, women from educated, well-established families set up the Syrian Women's Union of New York to help the poor, especially children and women. They held weekly sewing circles, giving their work directly to the poor, and auctioning off the more intricate pieces. Although at first they aimed to help the poor back home, they were made aware of the poverty among Arab Americans and later opened a nursery for mothers who peddled or worked in factories. In 1907, a similar group of women began the Syrian Ladies' Aid Society that employed a matron to help immigrant girls arriving at Ellis Island to find work in the United States. A Syrian Ladies' Aid Society was established in Boston. Women from all backgrounds helped to establish social, educational, and occasionally political clubs, as well as churches and mosques. They ran various events and parties to fundraise for these causes and were largely successful in their endeavors. For example, the Syrian Ladies' Aid Society raised $15,000 through holding bazaars and food sales to purchase the mortgage of the Orthodox Church in Worcester, Massachusetts. Women initiated the fundraising efforts for the creation of a mosque in Cedar Rapids, Iowa, in the late 1920s. Although there were Syrian American clubs run by men, these organizations allowed women to take public leadership roles within the community and to socialize with other women on the basis of shared ethnicity.

The wealthier women, who had the time and resources to help relieve the hardships of the less fortunate, developed some compassion for their co-ethnics throughout their charity work tempering their criticisms of peddling and working women. Today, similar class divides and critiques create distance between Arab American women. Women with few language skills or education, who need to work for the income, are the focus of these social critiques because they have to leave their children in the care of other family members. They are further disadvantaged by social mores that dictate the suitability of jobs. As mentioned, women rarely do manual jobs in the Middle East and North Africa. Other unskilled jobs, such as waitressing, are considered inappropriate in the United States because of the uniforms, hours, extensive interaction with men, and the handling of pork products and alcohol, which are forbidden in Islam. Therefore, depending on language skills, some women find work as secretaries in offices or in sales for major department stores and local shops. Some Arab American women work in fast food chains, especially teenage girls, who do so after school. At issue for Arab American women is achieving a balance between family responsibilities, upholding the family name, and finding fulfilling work. Some of the most desirable jobs for women are teaching and nursing, but they require education beyond high school. In areas with high unemployment rates, it is even more challenging to secure an appropriate job. In Dearborn, one study found that few immigrant women were employed despite their wishes to find a job.[19]

Despite these struggles for the less skilled and fortunate, many Arab American women enjoy full-time professional work in fields that range from accounting to zoology. Some of the pioneers in various fields are Arab American women. For example, Helen Thomas was one of the few female journalists in the White House Press Corps, the United Press International's chief White House correspondent for more than 30 years and is still working as a news columnist and correspondent. She is the daughter of a Lebanese peddler turned grocery store owner, and like other Arab American women, she has learned how to be successful in traditionally male-dominated fields in the United States. For some Arab American women, after struggling to finish an education and garnering family support for working outside the home, the climb to the top in U.S. corporations is just another step in a journey.

The ability of a woman to work full-time depends on the support she receives from her family and the division of labor in the home. Recent immigrant families from small villages or working-class backgrounds may have a stronger division of labor between men and women in the home. In such cases, women are expected to be the main caretakers of the family and to maintain the house (cooking, cleaning, and doing laundry), whereas men are the primary income earners. Women, who work full- or part-time in a family business, may not be remunerated at the same level as a waged worker, but if they work for a business not owned by a family member, presumably they would be paid, which may give them greater personal autonomy and the family a second income. The higher incomes paid in the United States than in the Arab world act as an additional incentive to work. Nevertheless, in more traditional families, working does not diminish the demands on women in the home, and if they are unable to fulfill their family's social expectations, their work may cause conflicts that may lead to a questioning of the roles within the family structure.

Arab Americans originally from urban areas or from highly educated or professional families arrive with their own set of expectations for women and men. Such families are unlikely to maintain a traditional division of labor in the home, and both parents are more apt to work outside the home and sometimes share domestic chores and childcare. This division of labor is both a reflection of their socioeconomic status in the Arab world and an adjustment to life in the United States. In the Arab world, children would be cared for by relatives when the mother was at work, but the breakup of the extended family with migration has forced many Arab Americans to find alternatives, including more paternal involvement in the home and child-rearing as well as nonfamily childcare options. Daycare in the United States, which is expensive, is often a tradeoff for many women. Whether the mother of small children works or not often depends on the available childcare options and the financial feasibility of such a choice for the parents.

Arab American women have been active in political and social organizations (see Chapter 6), and in the administration and fundraising activities in Arab churches and Christian charities. However, since 1965, the roles, activities, and positions of women in mosques has been curtailed and restricted by the influx of new immigrants and their imams, who want to establish stricter adherence to a form of Islam that conforms to patterns idealized in Islamic religious circles in the Arab world. American Muslim women are actively objecting to this trend, calling for mosques to be more woman-friendly, but they rarely call for the complete mixing of genders common in most Christian services. In many smaller mosques, women do not have a prayer area. The larger mosques, especially custom-built ones, have separate entrances and prayer sections for women. For now, the mosque remains the locus for public expression of faith and is "the province of men."[20] The rationale behind the separation of the sexes in worship, meetings, and other public gatherings is that women are more comfortable in their own space where they can interact in a more relaxing environment. The women's prayer areas are located on the side or at the back of the mosque because the sight of women prostrating themselves before God is considered distracting for men. The most traditional Muslim leaders and imams, who are always male, believe that women should pray at home and not attend the mosque, even for Friday sermons.

Islam calls for modesty of dress for both men and women. Although some religious Muslim men have distinctive beards, the men's requirements do not usually constitute any outward signs of religion. Women, however, have to dress modestly, and some Muslims believe that the Quran requires a woman to wear a veil when a man who is not a close family relative can see her. (See Chapter 1 for more discussion of what the Quran says about veiling.) The purpose of the veil, or *hijab,* is not to belittle a woman but to protect her from unwanted male attention by covering her hair and perhaps her body, depending on the interpretation of Islamically required dress. In the United States, many Americans see the veil as a symbol of oppression and degradation forced by Muslim men on women and consider the veil an endorsement of a backward culture and religion. In contrast, many veiled women report feeling full of dignity and self-esteem and enjoy that their physical, personal self does not enter into social interactions. As a result, many veiled women consider the *hijab* a symbol of freedom and liberation from men. One Muslim American woman said, "My husband didn't make me dress this way, and I'm not oppressed. I'm set free—free from the bondage of fashion, clothes, hair, shoes, and the like."[21] As a result of the rise of pride in the Muslim religion and the Islamic revival movement, more women are adopting the veil in their daily lives. About 70 percent of the people who convert to Islam in the United States are women, many of whom are well-educated professional women. Among these women, as well as Arab American Muslim women, some adopt the traditional *hijab,* others cover themselves with contemporary clothing and scarves, and others choose to not wear a covering at all. Some women are making a statement that they are Muslims when wearing the *hijab;* others are following what they consider to be religiously mandated clothing. However, "veiling" attracts attention in the United States and often prompts discrimination, harassment, and even hate crimes. Many veiled women have faced discrimination in the workplace and have been denied promotions, or even fired, from their jobs for wearing a *hijab.* Muslim organizations, such as the Council on American Islamic Relations (CAIR) and the American Muslim Council (AMC), have filed several lawsuits against major corporations and won on the basis that employers cannot discriminate on the basis of religion. In May 2004, the Department of Justice ruled that the Muskogee Public School District in Oklahoma must allow for religious clothing in its dress code and reinstate a Muslim girl who had been suspended twice for wearing a headscarf (or *hijab*) to school. The Department of Justice stated that the Oklahoma school had violated the constitutional rights of the girl and the Civil Rights Division of the Department of Justice continues to be involved in a number of religious liberty cases.[22]

Despite incidents of discrimination and hate crimes, the openness of U.S. society and dialogue available in the United States has allowed the voices of Muslim women to form and be heard. Muslim feminists believe that it is possible to be both a feminist and a Muslim without compromising either identity. Whereas many feminists argue that male/female differences are socially constructed, the dominant Islamic and Arab perspective is that women and men are different by nature, both biologically and psychologically. Both analyses conclude that gender defines life's parameters and believe that women have more hardships than men in life as a direct result of their gender. Muslim feminists are less focused on women's sexual behavior, the individual, identity, and exploitation by men; instead, they are more focused on politics, cultural identity, and the freedom and nonexploitation of the larger group. Feminists within Islam are working to reinterpret religious traditions in the Quran, arguing that men and corrupt states distorted the practice of Islam and the *hadith,* and that men and women are equal before God. Christian Arab American women have allied with other women in their churches and social organizations. Arab American feminists are members of non-Arab feminist organizations and movements focusing on issues such as equal pay, equal opportunities, and freedom from sexual harassment.

Arab Americans have worked to reform opinions about women in the Arab world and the perception of Arab women in the United States. Much of the Arab American feminist movement has formed at academic meetings and conferences in panels on Arab women, and the academic constructions of Arab American feminism tend to dominate the discourse. Arab Americans have established the Feminist Arab-American Network, the Union of Palestinian Women's Associations in North America, the Institute for Arab Women's Studies, and the Association for Middle Eastern Women's Studies to engage both the feminist and the academic circles in discussions on the situation of women in the Arab world and in the United States. Some Arab American academics, such as Therese Saliba, believe they have been marginalized by the mainstream American feminist movement and organizations such as the National Women's Studies Association. Pointedly, Saliba titled her 1999 article on the subject, "Resisting Invisibility: Arab Americans in Academia and Activism," arguing that Arab American feminists are ignored because they are classified as whites and therefore do not fit into panels on women of color where race and ethnic issues are discussed. In addition, many American feminists do not believe that there can be Arab feminism, assuming that the two terms are oxymoronic. As a result of their lack of success in American feminist circles, Arab American women have sought to change their own society. Even though feminism remains controversial in the Arab American community, feminists have made some inroads into Arab American organizations (notably the ADC and the AAUG).

However controversial the topic or identity of feminism is, homosexuality is even more so. Like other Arab Americans, homosexual Arab Americans have to combat the immediate assumption that Arabs are anti-Semitic or fall into one of the many U.S. media stereotypes of Arabs, and in addition, they have to combat possible rejection of their sexual identity by Arab Americans. Arab American lesbians and gays have expressed that they feel marginalized on two accounts: by the lesbian, gay, bisexual, and transgender community and by Arab American circles. Some families are accepting of their child's sexual preference and embrace their partners as members of the family but homosexuality is not widely tolerated in the Arab American community.

LANGUAGE

Arab Americans are similar to other immigrant groups in that the first generation is fluent in the spoken home language and learns English as a second language, sometimes before leaving the Arab world. English is easier to learn if a person is literate in one or more languages. Because illiteracy in Arabic is still a concern for those from urban and rural areas of poorer Arab countries such as Yemen, it is often hard for some first-generation Arab Americans, particularly the elderly, to learn English. The second language taught in Arabic school systems often reflects their colonial history, so some sending countries, such as Lebanon and Morocco, teach French; others, such as Palestine, Jordan, Egypt, and Yemen, teach English in school. Obviously, arriving in the United States with strong English skills helps the individual adjust to the country, but Arab community groups in Dearborn as well as in Chicago also teach English classes to recent arrivals.

The early Arab Americans who lived in ethnic enclaves used their mother tongue in the home and in the neighborhood, learning English for commerce purposes only. Eventually the scales tipped, and English began to be spoken at home as well as in public. When the third wavers arrived, they boosted the use and extent of Arabic spoken in the United States. According to the 2000 Census, roughly 615,000 Americans speak Arabic, and Arabic is ranked as the seventh most common foreign language spoken by school-aged children in the United States. Arabic *(fusha)* is a *linga franca* that all the peoples from the Arab world share in common, bringing together people who may not associate back home. Minorities from the Arab world who speak other languages, such as Berber, Assyrian, and Chaldean, may also communicate in Arabic.

In the Census 2000 statistics limited to the foreign-born and those of two Arab parents (who could be of any generation), 69 percent of Arabs aged 5 and older "spoke a language other than English at home."[23] This is high compared with 18 percent of the total population who spoke a language other than English at home. When native born and those of mixed heritage are factored into the Arab American grouping, it is found that Arab Americans speak only English in the home on par with the national level. This observation highlights that Arab Americans are more likely to stop speaking Arabic at home when they are born in the United States and/or are from mixed parents.

As residence in the United States is drawn out, Arab Americans increasingly use English in the home as well as in public. In casual conversations, the first and second generations may switch from English to Arabic in one sentence; this slang is sometimes known as "Arabish." Second- and third-generation Arab Americans usually have to take extra language classes to be fluent in Arabic. In larger communities, classes are offered by the local community center, mosque, or church. In smaller communities or out of personal preference, Arab parents may choose to hire private tutors from the foreign students at a local university.

The various dialects spoken in the Arab world indicate where a person or his or her parents originated. These dialects can differ so radically from one another that some people consider them to be individual languages (e.g., Lebanese or Egyptian), even though they share a written form of Arabic. The differences between written and spoken languages are additional challenges for Arab Americans learning to speak Arabic. Breakdowns of community by nationality indicate that Lebanese is probably the most widely spoken dialect among Arab Americans, and Iraqis are the most likely group to speak English less than "very well."[24]

FOOD

Some multigenerational Arab Americans describe their Arabic-language skills as "kitchen Arabic," meaning that they only know the Arabic words for dishes cooked by their family in the home. Indeed, there is a strong association between food, ethnic identity, and language for many Arab Americans. This has created a unique situation, highlighted by a book on the national, racial, and feminist identities of many different generations of Arab Americans, *Food for Our Grandmothers: Writings by Arab-American and Arab-Canadian Feminists* (1994). The progressive nature of the book may seem to be at odds with the inclusion of recipes for traditional Arab dishes, but in the world of multigenerational Arab Americans, food is a cultural product shared and passed down from generation to generation, generally by women.

Culinary dishes vary from country to country, even within a region, but Lebanese cuisine and particularly hummus, pita bread, and kebabs are the most popular Arabic foods in the United States. Arab Americans tend to cook in their homes, creating a demand for products typical of home. The long transport hauls from Lebanon and Syria to the United States in the early 1900s made the import of certain goods from home pointless, so food products (and dairy in particular) that mimicked the home versions began to be produced and sold by Arab Americans in the United States in the early 1900s. At first the industry was small, catering only to other Arab families who cooked their local cuisine in their homes daily. As mothers taught their children how to cook and passed down their preparation methods and recipes, demand among the Arab American community alone led to the establishment of Arabic grocery stores. There are now specialty grocery stores in most major cities across the country that cater to Arab Americans as well as to a wider audience of Americans. Lebanese dishes, such as hummus, tabbouli, fettoush salad, and shwarma, are often made on the premises and available for take-out.

Although these Arabic specialty stores may carry pork products, non-*halal* meat, and alcohol, other specialty stores cater to Muslims specifically by carrying only religiously permissible food. Shellfish, alcohol (in any form), and meat not slaughtered in the way prescribed by the Quran are not considered *halal* food. *Halal* grocery stores and butchers have increased in number in the last few years, mostly located in areas with concentrated Muslim populations. The demand for *halal* food by Muslim Americans not living in such areas has grown, and food production companies that offer frozen *halal* meat products have been established in the United States. Muslim dietary limits can restrict the ability of practicing Muslims to eat in restaurants or in the homes of non-Muslims, so some American Muslims have adapted by bringing a dish cooked with *halal* meat with them to non-Muslim potluck gatherings. Muslims have also adapted by eating kosher food because it is slaughtered in a similar fashion to *halal* meat and by carefully choosing vegetarian items from a restaurant menu. Some Muslims do not follow the *halal* food guidelines very strictly or only do so in *Ramadan* (the holy month) and on the feast days.

Since the 1970s, the growing interest in non-Western cuisine has fuelled the establishment of various types of so-called ethnic restaurants and eateries. The demand has spurred some of the first-generation Arab Americans to open up restaurants specializing in Mediterranean, Middle Eastern, or Moroccan cuisine that cater to mainstream American customers. Middle Eastern restaurants in major U.S. cities have capitalized on the appeal of the exotic side of their culture, as it is perceived by many Americans, by hiring belly dancers and by having patrons sit on the floor while eating from brass trays. This trend is part of a larger Orientalist view of the Middle East as backward, unitary, and foreign, but at least these restaurants show the hospitable and warm side of the Arab cultures to their American customers.

ARAB AMERICAN MEDIA AND COMMUNICATIONS

The Arab American media has grown and changed over the years, often reflecting the tensions and divisions among Arab Americans. The first publication, *Kawkab Amirka* (or Star of America), was founded in New York

City in 1892. Following that publication, the number of Arabic-language newspapers grew, each targeting specific subgroups. For example, *Meraat al-Gharb* was written for the Syrian Orthodox community, and *al-Hoda* (the Guidance) targeted the Maronite community. The early Arab American press used the U.S. freedom of press that it had been denied in its own countries, often writing about political issues and news from the homeland. Journalists, such as Afifa Karam, who wrote for *al-Hoda,* focused on the condition of Arab American and Arab women. By the 1930s, there were more than 50 publications, all in Arabic. In 1926, Salloum Mozarkel founded the first English-language publication aimed at the Arab American community, *The Syrian World.* This magazine, which gained a large following in the 1930s, helped to unite the community by reaching out to all Arab Americans rather than specific groups by focusing on national Arab and Arab American issues. After the success of *The Syrian World,* other publications were established that were bilingual or English-only, geared to the mainly English-speaking children of the first wavers.

In the 1960s, the new immigrants demanded news about the Arab world in Arabic, so Arabic-language radio programs were launched in Detroit, Chicago, Boston, and San Francisco, and many immigrants subscribed to Arabic newspapers published abroad. Arab American organizations produced their own publications, books, reference directories, and newsletters in Arabic and English—some geared toward in-group communications and some toward educating an American audience about the ongoing events in the Middle East.

By the end of 2002, the Arab American media outlets combined had reached members of the community with 45 printed publications, with a combined circulation of about 500,000.[25] Some of the largest circulating newspapers today are the *News Circle* and *Arab-American Business Magazine.* The last 30 years have witnessed a growth and diversification of Arab American media from printed publications and radio shows to local television programs, cable channels, and Web sites. Of note is the Arab Network of America (ANA)—the first Arabic-language cable television network to broadcast nationally in the United States as well as to Canada and to parts of Central and South America. ANA radio is syndicated in major U.S. cities. In 1995, the Arab Radio & Television (ART) network began broadcasting news and entertainment from California through local cable systems and direct satellite broadcasting.

The growth of the Internet as a medium of communication has brought the Arab world closer to the United States. Arab Americans can now read Arabic newspapers from home online and can have discussions in chat rooms.

Cell phone text messaging and e-mails are used to keep in touch with friends and family in the Middle East, making the maintenance of extended family networks easier. Arab Americans are using the Internet to educate others and bring together political activists from Europe, the Middle East, and the United States to create global networks. Three sites run by Arab Americans that focus on political issues are http://www.electronicintifada.net; http://www.mideastdilemma.com; and http://www.vestedowl.com. Arab Americans have formed their own community-based Web sites, such as http://www.cafearabica.com and http://www.arabamerican.net, where Arab Americans can post messages and discuss their issues and concerns. Whether they are religious or secular, national or local, some of the community organizations have well-maintained, extensive sites that present a variety of publications and viewpoints on the current state of Arab Americans. With a population spread throughout the 50 states and the national growth of home-based Internet access, the Internet will continue to grow as a tool for Arab American community activists in the coming years.

RELIGION

Christians

As Arab Americans settled down in the United States, their religious sect, as well as their religion, played a role in their assimilation and ability to maintain their ethnic heritage. To a large extent, the establishment and continuation of their own churches and mosques were pivotal in this experience because religious services bring together people at specified times and can encourage the sharing of friendship and pride in their commonalities. Religious institutions provide a locus for celebrations and rites of passage that signify life changes for individuals, such as baptisms, weddings, and funerals. Traditions and belief systems are passed down through religious institutions and provide continuity for the community. Religion is also a personal signifier for Arabs. Considering the importance of religion in the Middle East and North Africa, it is noteworthy that the first immigrants were reluctant to establish their own religious institutions. They clearly believed that their stay in the United States was a temporary sojourn and chose to emphasize individual independence over creating a sense of community. It was only when families began to join the single sojourners in the 1890s that they began to establish their own churches. Mosques would not be founded until the 1920s, possibly because of the small number of Muslims.

When the first and second wavers migrated, they brought with them the social delineations that existed at the time in the Middle East. In addition to socioeconomic and place-of-origin differentiations, people would identify by religion, and more specifically, by religious sect. Therefore, most of the first immigrants were not just Christian, but Melkites, Maronites, or Orthodox Christians. These immigrants arrived in the late nineteenth century to find that there were three main religious categories in the United States: Protestant, Catholic, and Jewish. This meant that to fully assimilate, they would have to give up their traditional religious identity and conform to one of these three recognized categories.

The Maronites and Melkites moved closer to Roman Catholicism. The Maronites came from a religious tradition that had shown its allegiance to the West, and to Catholicism in particular, and were eager to be recognized as Catholics in the United States. Although the Melkites were more closely allied with the Byzantines and shared distinctly Eastern Rites with the Orthodox, as another Uniate Church affiliated with the Vatican, they acknowledged the Pope's authority and were drawn to Roman Catholic Churches in the United States as well. Both groups felt pressured by the U.S. Catholic Church to conform their services and worship to the dominant religious services and traditions, which were largely defined by Irish traditions at the time. The official Roman Catholic Church did not give the Melkites and Maronites, both independent Catholic Churches, permission to establish their own dioceses in the United States until the mid-1960s, but they were able to establish their own parishes or churches soon after the arrival of their families—the Melkites in 1889 and the Maronites in 1891. These churches changed their rites and rituals to Latin to be closer to the Roman Catholic practices of other Americans, facilitating their assimilation and social mobility in U.S. society.

Some Maronites and Melkites chose to worship at other Roman Catholic Churches, while others persevered in preserving their own modified churches. By 1924, there were 33 Maronite Churches and 21 Melkite Churches in the United States.[26] Attendance in the same churches, coupled with similar religious beliefs, led many Maronite and Melkite youth to garner parental approval for marriages to non-Arab Roman Catholic spouses. Although families were able to maintain their Catholic identity, much of their Middle Eastern heritage and affiliation disappeared over the following generations. In recent years, there has been a movement to reclaim some of Maronite and Melkite religious traditions by newcomers from the Arab world. Today most Maronites and Melkites live in New York, Boston, Los Angeles, and Detroit, and there are large numbers of Maronites in St. Louis.

The Orthodox were better able than the Maronites and Melkites to maintain their churches and communicants in the long-term. Although some Orthodox joined Episcopal Churches, the first Orthodox Church was established in Manhattan in 1896, and by 1924, there were 22 Orthodox Churches in the United States.[27] Unlike their co-ethnics, the Orthodox did not have to conform to the U.S. Catholic Church. Instead, the Orthodox learned to mix with other Orthodox nationalities, such as Greeks and Russians. As with other Christians, the churches were the focal point for many community activities, and services were a social opportunity to meet potential spouses. The leader of the church was the priest, but this often did not translate into the priest becoming the leader of the community. The priest only led services on Sunday and restricted himself to the realm of religious guidance. Although the Church made concessions to the linguistic skills of the second and third generations by translating their liturgies into English, it kept its Eastern liturgical traditions and acknowledged its Arabic heritage and roots. Today, there are Orthodox communities in most major U.S. cities. The Orthodox community maintains a bimonthly newsletter, summer camps, and a local television program based in California. The Assyrians, who are not Arab in origin, are part of the Orthodox community. Founding their first church in the United States before World War II, they have a Patriarch in Chicago and churches in New York and the San Francisco Bay area.

Some Arab Americans come from families that were converted by missionaries in the nineteenth or twentieth centuries and were Protestant or Roman Catholic before arriving in the United States. On arrival, they usually chose a church that reflected their religious practices in the Middle East. Many of the Protestants joined Presbyterian, Lutheran, and Episcopalian congregations across the country and assimilated into U.S. society, sometimes maintaining secular Arabic traditions. Other Arab Christians choose not to join a church or participate in religious life in the United States.

Since 1965, Arab Christians have continued to immigrate to the United States. The Maronites, Melkites, and Orthodox have added to their numbers, and new groups have joined them. In the 1970s and 1980s, many of the new immigrants were Lebanese and Palestinian Christians displaced by war. They began attending established Protestant and Catholic churches whose parishes were mostly English-speaking and ignorant of the realities of the ongoing events in the Middle East. Some parishioners found it difficult to relate to the new arrivals, but others became more aware of the realities in the Middle East. Increased awareness of the distinct needs of the Orthodox in the United States led the church to establish a Patriarch in Hackensack, New Jersey, in 1999.

Iraqi Chaldeans and Egyptian Copts are recently transplanted denominations who have established their own churches and separate communities that usually do not identify as Arab American. Iraqi Chaldeans live in Chicago, Detroit, and California. Egyptian Copts have mostly moved to the New York/New Jersey area, Los Angeles, and Detroit. These new denominations have given extra diversity to Christianity as practiced in the United States. Table 4.2 provides the estimated numbers of Christians in various Middle Eastern churches in the 1990s.

The main adjustments that Arab Christians made in their churches in the United States in the last 115 years were in the language of the services, the recognition of holy days, and the mixing of genders. Whereas the language of the liturgy in the Arab world is usually Arabic, Aramaic, Syriac, or Assyrian, many Arab Christian churches chose to switch to Latin or English to be more in line with Roman Catholics and Protestants, respectively. An additional advantage of switching the liturgy to English is that those who are less familiar with Classical Arabic or Aramaic would better understand the religious messages conveyed. In addition, Arab Christian immigrants from South and Central America prefer to attend Spanish-language church services; there are such churches in Miami, Florida.

Most Arab Christian denominations celebrate major holidays according to the Eastern Orthodox calendar, but many congregations now celebrate Christmas according to the Western calendar. (see also Chapter 5.)

In the Arab world, men and women are usually separated on opposite sides or sections of the church. One accommodation that Arab Christians have made is to mix the genders, and it is now a widespread norm that men and

Table 4.2
Population of Christians from the Middle East in the United States

Denomination of Church	Number of Churches	Population
Orthodox Church*	192	unknown
Melkite Church	42	75,000
Maronite Church	62	150,000
Chaldean Church	14	100,000
Coptic Orthodox Church	29	unknown

* Includes Syrian Orthodox and Antiochian Orthodox Churches.

women sit and pray alongside one another in the same pew. Christian Arabs, who felt that they shared a religion with the people of the United States, were perhaps surprised to discover how differently people could worship within one faith. Over time, they chose to modify their services not only to conform to U.S. Christian practices, but also because the churches that firmly maintained religious traditions were losing members. Despite making concessions, the numbers of the Arab Christians have suffered from drastic out-marriage rates, estimated by one researcher to exceed 80 percent in the mid-1970s.[28]

Jews

The first Arab Jews arrived in the United States around 1900 from Aleppo and Damascus in Syria and spoke Arabic fluently. They chose New York City as their main center. They became peddlers, buying goods from the Arab wholesalers on Washington Street but living in predominantly Jewish areas. These Jewish immigrants defined themselves as Sephardic Jews, referring to their roots in North Africa and Arab Mediterranean Jewish communities, particularly in Spain (*Sephardim* is Spanish in Hebrew). These Sephardic Jews have characteristics that reflect their Arab history and experiences, distinguishing them from Ashkenazi (or European) Jews. For example, the Syrian Jews of Brooklyn follow the Syrian liturgical order, including the wording of prayers and music, but use the traditional ancient Hebrew language in their synagogues. Today, many of the Sephardic Jews who live in Brooklyn and throughout the New York City metro area identify themselves as Jewish Americans rather than as Arab Americans. Their prioritization of ethnic affiliation has made it difficult to include them in the Arab American community and the study of Arab Americans.

Druze

The Druze are sometimes considered Muslims but do not have mosques or any form of religious center in the United States or in the Arab world. Among the first Arabs to move to the United States, the Druze population now stands at 20,000. Many of the Druze have chosen to deemphasize their ethnic identity, and some have officially converted to Christianity, becoming Presbyterians or members of other Protestant denominations. There is a recent movement within the Druze community to reclaim their Druze identity and to include an affiliation with Islam within that identity. Although Druze originally settled in Virginia, West Virginia, Kentucky, Tennessee, and Washington State, the largest community is now living in Southern California.

Muslims

The first Muslims to come to the United States were slaves and ocean explorers from Africa who had been Christianized by the early decades of the nineteenth century and so the Muslims who arrived in the late nineteenth century found no mosques or fellow Muslims in the United States. Most of the Muslim first wavers were peasant farmers from the mountain areas of Lebanon. Like their Christian brethren, they arrived with few skills, education, or capital, and their biggest concern was basic survival, not religion. They believed that their stay in the United States was temporary, and the establishment of mosques would be a futile endeavor. Instead, they may have prayed at home. The earliest recorded group of Muslims gathering for communal prayer was in a home in Ross, North Dakota, in 1900.

Islam does not have a clergy or a central advisory or governing council, and prayer does not require a designated building, only a clean space devoid of images or portraits hanging on the walls, making Islam a rather "portable faith."[29] A mosque brings together Muslims in prayer, especially for Friday noon prayers, and so has a community purpose. It was incumbent on Muslims in a given area to decide that a mosque was needed, raise funds and buy a building, or commission an architect to build them a new, purpose-built mosque. Thus, the earliest mosques in the United States were built in the 1920s and 1930s; the oldest surviving mosque, built in 1934, is in Cedar Rapids, Iowa.

From the 1930s until the early 1960s, there was an acculturation period in which Muslims borrowed models for the foundation of religious communities from their local surroundings. Mosques often took a similar role for their community as churches did for Christians. Historically, the mosque only served as a place of worship, for prayer and religious orientation. However, in the United States, the mosque gained a social function, becoming one of the principal meeting places for men and women. Activities such as weddings, funerals, celebrations, and fundraisers were held in the mosque or the surrounding property. Bake sales, bazaars, and even dances and concerts, often organized by women, brought people together, and the mosque became the center of the local Muslim community. Some Muslim communities adapted to the U.S. workweek by swapping the day for community prayer and sermons, Friday, with the Christian day of worship, Sunday. Other Muslim communities held large Friday noon prayers in addition to Sunday schools and services. The children were instructed in the basics of Islam and the Arabic language during this prayer time. Women assumed an active role in teaching Sunday school and attending the

Sunday mosque services. The imam, or prayer leader, was chosen or hired by an elected committee from the congregation, who might arrange for the purchase of a building or a plot of land by obtaining a mortgage. In the United States, imams have a public role, representing American Muslims and explaining Islam to non-Muslims at interfaith gatherings, teach-ins, and conferences. If the mosque was purpose-built, the upper floor was dedicated to prayer and worship, while the lower floor was used for social events, separating the domains and making the mosque property more in line with Islamic traditions. All of these adaptations resulted in a distinct American influence on the architecture, function, and administration of the mosque. It was a place to declare and be comfortable with one's ethnic heritage and religious identity, much like an "ethnic" church. This served to give the American Muslims—a minority in an alien culture—a feeling of security and community.

The newcomers between 1957 and 1967 tended to be from the educated elites, some of whom were recently exiled and more concerned with Arab nationalism than with the practice of Islam. Most of these were "un-mosqued," meaning that they did not go to the mosque and were secular in outlook. Although they did raise political consciousness, especially after the 1967 Six-Day War, these intellectuals and professionals had a marginal impact on Islamic institutions in the United States.

In the 1970s, the sectarian civil war in Lebanon and the Islamic movement in Egypt forced some Muslims with an Islamic revivalist outlook to flee the Arab world. Some sought refuge in the United States. Upon seeing the way Islam was practiced in the United States, many expressed their dismay, believing that the innovations to the role and character of the mosque in the United States were not in keeping with their faith. They sought to restore the mosque as a place devoted exclusively to prayer and preaching and to limit the role of women in the mosques. To oust the U.S.-born imams, they ran for elections to the boards of the existing Islamic centers, coming into direct conflict with the earlier immigrants and their families, who had founded and funded the mosques. In one instance, the rules for the election to the governing board were changed so that a recently elected woman would be disqualified as a board member.[30] The newer immigrants then replaced the imams with religious leaders from the Arab world who were more inclined to concur with their point of view. In turn, the imams had a conservative influence on the congregation through their sermons and by acting as a counselor to members of the mosque, taking on a role similar to that of a Christian minister. As a result, some more liberal Muslims in the United States have called for a switch from foreign-born and foreign-trained imams to U.S.-born leaders who are better able to understand and advise the *umma* in a way that is grounded in the United States.

Since 1985, there has been a notable rise in Islamic consciousness among American Muslims, which is only partly due to immigrants and imams. The rise in conservative Islam has mirrored the growing Islamist movements in the Middle East as well as the evangelical Christian movement in the United States, and some believe that they fuel each other. This trend is a response to the appearance of declining moral-ethical principles in the United States and the oft-repeated call for family values imbued with religion by politicians, news commentators, and columnists. The growth of the number of Muslim religious schools is in line with a similar Christian evangelical movement for education. Organizations such as CAIR have responded to their members and advocated school voucher programs that divert funds from public schools into parochial schools. Increasing demands for public space for prayer in universities and workplaces, the vigorous building of mosques, and the revival of various forms of Islamic dress, particularly the *hijab* (headscarf), are perhaps indicators of a growing Islamic consciousness among American Muslims.

The revival of Islam in the United States has taken on a more national-istic and ideological meaning as more people claim that there is a clash of civilizations between the West/Christianity and the East/Islam. As a result, being Muslim in the United States is becoming more of a race, or an ethnic signifier, and the Muslim identity is overtaking ethnic affiliations such as Arab or South Asian. The events of 9/11 and the backlash against Muslim Americans and the rise in Islamic consciousness have accentuated the grow-ing rift between moderates and revivalists and between the generations. A few American Muslims have reacted to the current climate by converting to Christianity (usually through intermarriage) or becoming secular. However, the most common reaction is a regeneration of the moderate position and a reorientation of the mosques in most Muslim communities. To this end, there is a demand for more U.S.-born and/or U.S.-trained leaders, and so two schools have been founded: the School of Islamic Social Sciences in Leesburg, Virginia, for Sunni Muslims, and Imam Ali Seminary in Medina, New York, for Shia Muslims.

The Shia population in the United States, which was mainly Lebanese and Iranian, has grown substantially since the 1990s, with the influx of refugees from Iraq after the Second Gulf War (1990–91). It is estimated that the Shia constitute one-fifth of the U.S. Muslim population. There is a concentration of Arab Shia Muslims in the northwest area of Dearborn where they have their own mosques and Islamic centers.

Although Arab Americans only constitute approximately one-fourth to one-third of the American Muslim population, some Muslim communities are almost exclusively Arab, such as in the Detroit metro area. As the numbers of Christian and Muslim Arab Americans are now about equal, and the numbers of Muslim immigrants are surpassing the Arab Christian immigrants so most Arab Americans will soon be Muslim. There are concentrations of Muslims in and around major U.S. cities, including Chicago, Washington, D.C., New York, and Los Angeles. Muslims are estimated to constitute approximately 2 percent of the total U.S. population, around the same proportion as Jews (2%), and substantially less than Protestants (56%) and Catholics (28%).[31] The growth of the Muslim population through immigration, conversion, and procreation indicates the increasing importance of Islam in U.S. religious life, even though it remains a minority religion.

NOTES

1. Louise Cainkar, "The Deteriorating Ethnic Safety Net among Arab Immigrants in Chicago," in *Arabs in America: Building a New Future,* ed. Michael W. Suleiman (Philadelphia: Temple University Press, 1999), 193.

2. Barbara Aswad and Nancy Adadow Gray, "Challenges to the Arab-American Family and ACCESS," in *Family & Gender among American Muslims* (Philadelphia: Temple University Press, 1996), 230.

3. Barbara Aswad, "Attitudes of Arab Immigrants toward Welfare," in Arabs in America Building a New Future, ed. Michael W. Suleiman (Philadelphia: Temple University Press, 1999), 180.

4. Cainkar, 198.

5. Ibid.

6. Ibid., 205.

7. Arab American Institute Foundation, "Arab American Demographics," http://www.aaiusa.org/demographics.htm (accessed August 2005).

8. Paula Hajar, "Arab Families in New York Public Schools," in *A Community of Many Worlds: Arab Americans in New York City,* ed. Kathleen Benson and Philip Kayal (New York: Museum of the City of New York, Syracuse University Press, 2002), 141–42.

9. Arab American Institute Foundation.

10. Ibid.

11. Jane I. Smith, *Islam in America* (New York: Columbia University Press, 1999), 124.

12. Kristine Ajrouch, "Family and Ethnic Identity in an Arab-American Community," in *Arabs in America: Building a New Future,* ed. Michael W. Suleiman (Philadelphia: Temple University Press, 1999), 138.

13. An interesting study on Arab-Canadians found that teenaged girls were more likely to identify as Canadian than Arab in comparison with their male counterparts. The girls also reported feeling more comfortable with their Canadian friends than with Arab peers and more likely to have hidden their Arab identity at one time or another. See Baha

Abu-Laban and Sharon Abu-Laban, "Teens Between: The Public and Private spheres of Arab-Canadian Adolescents" in *Arabs in America: Building a New Future,* ed. Michael W. Suleiman (Philadelphia: Temple University Press, 1999), 113–128.

14. Quoted in Nadine Naber, "White but Not Quite? An Examination of Arab American In/Visibility," *AAUG Monitor* 13, no. 3 (December 1998): 9–10.

15. Evelyn Shakir, *Bint Arab: Arab and Arab American Women in the United States* (Westport, CT: Praeger, 1997), 186.

16. Naff, Alixia, *The Arab Americans,* (New York: Chelsea House, 1988), 237–38.

17. Yvonne Haddad and Jane Smith, "Islamic Values among American Muslims," in *Family and Gender among American Muslims* (Philadelphia: Temple University Press, 1996), 26.

18. Quoted in Shakir, 207, n.7.

19. Aswad and Gray, 237.

20. Smith, 110–11.

21. Quoted in Carol Anway, "American Women Choosing Islam," in *Muslims on the Americanization Path?* ed. Yvonne Haddad and John Esposito (New York: Oxford University Press, 1998), 153.

22. U.S. Department of Justice. www.usdoj.gov/opa/pr/2004/May/04_crt_343.htm (accessed September 2, 2005).

23. Angela Brittingham and G. Patricia de la Cruz, *We the People of Arab Ancestry in the United States, Census 2000 Special Reports* (Washington, DC: U.S. Census Bureau, 2005), 10; also available online at http://www.census.gov/population/www/cen2000/briefs.html#sr.

24. Ibid., 19.

25. Joseph R. Haiek, ed., *The Arab-American Almanac,* 5th ed. (Glendale, CA: New Circle, 2003), 188.

26. Gregory Orfalea, "Sifting the Ashes: Arab American Activism during the 1982 Invasion of Lebanon," in *Arab Americans: Continuity and Change,* AAUG Monograph Series no. 24 (Belmont, MA: Association of Arab-American University Graduates, 1989), 87–88.

27. Ibid., 87–88.

28. Philip M. Kayal, "So, Who Are We? Who Am I?" in *A Community of Many Worlds: Arab Americans in New York City,* ed. Kathleen Benson and Philip Kayal (New York: Museum of the City of New York, Syracuse University Press, 2002), 53.

29. The concept of a "portable faith" is from Yvonne Haddad, "Arab Muslims and Islamic Institutions in America: Adaptation and Reform," in *Arabs in the New World: Studies on Arab-American Communities* (Detroit: Wayne State University Press, 1983), 72.

30. Shakir, 115–16.

31. These estimates are from www.wikipedia.com and include 2 percent responding as "other religions" and 10 percent as "none."

Al-Hoda Publishing Company in New York City, no date. Al-Hoda (*The Guidance*) was one the earliest Arabic-language newspapers in the United States. Although the newspaper was first published in Philadelphia, the editor/founders moved its offices to "Little Syria" in Manhattan in 1903. This photograph of the company staff, family, and friends, was taken between 1903 and the early 1940s before "Little Syria" was demolished to build the Brooklyn Battery Tunnel. Courtesy of Mary Mozarkel Papers, Box 1, Folder 10, Immigration History Research Center, University of Minnesota.

Syrian Ladies' Aid Society at the golden anniversary banquet, Brooklyn, New York, 1958. Founded in 1917 in Boston, to assist those in need, The Syrian Ladies' Aid Society is one of the oldest, continuous Arab American organizations. Courtesy of Syrian Ladies Aid Society, Box 1, Immigration History Research Center, University of Minnesota.

A family-run business since 1895, Sahadi Importing Company, has been in its Brooklyn, New York location at 187 Atlantic Avenue for 54 years. In this photo, the 21-year-old daughter had opened her own carry-out section in the back of the store and was serving customers. Today, Sahadi Fine Foods runs a modern manufacturing plant that imports and distributes food all over the United States. Courtesy of Katrina Thomas/Saudi Aramco World/PADIA.

The Islamic Center of Cedar Rapids, Iowa. Cedar Rapids, Iowa, is believed to have the oldest existing purpose-built mosque in North America, which was abandoned when the Islamic Center pictured here was built in 1971. In 1990, some Muslims purchased the original site and rebuilt the mosque, which is now known as the "Mother Mosque of America." Courtesy of Katrina Thomas/Saudi Aramco World/PADIA.

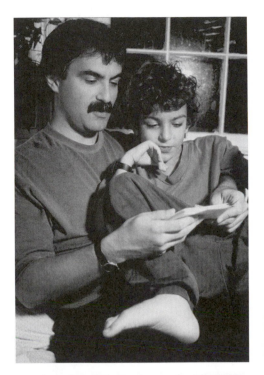

Father and son, third- and fourth-generation Palestinian Americans in their Washington, D.C. home, looking at photos. Courtesy of Najib Joe Hakim/Saudi Aramco World/PADIA.

Teacher reads to pupils at the Muslim Education Center, a private school for pre-school through 8th grade in Morton Grove, Illinois. The teaching of religion is barred in the U.S. public educational system, prompting the establishment of Islamic schools. Courtesy of Kathleen Burke/Saudi Aramco World/PADIA.

Arab American family members preparing food for a backyard barbecue in a suburb of Boston. Families often center around the kitchen table, preparing food and catching up on daily activities. Courtesy of the author.

Shish kebab, chunks of meat and vegetables cooked on skewers over an open fire, is one of the most popular Arab dishes in the United States. Here, it is being cooked for sale at an outdoor festival in Detroit. Courtesy of Katrina Thomas/Saudi Aramco World/PADIA.

Rashid Music Sales Company and the owner, Raymond Rashid, Brooklyn, New York, April 2005. Rashid Music Sales pioneered the importation of music and films from the Middle East into the United States, first through film showings in the 1930s and later through selling records to customers nationwide through mail-order and a store in Manhattan. The store moved to Brooklyn in 1947 and is now the largest and oldest distributor of Arabic music in the United States. Courtesy of the author.

Musicians playing together at the Arabic Music Retreat at Mount Holyoke College in South Hadley, Massachusetts. Since 1997, ethnomusicologists, amateur musicians, signers, dancers and composers have participated in a week-long intensive workshop that focuses on the theory and performance practice of classical Arabic music. The retreat is led by Simon Shaheen and Ali Jihad Racy, both renowned musicians living in the United States. Courtesy of Robert Azzi/Saudi Aramco World/PADIA.

Debkeh, a type of dancing popular in Lebanon, Palestine, Syria and Jordan, performed at an outdoor festival in Detroit. In debkeh, men and women clasp hands and dance in linear formations to the beats of drums and other instruments. Courtesy of Katrina Thomas/Saudi Aramco World/PADIA.

Islamic Society of North America (ISNA) Headquarters in Plainfield, Indiana, is an association of Muslim organizations and individuals that provide a common platform for Muslims in the United States. ISNA holds annual conventions, a variety of training workshops, and a Summer Leadership Institute and produces publications for its members. In 2005, the ISNA projected that 35,000 people would attend and participate in the annual convention held over Labor Day weekend in Chicago, Illinois. Courtesy of Charlie Nye/Getty Images/Saudi Aramco World/PADIA.

Association of Arab-American University Graduates (AAUG) conference in Novi, Michigan, October 1998. Conferences such as the 31st annual AAUG convention bring together Arab Americans from across the United States on a regular basis. Courtesy of the author.

"Palestine: Fifty Years of Dispossession, 1948–98" rally organized by the National Arab American Organizations to highlight the plight of Palestinians in front of the Capitol building, Washington, D.C., June 1998. Courtesy of the author.

Ralph Nader, Lebanese American attorney, public interest advocate, corporate critic, presidential candidate, and author addresses news conference at the National Press Club, February 2004, during 2004 run for President. AP/WIDE WORLD PHOTOS

Culture Fest at Tufts University, Boston, Massachusetts, Spring 2004. Arab and Arab American students meet and work together on U.S. campuses to organize political and social events. Courtesy of Abdul-Wahab (Kayyali).

"Yalla Vote" rally at the Henry Ford Center for the Performing Arts in Dearborn, Michigan, February 2004. The "Yalla Vote" (Come on, Vote!) campaign was organized by the Arab American Institute to get every Arab American to vote in elections. The campaign encouraged volunteers to post or pass out fliers at Arab American community centers, mosques, churches, universities and student clubs, grocery stores, restaurants—any place frequented by Arab Americans. Photo by Dave Weatherwax, The State News © 2/6/2004.

On Sunday October 24, 2004 dozens of Arab Americans in Dearborn, Michigan, walked along Warren Avenue posting "Yalla Vote" signs at local restaurants and stores. Photo permission granted by the Arab American Institute.

5

Identities within the Community

Although Arab Americans only form approximately 1.2 percent of the overall U.S. population, the numbers of Arab immigrants between 1990 and 2000 swelled the Arab American population. The diversity of today's community can partially be understood through an in-depth examination of national origin and religion, but the strong tendency of Arab Americans to live in metropolitan areas means that there are significant clusters of Arab Americans in some major U.S. cities.

Within these cities, many Americans, including Arab Americans, delineate their community by residential location as well as socioeconomic status. Arab Americans live in diverse areas from inner cities to suburbs, although a few Arab Americans live in rural areas. Beyond physical location and material wealth, there are many ways in which the community is divided philosophically. The pan-Arab label gained popularity among Arab Americans after the 1967 Six-Day War. Since then, most national organizations have used the term Arab American to indicate their ethnic affiliation to outsiders, and this has, in turn, reinforced the label within the community. The rise in Islamic consciousness among Arab American Muslims has mirrored the increased emphasis on the role of religion on identity in U.S. society, but it also reflects the increased profiling of the Muslim community for discriminatory treatment and suspicion. Identity as an Arab American and as an American Muslim may contend for prioritization, and, as with Christians, religious affiliation can divide Arab Americans. Another major division is generation or length of time in the United States, which is commonly, but inaccurately, thought to be directly tied to the degree of assimilation in the United States, and thus the distance between the individual and his or her ethnic heritage. These perceived divisions are well articulated in social networks and organizations. From the 1890s onward, Arab Americans formed, reformed, and disbanded organizations that reflected their interests and priorities as smaller communities. Arab Americans have adapted their celebrations and holidays to life in the United States. The many facets and layers of the contemporary Arab American community are the focus of this chapter.

DEMOGRAPHICS

The number of people of Arab heritage living in the United States is estimated by Arab American organizations and polling companies to be approximately 3.5 million strong. This estimate includes U.S. citizens, permanent residents, and Arabs living in the United States (e.g., students, aliens, and people in the midst of the immigration process).[1] Although the 2000 Census figures were substantially lower (see Chapter 3), both the census and estimates by Arab American organizations record that the decade of the 1990s saw a huge increase in the number of Arab Americans—more than 30 percent between 1990 and 2000 (see Appendix A). This increase was partially because of the influx of new immigrants from the Middle East and North Africa.

Between 1990 and 2000, U.S. Citizenship and Immigration Services estimated that 328,712 Arabs immigrated to the United States (see Appendix C). Of these immigrants, most are Muslims, with the largest number from Egypt. The 1990s also saw a continued influx of Lebanese and Jordanians, some of whom are Palestinian residents of those countries. The number of Iraqis immigrating increased after the end of the Second Gulf War (1990–91), and the number of Somalis and Moroccans moving to the United States has increased substantially since the mid-1990s.

As Table 5.1 indicates, despite the influx of other nationalities, Lebanese continue to constitute the largest demographic by national origin, making up one-third of all Arab Americans. The influx of immigrants has changed the composition of Arab Americans, and Egyptians are now the second-largest national group, closely followed by Syrians.

Although Arab Americans live in all 50 states, more than 90 percent live in metropolitan areas, with the top five cities being Los Angeles, Detroit, New York City/New Jersey, Chicago, and Washington, D.C. Since the 1960s, recent immigrants have flocked to areas that already had high concentrations of Arabs. One-third of Arab Americans live in California,

Table 5.1
Arab American Community by National Origin

Nationality	Arab American Population (%)
Lebanese	34
Egyptian	11
Syrian	11
Chaldean/Assyrian/Syriac*	7
Palestinian	6
Iraqi**	3
Moroccan	3
Jordanian	3
Arab/Arabic	15
Other Arab***	7

* Chaldeans, Assyrians and Syriacs are not Arabs but were included as such in this Census survey. This number is miscalculated on the AAI website.
** Excludes persons who identify as Chaldeans, Assyrians or other Christian minorities in Iraq. (see above note)
*** Includes those from Algeria, Bahrain, Comoros Islands, Djibouti, Kuwait, Libya, Oman, Qatar, Saudi Arabia, Tunisia, the United Arab Emirates, and Yemen. Does not include persons from Sudan, Somalia, or Mauritania.

New York, or Michigan, where cities have thriving, diverse communities. In the 1990s, the Arab American population doubled in Virginia, North Carolina, Connecticut, Alabama, and New Mexico, but the biggest growth in population occurred in Illinois, Pennsylvania, and Michigan. Decreases of Arab Americans in Maryland, Rhode Island, Louisiana, West Virginia, and Mississippi may correspond to intrastate migration and reflect the aging of older Arab American communities and their populations there.

The Lebanese are the largest group of Arab Americans in most states except New Jersey, where Egyptians are the largest nationality. Egyptian Americans, who live throughout the New York City area, are heavily represented in Jersey City, in particular. There are also large populations of Syrians in Rhode Island and Yemenis in Michigan (especially in Dearborn) as well as in the New York City area. Palestinians and Iraqis maintain notably large numbers in Illinois, Michigan, and California. In the last few decades, Moroccans have settled along the East Coast and mostly reside between Boston and Washington, D.C. About half of the 60,000 Jews of Arab descent live in New York City.

There are many debates on the breakdown of Muslim and Christian Arab Americans, and some Arab American organizations estimate that 63 percent of the population is Christian, (18 percent Eastern Orthodox, 35 percent Roman/Eastern Catholic, and 10 percent Protestant) 24 percent Muslim; and 13 percent other religion/no religious affiliation.[2] Others approximate the breakdown of the population closer to 50 percent Christian and 50 percent Muslim.[3] Despite these differing numbers, it is clear that the second- and third-generation descendents from the first wave of Arab immigrants—mainly Christians from Lebanon and Syria—still constitute a major proportion of Arab Americans.

A high percentage (80%) of Arabs living in the United States are citizens, and although most Arab Americans are native-born Americans, about 40 percent are first-generation immigrants who were born abroad and were naturalized in citizenship ceremonies across the country. One of four of these foreign-born Arab Americans arrived in the 1990s, yet the citizenship percentage remains stable due to the higher naturalization rate of Arabs (54%), compared with the overall foreign-born population (40%). The reasons for the stronger propensity of Arab Americans to become citizens than that of other ethnicities in the 1990s have not yet been explained by in-depth research.

There are some interesting demographic differences between Arab Americans and the U.S. population as a whole. As Table 4.1 indicated, the median age of Arab Americans compared to the general U.S. population was lower and the male to female ratio higher, although the married percentages were slightly higher for Arab Americans. The implications of these numbers will be examined in the next chapter. However, the statistics do give a preliminary indication that the Arab American population is healthy in gender and age terms, and the natural growth of the community has a positive outlook.

WORK AND ECONOMIC PROFILES

After the release of the 2000 Census, journalists from the *Washington Post* wrote that the "demographic portrait [was] at odds with recent images in the news of young, single, unsettled immigrants," and they expressed surprise that the results found that the "typical Middle Easterner in the Washington area and nationally" was "a suburban, professional family man."[4] In fact, the 2000 Census, like 1990 Census, found that Arab Americans are wealthier and better educated than most Americans. Today, Arab Americans can be found in every profession, although most (88%) work in the private sector.

The one distinguishing feature of the national Arab American workforce is that many Arab Americans have their own businesses. As the demand for peddlers bringing goods door-to-door diminished between 1900 and 1920, Arab Americans opened their own convenience and dry goods stores. Others who were employed in factories and textile mills worked long days and saved to purchase their own business. Many of the second generation who settled in the United States gave up their parents' thoughts of postponing improved material and social status until they returned to the Middle East and instead aspired to become middle class in the United States. With the example of their forefathers, some ran small family-owned businesses that they inherited or founded themselves. In a revolving cycle that continues to this day, the new arrivals from the Middle East filled vacancies left by the older immigrants and bought the business when the owner was ready to move on. Although the work patterns have changed, the strong entrepreneurial traditions have remained constant.

Vibrant family networks are often the backbone of business enterprises and important in the accomplishments of many Arab Americans.[5] In grocery stores, it is common to find many family members, even generations, working together. Family members help one another to find employment outside of the family business and often lend money and give advice to help other relatives start their own enterprise or make career changes. Some second- and third-generation Arab Americans have chosen not to open their own businesses and instead joined a diverse array of professions and industries as employees. Today, Arab American parents support their children in becoming professionals, in particular, doctors, businessmen, pharmacists, and engineers. They usually discourage their children from being artists because it is a riskier choice than careers with "guaranteed success." The 2000 Census found that 73 percent of Arab Americans work in managerial, professional, technical, sales, or administrative fields—many are clearly listening to the advice of their parents. In these ways, family and work are not individual undertakings; the two realms are often related, if not intertwined, for Arab Americans.

Arab Americans of all educational levels and generations have invested in businesses such as restaurants, bakeries, specialty food stores, hotels, medical and law offices, tobacco and grocery stores, as well as in import/export companies. More recently, immigrants have bought franchises in national chains, especially in gas stations, convenience stores, auto repair shops, as well as real estate and insurance branches. Education-focused Arab Americans are teachers in schools, universities, and community colleges. More recently, there has been a large presence in the high-tech industry as owners, programmers, and technicians.

The full- and part-time work undertaken by Arab Americans often reflects the economic strengths of their locality. The wealthiest Arab American community is in Washington, D.C., and Northern Virginia where many Arab elites moved and settled, particularly in Fairfax County. In Anaheim, California, and Cleveland, Ohio, there are Arab American salespeople. Arab Americans work in the health care and education fields in Boston; administrators predominate in Bergen-Passaic, New Jersey, and many Arab Americans work in manufacturing in Detroit and Chicago. In some cases, Arab American communities developed where there were economic opportunities, such as the automotive industry in Detroit. When the Ford Motor Company moved its production plant from Highland Park to Dearborn, Michigan in 1913, the Arab community moved with it so that they could walk to work. Arab Americans are active in the labor movement; one Arab American, Steve Yokich, was the eighth president of the United Auto Workers (UAW) labor union.

Newly arrived immigrants may have difficulties finding jobs in the same fields in which they were employed previously in their own countries. Those with fewer language skills and lower levels of education work for minimum wage in factories, convenience stores, or as farm workers. Immigrants with college educations, especially those with foreign college degrees, have found it hard to find jobs appropriate to their qualifications and have resorted to working in positions for which they are overqualified, including jobs as hotel receptionists, clerks, cab drivers, bartenders, and wait staff in restaurants. However, those Arabs who immigrate to attend college or graduate school in the United States tend to find employment in their fields. Of course, these Arab immigrants who opt for additional education are likely to have attained a high-school education level or higher in the Arab world. Equipped with a degree, or degrees, from a U.S. university, many of the educated, newly arrived immigrants continue to live in the same city as their universities after graduation. For example, Boston has a population of 3,000 to 5,000 Arab students, as well as an established Arab American community estimated to be between 100,000 and 150,000.[6]

The sojourners and the settlers both send money back home to family and friends and repay loans that may have been extended to them for their journey. Unless they are joining a relative, sojourners who are men come without their families and plan on returning to their home country within a short time frame. One researcher found that Yemenis, who have a tradition of sojourning in the United States, remit one-fourth to one-sixth of their gross monthly earnings back to relatives and creditors in Yemen.[7] Many countries such as Egypt, Yemen, Lebanon, Jordan, Syria, and Morocco rely on remittance income to infuse capital into the economy. Palestinians in the West Bank and Gaza Strip are dependent on money from abroad as unemployment rates have been high since the late 1980s. To save money and maintain their primary affiliation with their home country, these sojourners tend to keep their costs and social activities to a minimum, postponing their social mobility and material gratification until they return home. Therefore, sojourners generally do not set up businesses, institutions, or organizations in the United States.

The settlers who decide to stay in the United States save their money to buy or start their own business and to send for family members from home. The two goals are often interrelated. Many small business owners hire their own relatives whom they feel they can trust. This has been the case in California where migrant farm workers from Yemen, Jordan, Egypt, Lebanon, and Morocco have bought convenience and gas stores and franchises in Oakland, San Francisco, Bakersfield, and Fresno. The storeowners send for their relatives who help them in the store and who work for low wages, sometimes at great personal risk if the store is located in a high-crime area. These newer immigrants save their wages so they can purchase their own business, buy their relative's store, or return home in the future with more social and material possibilities. As an immigrant brings over more family members, the levels of remittances may decrease as levels of investment in their businesses and/or residences in the United States increase. Regardless, many maintain strong emotional connections and return back to their country of origin to get married or for family weddings and visits, usually in the summertime.

In the contemporary United States, Arab immigrants from all socioeconomic levels are moving to both urban and suburban locations. The obvious advantages of urban living are convenience and the availability of public transportation, so many students and young professionals choose to live in major urban centers, such as New York City, Boston, Washington, D.C., and Chicago. Working-class families live near the factories and convenience stores where they work, as is the case in areas of Chicago and Detroit. Both the less privileged and the elites from the Middle East often move directly into the suburbs to be near relatives already located there for business opportunities. The Washington, D.C., area is one of the most popular destinations for immigrants from the Middle East. From 1990 to 2000, most of the 125,000 immigrants to Washington, D.C., moved to the suburbs.[8] It is estimated

that 180,000 Arab Americans live in the Chicago area.[9] Although suburban residences are less concentrated than urban areas, these suburbanites
generally own cars and are often in daily contact with one another. Physical
dispersal does not translate into a breakdown in the bonds or networks
between members of the community. However, the distance does mean that
an individual has to make an effort to keep in touch with friends and family
as daily interaction with other Arab Americans is no longer inevitable. The
typical distancing of neighbors in the suburbs has meant that an individual
has more freedom to choose friends and acquaintances, and if the location
is based on that of family and friends, socializing is clearly a priority. The
tendency of family and friends to cluster has resulted in some areas becoming
affiliated with certain subcommunities. For example, in the Detroit suburbs,
the Lebanese and Syrian Christians moved to the east side (toward Grosse
Pointe); the Yemenis, Palestinians, and Lebanese Muslims to the west side,
and ultimately into the suburb of Dearborn; a Yemeni community formed in
Highland Park near Daimler-Chrysler/Dodge main automobile plant; Iraqi-
Chaldeans live on the north side; and the Palestinians (mainly Christians)
moved into the western suburbs, and then to Cleveland, Ohio.

Although some of the wealthier neighborhoods, such as Gross Pointe,
are not predominantly Arab American, other less-affluent suburbs, such as
Dearborn, are visibly ethnic with Arabic restaurants, bakeries, and gas stations that have signs in Arabic. The example of Detroit illustrates how the
community is physically divided along socioeconomic and religious lines
with the more established and wealthy subcommunities living in more affluent neighborhoods that are not predominantly, or visibly, Arab American.
A social service organization, ACCESS, brings members of each subcom-
munity in the Detroit area to work together as one community, underlining
that, despite these divisions, there are some commonalities.

INTRAGROUP DIVISIONS AND ISSUES

Philosophical differences divide the community further beyond the occu-
pational, socioeconomic, and geographic divides. Although intragroup relations ebb and flow according to reactions to the contemporary political and
social realities, the differences that Arab Americans make among themselves
are important in helping to understand the community's many voices and
faces. Three main internal dividing lines are highlighted here: the broad
pan-Arab affiliation, Muslim and Christian identities, and the differentiations
between new immigrants and the older generations of Arab Americans.

Pan-Arab Identification

Until 1967, Arab Americans identified themselves mainly by their country, city, village, or town of origin and by their religious affiliation. The pan-Arab movement that swept across the Middle East had little impact on Arab Americans who, by World War II, were generally assimilated into the mainstream American culture at least in public. After 1945, some Arabs from elite backgrounds moved to the safety of the United States, arriving with strong opinions about politics in the Middle East and affiliations with the pan-ethnic label of *Arab*. *Pan-Arabism* or Arab nationalism, is an ideology that believes that all Arabs are one nation, that the boundaries between the Arab countries are false, and that they were imposed by colonial powers to divide the Arab population. With the dissolution of the United Arab Republic in 1961 and the Arab defeat in the Six-Day War, Arabism began to decline in popularity in the Middle East. Ironically, the failure and shame felt by Arabs as a result of the 1967 war acted as a catalyst for Arab Americans to coalesce and form a community.

As the popularity of pan-Arabism waned in the Middle East, it increased in the United States. The alignment of U.S. foreign policy with Israel in the 1967 Six-Day War created negative images of Arabs in the U.S. media; people of Arabic heritage who had kept a low profile, assimilating and hiding their roots, found themselves targets of discrimination and negative comments in public spaces. To defend themselves, many of the more assimilated Arab Americans reacted by learning more about the Middle East and befriending the newer immigrants, who taught them about the political and economic situations in the Arab world from a personal perspective. The newer immigrants, who considered themselves Arabs before migration, settled down in the United States and began to identify as Americans. Through exploring their commonalities of location and discrimination, the newer immigrants and the more established co-ethnics began to mesh the two identities into a primary identity of Arab American. A collective ethnopolitical consciousness was raised as leaders worked together under a new Arab American banner to balance the negative connotations of the word *Arab* in the United States. These efforts were further aided by the discourse of ethnic revival in U.S. pop culture in the late 1960s and 1970s that encouraged people to reclaim their heritage and speak out as members of a collectivity, or an ethnic group. With the civil rights victories and the protests against the war in Vietnam in the background, many also spoke out, as Americans, on behalf of Palestinian rights to self-determination and nationhood.

As a result of this new in-group cohesion and shared political convictions, three major organizations were established in the late 1960s and early 1970s: Arab-American University Graduates (AAUG) in 1968, Arab Community Center for Economic and Social Services (ACCESS) in 1972, and National Association of Arab-Americans (NAAA) in 1973. The AAUG is the oldest Arab American organization because it first used the moniker Arab American. The choice of the names of these organizations reinforced a pan-Arab identity to their members and labeled their outreach work as ethnically based. By using a broad identifier, Arab American organizations are also able to claim to represent a larger population for elections, census taking, and public services purposes.

One of the shared interests of the more politically inclined Arab Americans as well as most of the national organizations has been the role of U.S. foreign policy within the Middle East. Particularly at issue is the Palestinian-Israeli conflict which has engendered much debate and controversy within the Arab American community. Some believe in a one-state solution, and others in a two-state solution. A one-state solution refers to the proposed resolution of the Israeli-Palestinian conflict by the creation of a secular, democratic, bi-national state that would include Arabs and Jews with equal rights. The two-state solution advocates the creation of a Palestinian state for Arabs alongside present-day Israel. As advocates of Palestinian rights and justice, some Arab Americans drew the ire of pro-Israeli groups and individuals, which led to greater stereotyping and discrimination against Arab Americans in the 1970s. The backlash, as well as personal political inclinations, led some Arab Americans to charge that national-level organizations were too focused on the Arab world and the Palestinian issue in particular; others disagree. The founder of the ADC, Senator James Abourezk, described the Palestinian-Israeli issue as "a conflict, which has created social and political havoc with our community."[10]

Three of the national-level organizations (with the exception of ACCESS) devote substantial time and effort to U.S. foreign policy, so the politics and divisions in the Middle East heavily impact the Arab American community. Although other events have rocked the veneer of unity, the Second Gulf War (1990–91) was perhaps the most divisive as different organizations took opposing stands—some supporting Desert Storm and others preferring a peaceful resolution to the invasion of Kuwait. Just as in the Middle East, citizens from one country did not always follow their government's positions; for example, some Egyptian Americans supported Desert Storm and others did not. In that case, the community was not split according to national origin but divided by positions of consent or dissent to U.S. government policy.

However, country of origin affiliations can divide the Arab American community under different circumstances. In the late 1970s, some Egyptian

Americans felt alienated from national Arab American organizations, most of which criticized Egypt for signing the Camp David Accords. Marginalized by Arab American organizations, some Egyptian Americans let their memberships in these national organizations lapse and distanced themselves from the broad identifier of Arab American.

Christian and Muslim Identities

Many people originally from Arab countries prefer to be identified by a religious moniker rather than as Americans of Arab ancestry or Arab Americans. Christians from the Middle East—Maronites, Orthodox, Assyrians, Copts, and Chaldeans—practice their faith in unique ways and in different languages that predate Islam and the Arab conquests. This pre-Islamic heritage and the discrimination that many have suffered in modern times have caused them to shun the label *Arab*. Many Christians maintain their own churches that act as focal points, spiritually and socially, in their own communities and have strong community affiliations that are separate from other Christians of the Arab world. Oftentimes, the church leaders consider themselves as part of a larger Christian community and reach out to mainstream U.S. Christians to help fellow Christians in the Middle East.

These religiously based identifications can conflict with the policies and success of national community organizations. For example, in 1980, the Maronite Church forbade its members from joining the Arab-American Anti-Discrimination Committee (ADC) because it was perceived that the organization was not politically aligned with the Phalange. The Phalange were members of the Kateeb Party in Lebanon which was a right-wing political party dominated by the Maronites that often allied with Israel against the Palestinians and Sunni Lebanese in the Lebanese civil war. Although the impact of this choice on the organization's effectiveness is unclear, it divided Arab Americans and undermined ADC's stance as a grassroots, community organization.

Other Christians from the Middle East have also sought to distance themselves from inclusion as Arab Americans. The Egyptian Copts have formed their own organizations and charities as well as churches. Since 9/11, Middle Eastern Christians have become more vocal about their desire to be excluded from statistics on Arab Americans. In October 2001, an ad hoc coalition of Assyrians and Maronites mounted a campaign against the Arab American Institute Foundation (AAIF) to protest their inclusion in the statistical calculations of Arab Christians in the United States. The groups built on age-old arguments from the Middle East to disassociate themselves from Arab Americans and, by extension, the smear of ethnic affiliation that the 9/11 terrorists left on the community. The AAIF's Executive Director, Helen Samhan, recognized their concerns and responded in an open letter to the coalition and countered that "identities that are carefully maintained within a group do not always correspond with how the group is perceived in the broader society."[11] She recalled that the backlash that followed 9/11 was indiscriminate and "founded in fear or ignorance"—meaning that those who were involved in the backlash did not distinguish between an Arab, an Assyrian, or a Maronite. After it was revealed that the Census Bureau had released the ethnic breakdowns only of people of Arab descent to the U.S. Department of Homeland Security, many Arab Americans feared being profiled and targeted for collective punishment, if they were identified as Arab on official forms. There is a common fear, even paranoia, among Arab Americans that to identify as an Arab makes one a target in the United States and to participate in political movements, even majority non-Arab ones, could lead to the loss of one's business or immigration status. This fear of backlash silences many Arab Americans from expressing their views and pride in their ethnicity, therefore undermining their civic engagement in Arab American organizations and in U.S. society. The backlash has strengthened the resolve of other Arab Americans to speak out by embracing their heritage and its meaning in the United States.

Politics in the Middle East has directly affected Arab Americans through the Islamic revivalist movement that embraces a pan-Islamic identity, which overrides other localized affiliations. The renewed vitality of this movement began during the Iranian revolution in 1979 when the Ayatollah Khomeni took power and ousted the Shah in an Islamic revolution. Although many vehemently disagreed with Khomeni's government, the success of the overthrow helped to create a popular Islamic upsurge at a time when pan-Arabism was waning in the Middle East. At first only a handful of the newest immigrants identified themselves as Muslims above their national or pan-ethnic affiliation. As they became active in mosques and Islamic activities, they encouraged other Muslim Americans to make Islam a focal point of their lives and their identity. The growing religiosity in today's American pop culture has increased religious identification for all religious groups, and Muslims are no exception to this trend. However, the Muslim community is not monolithic, and there are tensions among groups of Muslims. The range of opinions from "secular to scarfed" divides the Muslim community in many complex ways.

In the United States, Arab Christian and Arab Muslim institutions do not openly clash, but there is a lack of communication. Although Arab Americans may have strong personal relationships, based on their common language, cultural values, and history, their leaders often consider their religious communities as separate. For example, when the Brooklyn-based Islamic Society of Bay Ridge invited the pastor of the Salam Arab Lutheran Church to speak at a Ramadan event, in December 1999 the reverend said: "I have to confess [that] your invitation came to me as something of a surprise. I'm deeply humbled to be here tonight to share with you this special month. And I thank you for this gesture of reaching out so that out two communities may come closer together for the benefit of all."[12]

Generational Differences

Intragroup relations are often based on stereotypes. First-generation Arab Americans and Arabs living in the United States without citizenship or residency are sometimes derogatorily called "boaters." The term refers to the historical migration of the early Arab American settlers who arrived in the United States by sea, and it still denotes someone who has recently migrated from the Arab world. According to the stereotype, first-generation Arab Americans speak English "with an accent," preferring to converse in Arabic, and they do not understand U.S. institutional systems and feel "betwixt and between" countries and cultures. This sense of estrangement, of not fully belonging to American society, gives rise to a sense of nostalgia for their homeland and a longing to return to "where they were born." The stereotype extends to the issues of concern to these first-generation Arab Americans and the corresponding focus of organizations that represent them. Pertinent issues to first-generation Arab Americans are considered to be school choice (mostly so that children can attend Islamic or Catholic schools), discrimination issues, immigration policies, and U.S. foreign policy in the Middle East.

In turn, second-, third-, and fourth-generation Arab Americans are stereotyped by first-generation Arab Americans. The first stereotype is that the more acculturated Arab Americans always speak in English and have poor Arabic skills. Two terms have been coined to describe their language skills: *kitchen Arabic,* when a person only knows Arabic kitchen- and food-related words, as food was the one cultural element that many Lebanese descendents kept; and the more fluent *Arabish,* a slang mix of Arabic and English. The second stereotype assumes that these Arab Americans know and care little about the Arab world, and so in the political realm are only concerned with

U.S. domestic politics and government policies toward small businesses in particular. A second- or a third-generation Arab American is stereotyped as a fully integrated American, who knows how the U.S. system works and can pass as an American of European ancestry. On a personal level, Arab heritage is more of a social and religious affiliation than a political tie. Therefore, *haflas* (parties) and political events focused on elections or other domestic issues are considered to be more important than issues pertaining to politics in the Middle East.

Despite these strong forms of labeling the "other" within the community, there is substantial interaction and affinity among different generations of Arab Americans. Most Arab Americans are concentrated in cities and work with other community members on various projects, as members of local chapters of national organizations, university clubs, or in grassroots organizations. These interactions serve to form bonds of friendship that diffuse and discredit stereotypes.

The divisions within the Arab American community are evident at both the local and national levels. Occasionally, the leadership even vocalizes these stereotypes by declaring the type of supporters or members they desire for their organization. In his resignation speech in 2003, Ziad Asali, the former president of the largest Arab American organization, ADC, described three distinct types of people in his constituency:

> We have Arabs in America who live in a self-imposed ghetto with little contact with other citizens of their community. They watch *Al Jazeera* and know more about Gaza than they do about their own school districts, or the names of their congressman. Then, we have Americans of Arab heritage who have a vague familiarity with *kibbeh, debkeh* and Arabic music with dim memories of their immigrant grandparent's accents. Then there are Arab Americans who share affection for both America and the Arab world and are trying to play an active role as a bridge between these two cultures.[13]

Asali clearly preferred what he described as "Arab Americans" to play an active role in the organizations that act as a bridge between the Arab and U.S. cultures. Later in this speech, Asali said that the community's diversity was overwhelming, almost a cause for failure, and it was "not always possible for one voice to speak on behalf of the all these groups on all issues." He called for the establishment of more organizations to address the divergent concerns and increasingly important issues facing Arab Americans. The multifaceted nature of the community and Arab American identity is clearly a challenge for the leadership—a situation not eased by divisions and the use of stereotypes within the community.

SOCIAL CLUBS AND NETWORKS

One of the strongest criticisms of national Arab American or Muslim American organizations is that they are dominated by one type of Arab American or American Muslim. The validity of such accusations depends on the assumptions made at the time. It would be more accurate to say that the establishment and development of Arab American societies and networks reflect the fluidity of ethnic identification and the multifaceted nature of the Arab American community.

The Arab American organizations range from serving in-group needs to outreach to non-Arab groups. The first Arab American organizations tended to help the fledgling small Arab American community. The goal of one of the earliest societies, the Syrian Society, was to provide "an educational and industrial institution for natives of that [the Syrian] race, by which they shall be taught the English language and such branches of learning and industry as may assist them to support themselves, and to become intelligent American citizens."[14] The Syrian Ladies' Aid Society helped early newcomers when they arrived at Ellis Island and New York City. Both organizations explicitly wanted the new immigrants to stay and succeed in the United States. Other early churches and organizations focused on providing charitable help to those left back home.

During the breakup of the *haras* and the dispersal of Arab Americans to the suburbs, there was a need to bring together people for events. In the 1920s, there was an abundance of women's and men's clubs in each locale where Arab Americans lived. Churches sometimes acted as agents that brought members of the community together, but the growing popularity of *mahrajans,* or festivals, crossed sectarian lines during their heyday, between the 1930s and 1960s. These *mahrajans,* which will be discussed further in the next chapter, were outdoor festivals held in municipal parks. Lasting up to three days, they would draw hundreds, even thousands, of Arab Americans toward the end of their era. Although these *mahrajans* served to energize and retain Arabic arts, they were in essence social events that provided forums for young and old to meet and talk.

In the South, the men's local athletic clubs formed autonomous basketball and baseball leagues that brought together Arab Americans from various towns to the games to play and socialize. On July 4, 1931, a two-day ball game in Port Arthur, Texas, was organized that brought together these informal leagues. Two months later, a small group of leaders formed a committee in Austin, Texas. They drafted a working constitution for the Southern Federation of Syrian Clubs, inviting local clubs across 13 Southern states to join the federation and sign the constitution. The organization was later renamed the Southern Federation of Syrian Lebanese American Clubs after Lebanon gained independence. The traditions and influence of the first meeting can still be seen in their annual Fourth of July meeting today. A researcher described the weekend event in 1989 as such:

> The federation is defensively patriotic and loyalty and allegiance to America are loudly proclaimed at meetings, as was characteristic in the advocacy of [the] federation in the 1920s. The national anthem is played at the banquets and the pledge of allegiance is not neglected. Music, food and activities during the convention are basically those of popular American culture, although some symbols representing heritage—"emblems"—of shared identity are projected.[15]

Although little Arabic is spoken, the attendees do share some cultural emblems, including dancing *debkeh* (a form of dance that will be discussed in Chapter 6) at the parties that follow the presenting of debutantes. These annual events are distinctly American and social in nature—with the only politics being an American patriotic theme. The event brings together single Arab Americans to socialize and possibly to find a partner. Without such a networking opportunity, these Arab Americans would probably have little interaction, and future generations might lose a sense of grounding and connection with their heritage.

The Midwest Federation of American Syrian-Lebanese Clubs was established in 1936. Similar to its counterpart in the South, the Federation comprises a number of regional clubs, including the Phoenician Club of Chicago, the Sands Club of Detroit, and the Ladies Cedar Club of Flint, as well as member organizations in Des Moines, Milwaukee, and Cleveland. The main event is its annual convention, and its goal is to promote the people's culture and heritage. Although its focus is "philanthropic, educational and informative," the annual conventions and board meetings "also provide a forum for all to speak and thus present a united voice for peace, harmony and opportunity to voice middle eastern [*sic*] concerns." The choice of wording indicates that they are consciously distancing themselves from an Arab American identity, as they refer to themselves as "Middle Eastern individuals."[16]

Arab Americans have been active in non-Arab social clubs and organizations from the Junior League to the American Civil Liberties Union. In the 1930s, some Arab Americans wanted to join the Shriners and the Rotary Clubs in their area with mixed results. Their status as whites was found to be partial and, like Jews, many were not admitted as members. This also happened at exclusive clubs. For example, the Lebanese of Vicksburg, Mississippi, were excluded from the local country club until the 1950s. In 1988, the president of the same Vicksburg country club was of Lebanese descent, leading one to believe that their acceptance into that society is now complete.

By the 1940s, second-generation Syrian Americans showed their heritage and made public their ethnicity only when they felt it was safe to do so, in ethnic fairs or fashion shows, for example.[17] Seeking approval by the American public, they projected an image that showed others their differences in palatable ways. They established clubs with logos and names that were exotic to Americans, such as the Caravaneers, a club that had as its logo an image of sand dunes and oases, even though the members were from Lebanon—a country of lush mountains, seacoasts, and fertile plains, not the desert climate of camels, oases, or sand dunes. Non–Arab Americans had clearly framed how these Middle Easterners portrayed themselves as a group and perhaps how they thought of themselves. Sensitivity to the perceptions of outsiders impacted local and national social networking and activities.

In comparison with the majority of the first and second wavers, many third wavers were more educated, spoke better English, and were more likely to be fleeing political persecution. They were more diverse in terms of region of origin, and many were Muslim. They arrived in the United States during the civil rights era and continued to immigrate at a time when multiculturalism was the norm. Appreciative of the political freedoms available in the United States, they expressed their personal identities and their attachment to the Arab world. After the 1967 defeat, angered by the Arab political regimes that had forced them to flee, they formed national organizations with more overt political aims—to build unity for political purposes and to improve the image of Arabs and Arab Americans in the United States.

Although established for mostly political purposes, almost every Arab American national organization holds an annual convention or black-tie dinner that is mainly social in nature. The main purpose of these events is fundraising, but they secondarily serve the same purposes as the federations—to create informal networks of Arab Americans. In particular, the Saturday evening *hafla* at the annual ADC convention is attended by hundreds of Arab Americans, and an Arabic band or DJ plays contemporary

Arabic music. The moves on the dance floor reflect the different dance forms of the Middle East with *dabkeh* –(and Raqs Arabi) as well as contemporary popular dancing.

Most of the 104 Arab American organizations listed in the *Arab-American Almanac* represent a narrow member base or a specific interest. Many of the organizations founded in the 1920s and 1930s, which only had members from a certain village, are still in existence. For example, the Syrian Women's Ferouzi Club, founded in 1935, represents members, mostly women, from the village of Ferouzi near Homs, Syria. As with other village- and town-based member organizations, its activities are to fundraise and help the poor and orphans in Ferouzi. Other organizations strive to help those from their own community in the United States, such as the Yemen American Association, which has a recreation center and language and translation services. Other organizations help the less fortunate in the Middle East, not necessarily from one particular area.

Since the 1970s and 1980s, there has been an increase in professionally based organizations, such as the Arab Bankers Association of North America, Arab American Press Guild, and the National Arab American Medical Association. Organizations focusing on the arts have gained popularity among artists and art-lovers, such as turath.org, Kan Zamaan Community Ensemble, the Radius of Arab American Writers (RAWI), and the Arab film festivals that take place across the country. However, many Arab American organizations exist solely for socializing and throwing parties, especially the U.S. city–based organizations. There has been a recent movement initiated by ACCESS to reorient some of the mostly social groups to help the less fortunate and provide social services to needy Arab Americans.

Most Muslim organizations strive to reach beyond ethnically based boundaries and stress the commonality of a shared faith. Although American Muslim organizations can be dominated by one ethnicity, such bias is not mentioned in their mission statements. There are few, if any, explicitly Arab Muslim organizations even though there are scores of Muslim organizations in the United States. The first association that provided a vehicle for American mosques to coordinate and collaborate in the middle of the twentieth century was the Federation of Islamic Organizations in the United States and Canada. In 1963, the Muslim Student Association (MSA) was formed to bring different nationalities on university campuses together under the banner of Islam. The MSA chapters in the United States and Canada continue to be a strong influence on the youth by planning religious and social activities for international Muslim students as well as American Muslims (MSA of the United States and Canada). The national MSA holds an annual conference where approximately 3,000 Muslim students meet and air their concerns as well as socialize. Other large, faith-based organizations are the Islamic Society of North America and the Islamic Circle of North America, which hold regular meetings and huge annual conventions.

More recently, the information age has had a tremendous impact on Arab Americans as well as the rest of society. The Internet has created new networks for Muslim and Arab Americans within the United States and across national borders. Web sites have supplemented the social gathering places for interactions between Arab Americans. Although the Arab American community has used the World Wide Web and its associated technologies for activist and informational purposes, the Muslim community has gone one step further and formed voluntary social networks through sites such as http://www.IslamOnline.net and http://www.naseeb.com. The Internet in general has a professional, middle-class bias, and many of the Muslim sites cater to the tastes and inclinations of this class. Naseeb.com, for example, states that it "is an online community that connects young, educated, professional Muslims through networks of friends," conveying to its readers that on its Web site, they will meet like-minded "people with similar backgrounds." As with some of the mainstream U.S. Web sites, matches and marriages can result from online introductions, and in Muslim-based Web sites, these matches may be transnational as well as faith-based choices.

HOLIDAYS AND CELEBRATIONS

Arab Americans celebrate major life events and religious holidays as well as some American holidays. Holidays are often an opportunity to get together as a family and to reinforce shared cultural and religious values with food, dance, music, and conversation. The choice of how, when, and which holidays to celebrate can identify the degree of assimilation, religion, and cultural traditions that a family follows.

Arab Americans share in the revelry of occasions that signify life changes such as weddings and births. The importance and size of festivities surrounding a wedding have been transferred from the Middle East to the United States. Although the religious ceremonies differ—Christians holding their marriages in churches and Muslims in small family-only gatherings with an *imam* in a home or perhaps in a mosque—both hold large wedding receptions. Receptions may be held in a hotel, banquet hall, or home and may last more than one night, although these celebrations have been truncated from the weeklong festivities common in the Middle East, especially in villages.

Lavish occasions with huge displays of food honor the guests, including friends and relatives, who have sometimes traveled from the Arab world to share in the festivities. In some Arab American weddings, musicians may lead the bride and groom into the wedding hall, and there may be an Arabic DJ or band, with dancing and singing until late into the night. Guests may throw money to help the dancing bride and groom in their future. However, in most areas of the United States, there are few Arabic musical resources, limiting the choices available to the bride and groom. Instead, they may hire an American band and DJ. Conservative Muslims do not serve alcohol, and some may eschew music and dancing, choosing to focus the celebrations on food and the company.

A tradition that is practiced in some Arab American communities (Yemeni, Egyptian/North African, Sudanese, and Palestinian) before the wedding is the *henna* night. Henna, made from the leaves of the henna tree, is a natural dye that is painted onto the body, especially the hands and feet, of the bride and her female friends and cousins. The henna designs look to an American eye like a tattoo, but they fade completely after about three weeks. The purpose of the henna night is to bring together the women, and sometimes the men as well, to kick off the wedding celebrations. The application of henna is supposed to make the bride more attractive to her groom on their wedding night.

Children are considered blessings from God, and so births are usually celebrated with much gusto in the Arab American community. After a birth, relatives and friends come to the hospital or later the home of the parents to bring gifts to the baby. The traditional gifts are a cross (for Christians), a small Quran (for Muslims), a blue bead (an amulet that wards off the evil eye), or a gold coin. These gold pendants are pinned onto clothing or put on necklaces for the baby. A special pudding made of spices and nuts is made and served to guests. It is believed that a new mother takes 40 days to recover from childbirth, so her own mother will usually stay with the family for that duration to help with the new baby and other children, if there are any. Birthdays and graduations are celebrated in most Arab American families, although pious Muslim families believe that extravagant birthday celebrations foster "a sense of self-centeredness in children that may not be advisable."[18]

When Arab Americans first arrive, they are likely to observe the same holidays that they celebrated back home, as these dates still signify the celebrations more vividly to them. Therefore, newcomers consider Mother's Day to be on March 21 rather than the U.S. Mother's Day, the first Sunday in May. Other holidays that are new to them may take some adjustment. Many Arab Americans consider the Fourth of July a time for patriotism and family celebrations. In fact, most Arab Americans have their large annual family reunions on that weekend, perhaps as part of the larger regional conventions. On that weekend, the descendents of Arab Americans from Ramallah, Palestine, gather, and 3,000 to 5,000 people attend their family reunion/convention. Thanksgiving is celebrated as a family- and food-focused holiday. For some Arab Americans, other holidays are harder. Muslims may believe that Valentine's Day promotes cheap, commercialized romanticism in boys and girls, but they may allow their children to exchange cards with their friends. Halloween is another holiday that is opposed by some Muslim families, as it is seen as a celebration of witchery. Other Muslims see the holiday as harmless and allow their children to dress up and trick-or-treat with adult supervision.

Muslim holidays are often mistaken to be Arab holidays in the United States, but Arab Christians obviously do not share the same religious beliefs and so have different days and traditions for celebrations. The dates of the Muslim holidays rotate, further confusing Americans. The Muslim calendar is calculated according to the moon's cycles and so differs from the calendar used by most of the world, the Gregorian calendar, based on the movements of the sun. The lunar year has 354 days, and the solar year has 365 days. Although Muslim holidays are always on the same date in the lunar calendar, they fall about 11 days earlier each year in the Gregorian calendar. Therefore, the lunar month of *Ramadan* begins 11 days earlier each year, and so, the season and the dates of Ramadan, and Muslim holidays, change according to the sightings of the moon.

Ramadan is not actually a holiday but rather a month in which Muslims fast from sunrise to sunset. Fasting during Ramadan, the holiest month for all Muslims, is one of the pillars of Islam, so practicing Muslims in the United States consider the observance of Ramadan a central religious activity. Muslims are expected to spend more time reading the Quran and praying at the mosque during the month. At sunset, Muslims, often "break the fast" or have *iftar*, a sunset meal, and pray together. On university campuses, Muslim students will often arrange to meet and eat together in the cafeteria at sunset or cook an early dinner for one another in their dorms. In the United States, members of the local mosque or Muslim community meet at homes to share *iftar*, and families often wake up early to have some food together before the sun rises. Each Arab country has different culinary traditions, and the traditional foods served at *iftar* differ according to country of origin. Many recent immigrants report that it is much harder to fast in the United States than in the Arab world, where schedules and timetables are rearranged for Ramadan. In the United States, Muslims are expected to work and go to school as normal, and they are surrounded by people eating during the day and may not have time to eat *iftar* when the sun sets. Ramadan may make practicing Muslims feel isolated because their patterns differ from their non-Muslim friends for those 30 days. Some U.S. schools have shown sensitivity to practicing Muslim students by setting aside a special study hall for them and not insisting that they go to the cafeteria at lunchtime. Some Muslims have found ways to celebrate Ramadan with their non-Muslim friends by sharing the *iftar* meal together. Ideally, Ramadan gives Muslim Americans a feeling of belonging to a group when they are able to share in the rituals together.

Muslims celebrate two major holidays, *Eid al-Fitr* and *Eid al-Adha*. Although the lesser of the two holidays, *Eid al-Fitr* is the most publicized holiday in the United States, as it takes place at the end of the month of fasting, Ramadan. It is a happy occasion; children are given new clothes and all receive gifts and money from friends and relatives. During *Eid*, Muslims are expected to pray at the mosque more, read the Quran, and visit Muslim friends, neighbors, and family. Yemeni children celebrate this holiday by walking around the neighborhood, collecting candy, gifts, and money. Although the other activities around *Eid al-Fitr* can easily be adapted to life in the United States, Yemeni Americans not living in ethnic neighborhoods may not be able to go from door-to-door in the same manner as in Yemen. More important to Muslims is *Eid al-Adha*, a lamb feast that commemorates Abraham's attempted sacrifice of his son, whom Muslims believe was Ishmael rather than Isaac. This *Eid* falls at the end of the *hajj* period of pilgrimage to Mecca. The only way in which the celebration of this *Eid* differs from *Eid al-Adha* is that *halal* lamb is always cooked and shared with their family and friends. Muslim families donate the monetary value of half of the lamb or cow to the mosque, which then buys meat and distributes it to the poor and needy.

Shia Muslims observe the first 10 days of the month of *Muharram*, which is a mourning period for the Prophet Mohammed's grandson, Hussein, who was martyred in Kerbala, Iraq. In the United States, religious Shia pray at the mosques, chant religious songs, and read verses from the Quran. During this mourning period, women cannot wear makeup and all dancing, music, television, and parties of any sort are prohibited in many practicing Shia households.

Arab Christians celebrate three major holidays: Easter, Palm Sunday, and Christmas. The Arab Christians who are the descendents of the early pioneering families have adjusted their celebrations in the United States. Although churches in the Arab world celebrate Christmas on January 7 when they believe that Jesus Christ was born, many Arab American churches celebrate Christmas on December 25 with services on Christmas Eve, as well as January 7. The Egyptian Coptic Church, and a few Eastern Rite Churches, continue to hold Christmas services on January 7. In the Middle East, the children, and perhaps the elderly, receive presents for Christmas, but the tradition of gift giving is muted. In the United States, Arab Christians have adjusted by giving more expensive and numerous gifts to all the adults and children in the family on Christmas Day. Some Muslim American families may give gifts on December 25, mostly for the children's sake. Arab Americans tend to merge the cuisines and traditional foods on Christmas Day, serving turkey as well as lamb, rice, grape leaves, and other Arabic dishes.

In the days leading up to Easter, many practicing Christians abstain from certain foods. Chaldeans and Assyrians fast for three days and abstain from meat and dairy products in the period known as the Rogations of Nineve. Some Arab American Christians observe Lent, the period before Easter, by avoiding dairy products, meat, and eggs, or by giving up one food item that they enjoy a great deal. During Lent, churches hold special services or masses, and families cook special foods, often socializing together over meals on the weekends. On Palm Sunday, parents buy their children new clothes and enter church with candles decorated with ribbons and palm branches with flowers. As Easter is the most important Christian holiday, families attend church and then serve elaborate meals to mark the transition from the simple meals of Lent. As Americans do, Arab American Christians color eggs and serve baked ham at the big Easter meal, alongside various Arab dishes and traditional date and nut cookies.

Arab American Christians have adjusted some of their traditions in the United States, just as Muslims celebrate Ramadan while going to work or school for the entire day. One issue that surfaces regularly is whether institutions, such as corporations, universities, and schools, should recognize the two *Eids* and the January 7 Christmas as days off for their practicing employees and students. This debate is part of the balance among accepting diversity, insisting upon cultural homogenization, and making room for minorities within schedules and curriculums. Different U.S. institutions have found ways in which to accommodate ethnic minorities and religions, while maintaining an orderly system that continues to produce harmonious work and school environments.

NOTES

1. The demographic information on Arab Americans used in this book derives from the Arab American Institute Foundation, Zogby International, and the Allied Media Corporation, in addition to the *2000 Census Reports*. www.census.gov/prod/2003pubs/c2kbr-23.pdf; www.census.gov/prod/2005pubs/censr-21.pdf.

2. Based on a 2002 Zogby International survey for the Arab American Institute Foundation, "Religious Affiliations of Arab Americans," handout transmitted to author, on June 30, 2004.

3. Anan Ameri and Dawn Ramey, eds., *Arab American Encyclopedia* (Detroit: UXL, 2000), 3.

4. D'Vera Cohn and Sarah Cohen. "Statistics Portray Settled, Affluent Mideast Community," *Washington Post,* 20 November 2001, A04.

5. Louise Cainkar, "Immigrant Palestinian Women Evaluate Their Lives," In *Family & Gender among American Muslims* (Philadelphia: Temple University Press, 1996), 196.

6. Ameri and Ramey, 59.

7. Abraham Nabeel, "The Yemeni Immigrant Community of Detroit: Background, Emigration and Community Life," in *Arabs in the New World: Studies on Arab-American Communities,* ed. Sameer Abraham and Nabeel Abraham (Detroit: Wayne State University Press, 1983), 123.

8. Cohn and Cohen.

9. Ray Hanania, "How Many Arabs Live in Chicagoland?," http://www.hanania.com/profiles/arabvote.htm.

10. James Abourezk, "Remarks to AAUG National Convention," quoted in *Arab American Voices,* ed. Loretta Hall (Detroit: UXL, 2000), 152.

11. Helen Samhan, letter dated October 31, 2001 given to the author on June 30, 2004.

12. Louis Abdellatif Cristillo and Lorraine C. Minnite, "The Changing Arab New York Community," in *A Community of Many Worlds: Arab Americans in New York City,* ed. Kathleen Benson and Philip Kayal (New York: Museum of the City of New York, Syracuse University Press, 2002), 124.

13. Ziad Asali, "Farewell Address from Outgoing ADC President Ziad Asali," ADC Press Release, e-mail to members, 15 June 2003.

14. Alixa Naff, "New York: The Mother Colony," in *A Community of Many Worlds: Arab Americans in New York City,* ed. Kathleen Benson and Philip Kayal (New York: Museum of the City of New York, Syracuse University Press, 2002), 10.

15. Ann Louise Bragdon, "Early Arabic-Speaking Immigrant Communities in Texas," in *Arab Americans: Continuity and Change* (Belmont, MA: Association of Arab American University Graduates, 1989), 95–96.

16. Midwest Federation of American Syrian-Lebanese Clubs Inc., "Who We Are," http://www.midwestfederation.org/whoweare.asp. In spite of the Federation's positionings, on the afternoon of September 11, 2001, the Des Moines Marriott Hotel allegedly revoked its offer to host their 2002 convention. In 2002, under a Justice Department settlement agreement, Marriott International agreed to pay the Midwest Federation $115,000, with $100,000 of it designated as scholarship money. U.S. Department of Justice, Civil Rights Division, "Enforcement and Outreach Following the September 11 Terrorist Attacks," 2002, http://www.usdoj.gov/crt/legalinfo/discrimupdate.htm.

17. Evelyn Shakir, *Bint Arab: Arab and Arab American Women in the United States* (Westport, CT: Praeger, 1997), 82.

18. Yvonne Haddad and Jane Smith, "Islamic Values among American Muslims," in *Family & Gender among American Muslims* (Philadelphia: Temple University Press, 1996), 31.

6

Impact on U.S. Society

Throughout the last 125 years, American audiences have been exposed to images and stereotypes of Arabs that directly influence how Arab Americans are perceived by the larger U.S. society. In the 1920s, "the Orient" was popular as an image for commercial products aiming to be exotic, and some of these products, such as Camel cigarettes, still bear the signs of this trend. Before 1967, Hollywood served to perpetuate the Orientalist images of the Middle East in the form of belly dancers, harems, rich sheikhs, and water pipes through movies such as *Lawrence of Arabia.* Museums, art galleries, and antique dealers collected and sold fine art made in the Middle East, as well as paintings, mostly done by Europeans, that depicted Orientalist images and themes. Then, as now, these articulations of the Middle East and Arabs were created by people who had little or nothing to do with the realities of the region and were constructed mainly for non-Arab, American audiences. Although these Orientalist images allowed for some expression of Arab culture in the public sphere, most Arab Americans could not relate the images to their everyday lives.

Since the 1970s, the image of Arabs presented by Hollywood and the media has turned for the worse. Although there are other images, two main, gendered stereotypes prevail—Arab men as terrorists and Arab women as submissive, veiled shapeless beings. As a result of these images and real events in the news, such as 9/11 and the war in Iraq, Arab Americans have suffered from discrimination and harassment. However, Arab Americans continue to have a positive relationship with, and impact on, U.S. society in the form of music, dance, literature, and art, on which the first section of this chapter focuses. The latter half of the chapter examines the complex relationship between Arab Americans and the larger U.S. society.

MUSIC, FESTIVALS, AND DANCE

The early settlers brought their musical instruments with them on the long sea voyage, playing for their friends at the informal and usually impromptu evening gatherings called *sahras* in the United States. Among these instruments was the *durabakkeh,* a goblet-shaped drum, and the *oud,* a fretless stringed instrument with a wooden face and a pear-shaped back. The *oud* is played by plucking the strings with a pick traditionally made out of an eagle's feather or a gazelle's horn. The amateur musicians played traditional village songs as fellow partygoers clapped and danced the *debkeh*—a line dance in which women and men clasp hands and dance rhythmically together. These *sahras* were opportunities for the early, mostly male, settlers to share memories and cultural expressions in a relaxed atmosphere in a boarding house or private home.

As more women immigrated, there were more weddings and parties, or *haflas,* that brought financial opportunities for musicians and singers. As the *haflas* became bigger, they moved out of smaller spaces into churches or social halls that could accommodate greater numbers of people, such as Masonic lodges, Knights of Columbus halls or, later, the ballrooms of local hotels. Singers were often hired and paid by the party organizers and given free reign to organize an accompanying ensemble. The vocalists thus became important in the early entertainment structure of Arab American music. At these gatherings, the lead singers sung in Arabic, accompanied by traditional instruments, such as the *oud* and *durabakkeh.* Most of the musicians played without sheet music, memorizing the scales and tunes by ear. Although the musicians were paid, dancers were rarely hired. Instead, the women in the community would come up one at a time to dance in front of the audience, and family and friends would toss money over their heads to show appreciation for the dancer's skills. The money was donated to the church, a philanthropic cause, or given to the new bride and groom. Called *Raqs Arabi* (or *Raqs Sharqi*), this type of dancing was later known in the United States as solo "Oriental style" dancing, or belly dancing.

As the Depression set in, Arab American communities organized weekend festivals, celebrations with singing and dancing, called *mahrajans.* Between the 1930s and 1960s, *mahrajans* usually were centered in a church, and some grew to be three-day-long festivals. There were grand stages with many singers and ensembles playing all day and into the evenings. Attendees would dance in marathon dances and learn how to play the Arabic drum, the *durabakkeh.* Local religious and community leaders gave speeches, and people recited poetry on stage. However, as the numbers of attendees increased, the costs for holding the *mahrajans,* originally covered through the sale of homemade dishes and delicacies, became prohibitive.

Although few non-Arabs attended these *haflas,* American recording labels geared to mainstream audiences produced a few instrumental recordings of Arab American musicians. Arab American entrepreneurs then decided to produce music for sale to a mostly Arab American audience. Between the 1920s and 1940s, recording companies such as the Macsoud, Malouf, Maarouf, Ash Shark, and Alamphone were established. The tracks of the subsequent 78rpm records included vocals in Arabic. The musicians followed the trends prevalent in the Middle East but added their own embellishments that reflected their situation in the United States. The songs recorded were a mix of ballads and more upbeat tunes that conveyed the hardships of immigrant life and feelings of longing and nostalgia for the homeland or had lighthearted themes and comedic elements. Toward the end of the 1940s, the musicians used more English in their live performances as well as in their records, reflecting the shift in language spoken within the community. Despite the switch in language preference, musical influences from the Middle East continued.

The Rashid Sales Company in particular facilitated the import of Middle Eastern musical tastes and trends into the United States. Through organizing showings of Egyptian films at the Brooklyn Academy of Music in 1934 and at a Brooklyn movie theater at the end of the regular Sunday feature in the 1940s, Albert Rashid kept American film buffs and Arab American factory workers up to date with the newest films from Cairo, replete with their musical and dance themes. As a result of the demand from his New York customers, Rashid began to import and sell records of Arabic music. In 1944, Rashid Sales opened a storefront in Manhattan and sent records by mail order to customers nationwide, particularly Arab Americans outside New York. In 1947, the store moved to Atlantic Avenue in Brooklyn and later to the Cobble Hill section of Brooklyn where the Rashid family continues to operate their specialty store today.

Music produced and recorded in the Middle East remains popular with Arab American audiences. On occasion, singers from the Middle East come to the United States to give concerts. Fairouz, the popular older Lebanese singer, on May 15, 1999, sang to a sold-out audience of 13,600 in Las Vegas. Younger Egyptian artists, such as Hisham Abbas, Hakim and Mohammed Mounir, have performed to smaller sold-out crowds in the United States. Recently there has been a surge in popularity of rai music from North Africa by way of France, particularly by Cheb Khaled, Rachid Taha, and Cheb Mami, the latter of which sang with sting in the 2001 super Bowl. Arab music is sold on the Internet through various channels and at large Arab American gatherings. Younger Arab Americans dance to contemporary Arabic music at nightclubs in New York, Washington, D.C., Detroit, Los Angeles, Boston/Cambridge, Chicago, and Orlando, where Arab American DJs mix music on location.

Another public venue for Arab and Arab American music and dancing were *mahrajan*s, or outdoor festivals, which acted as a social networking opportunity. In the 1990s, the *Mahrajan Al-Fan* (Festival of the Arts) revived the tradition of the *mahrajan* and simultaneously focused the event on the arts and reached out to a non-Arab American audience. The festival, which took place in 1994, 1995, 1996, and 1998, was initiated by the Ethnic Folk Arts Center in New York City, and later organized by Simon Shaheen, a prominent Arab American *oud* player and composer. As "the most elaborate cultural event produced by New York's Arab community in many decades," the *Maharajan Al-Fan* included performances by musicians and dancers as well as lectures, panel discussions, and demonstrations by ethnomusicologists and performances by Arab American poets and writers.[1] Arab American families from New Jersey, New York, Connecticut, and Maine attended, and the Arab Network of America cable television station broadcast the 1995 festival to its viewers in Europe and the Middle East.

Mahrajan Al-Fan prominently featured its organizer, Simon Shaheen, and his band, the Near East Music Ensemble, which uses traditional Arab instruments. Shaheen is perhaps the most well known Arab American musician; he has made five recordings and composed music for two movie soundtracks, *Malcolm X* and *Sheltering Sky.* Shaheen also runs the Arab American Arts Institute in Brooklyn, New York that organizes retreats and concerts. Hamza El Din, Hassan Hakmoun, and Ali Jihad Racy are other famous Arab musicians who reside in the United States. Simon Shaheen and Ali Jihad Racy, professor of ethnomusicology at the University of California in Los Angeles, cofounded the Arabic Musical Retreat held at Mount Holyoke College every summer since 1997. Their combined work has created a new appreciation for Arabic music in the United States and spurred studies of Arabic music in ethnomusicology departments in U.S. universities. One ethnomusicologist said, "Jihad Racy and Simon Shaheen have single-handedly effected a return to traditional classical Arab music."[2]

The revival of festivals in the 1990s was not limited to *mahrajans*. Arab Americans have participated in and organized other festivals across the United States, such as the *Ana Al-Arabi* (I am an Arab) festival in Washington, D.C., the Arabic Festival in San Francisco, the East Dearborn International Festival, the Arabian Festival in Milwaukee, Wisconsin, and the Arab World Festival in Detroit. These festivals, which usually feature traditional Arabic food, clothing, art, films, music, and dance, reach out to Arab American as well as non-Arab audiences. The World Music Institute holds an annual festival that features various dance and music groups from the Middle East and North Africa. Through its Cultural Arts program, ACCESS in Detroit is one of the largest supporters of Arab American music and arts in the country and often puts cultural event organizers in touch with artists and helps to organize events such as the 2004 Concert of Colors in Detroit.

Part of the revival of Arab arts can be seen in the field of dance. As expressions of ethnic identity became more popular in the 1960s, many non-Arab American women took up belly dancing, first in San Francisco, and as the craze took off, across the United States. Today there are belly dancing classes offered in most U.S. cities and some suburbs. There is an extensive network of dancers, equipment suppliers, and competitions. Three dominant forms of belly dancing have developed over the years in the United States: tribal fusion, American nightclub, and *Raqs Sharqi,* which literally means "Eastern dance." The links between the Arab world and the American forms of belly dancing can be seen in the music and the dance moves, particularly in the *Raqs Sharqi* style inspired by the Egyptian nightclub dancers. Although most belly dancers and the bands that cater to them are not of Arab origin, this form of art has become part of U.S. pop culture.

LITERATURE

Arab American literature addresses a variety of topics, only some of which are recognizably Arab or ethnic in content. The location of these artists in both the Arab and American realms is what creates Arab American art. As one literary critic wrote, "The art that results is Arab-American because it arises from the experience of Arab-Americans—personal or public, 'ethnic' or not."[3] There are some recurring themes in the art of Arab Americans, particularly displacement, diaspora, and cross-cultural identity. One theme that is shared with other immigrant groups in the United States is the feeling of isolation and the yearning to find a place in U.S. society. Arab Americans tend to focus on personal tensions between U.S. foreign policy and their personal views on issues such as Palestine and Iraq, and the presence of their relatives living in those areas. These artists often articulate family interconnectedness, especially the sharing of food, music, and dancing in their work. Arab Americans have created a few ethnically based organizations that bring together Arab American writers, thespians, and visual artists. *Mizna* is the only literary journal devoted wholly to Arab American issues, but other journals published in the United States, such as *Al Jadid* and *Jusoor,* which focus on Arabic literature, often include Arab American issues, writers, and themes. New York City is particularly rich in Arab American cultural organizations. The Radius of Arab-American Writers, Inc. (RAWI), a national organization, brings together Arab American creative and prose writers, including novelists, poets, and journalists in a national organization. RAWI, which has organized various events, held a national conference in New York in June 2005. Other Arab-American writers' conferences have included the 1999 Professional Conference on Arab-American and Ethnic Writing, organized by journalist Ray Hanania. *Ziryab,* also based in New York City, holds a monthly reading series geared to Arab American writers, poets, and playwrights who read to the audience from their own writings. The arts organization *Diwan* also promotes Arab music, storytelling, films, and book parties as well as art exhibitions in New York.

Arab American literature began in the late nineteenth century when the first Arab American newspapers began publishing articles and literary pieces by Arab Americans. The most famous Arab American literary figure is Kahlil Gibran (1883–1931). Gibran came to the United States at the age of 12 and wrote in both English and Arabic. In 1923, he wrote and illustrated *The Prophet,* a book of mystical poetry, in English, and shortly thereafter, he became a celebrated writer. *The Prophet,* in print continuously since its publication in 1923, has sold more than 9.5 million copies and has been translated into 20 languages. Gibran was part of an Arab American literary group called the Pen League founded in New York City in 1920. The Pen League included writers such as Elia Abu Madi (Madey), Mikhail Naimy, and Ameen Rihany, who wrote the first English-language Arab American novel, *The Book of Khalid* (1911), which traces the journey of an immigrant from Lebanon to the United States and back home again. The members of the Pen League, who traveled between Lebanon and the United States, wrote in English as well as Arabic, often consciously trying to bridge cultures and positing the United States as a land of opportunity and freedom.

Since 1965, Arab American writing has reflected the greater sense of security Arab Americans feel, as well as reflecting more nearly than earlier texts, the social and literary trends taking place in the United States. Contemporary Arab American writers generally tend to be more critical of the U.S. role in the world as well as more focused on domestic issues, such as poverty, racism, and injustice than were the Pen League writers. There was a shift in the use of language; post-1965 Arab American writers compose their poetry, short stories, and novels almost exclusively in English. Poetry is the most popular literary form, and many Arab American published books are collections of poems. Earlier collections of poetry include Naomi Shihab Nye's many collections, books by David Williams, Khaled Mattawa, Gregory Orfalea, Samuel Hazo, Sam Hamod, D. H. Melhem, Etel Adnan, Nathalie Handal, and others. Suheir Hammad, author of the poetry book *Born Palestinian, Born Black* and the memoir *Drops of This Story,* is well known for her role as co-writer and performer in the 2003 Tony Award–winning Broadway show and HBO series "Def Poetry Jam on Broadway." Recent poetry books include Hayan Charara's *The Alchemist's Diary,* Mattawa's *Zodiac of Echoes,* Mohja Kahf's *E-mails from Scheherazad,* and Nathalie Handal's *The Lives of Rain.*

Arab American writers, like many Arab writers, have chosen to write novels, a genre that is not in Arab literary traditions. William Peter Blatty wrote *The Exorcist* in 1971. His 1960, less famous, book, *Which Way to Mecca, Jack?,* was an autobiographical novel. Similarly, Elmaz Abinader's *Children of the Roojme* (1991) and Vance Bourjaily's *Confessions of a Spent Youth* (1960) were based on autobiographical material. Since 1990, there has been a relative boom in the number of Arab American novels. Patricia Serrafian Ward's *The Bullet Collection,* Rabih Alameddine's *I, the Divine,* Laila Halaby's *West of the Jordan: A Novel,* and Diana Abu-Jaber's *Crescent* are among the newest Arab American novels. Diana Abu-Jaber published a memoir, *The Language of Baklava,* in 2005. Author and editor Naomi Shihab Nye has won numerous awards for her poetry and children's literature and particularly for her novel, *Habibi,* which follows a young Arab American girl's journey with her family back to their Palestinian village.

To date, several anthologies of Arab American writing have been published. The editors of the 1990s anthologies alluded to the exclusion from writing circles and publications felt by Arab Americans as a group, but in the twenty-first century, Arab American writers are becoming more widely read. *Grapeleaves: A Century of Arab-American Poetry* included the works of 20 poets who wrote from the early 1900s until the 1990s. First published in 1988, the anthology was reprinted in 2000. The editors of *Grapeleaves* described the state of Arab American poetry in the introduction, "Arab American poetry is an especially rich, people-involved, passionate poetry. At the same time, it has been spawned, at least until recently, in isolation from the American mainstream. If art intensifies on the peripheries, then this is art."[4]

The editor of the 1994 publication, *Food for Our Grandmothers: Writings by Arab-American and Arab-Canadian Feminists,* called Arab Americans "The Most Invisible of the Invisibles." In this specifically woman-centered volume, the editor gathered poetry and essays by more than 40 women, including the works of younger writers, partially to encourage and publish more writing by Arab American and Arab Canadian women writers.[5] In the introduction to *Post-Gibran Anthology of New Arab American Writing* (1999), the co-editors pointed out that no literary journal has devoted an issue to "our literature," implying through their use of the pronoun "our" that they assume that the readers are mostly Arab Americans or Arabs. The stated goal of this anthology was "to infuse a new energy into this area of writing" and as such, the co-editors encouraged Arab American writers to write for themselves.[6]

Since 2000, an increasing number of novels, collections of poetry, and anthologies by Arab American writers have been published. Two recent anthologies include *Dinarzad's Children: Anthology of Arab American Fiction,* edited by Pauline Kaldas and Khaled Mattawa, and *Scheherazade's Legacy: Arab and Arab American Women on Writing,* edited by Susan Muaddi Darraj. This latter collection follows the publication of an earlier anthology of women's poetry, *The Poetry of Arab Women,* edited by Nathalie Handal. Arab American women writers have taken a prominent place in the field of writing; Naomi Shihab Nye, Nathalie Handal, and Diana Abu-Jaber combined published six books in 2005 alone. The future of Arab American writing and publishing is promising.

VISUAL ARTS

Arab American artists tended to show their art in solo shows but since 9/11, there has been an increase in exhibits of Arab American artists, particularly in the Detroit area. This rise in collective art exhibits was mainly because of the work of the Arab Community Center for Economic and Social Services (ACCESS) and the Center for Arab American Studies at the University of Michigan, Dearborn, to educate and bring together a multicultural community. In 2002, the exhibit, "Perceptions: An Exhibit of Four Arab American Artists" was followed by "Diversity in Harmony: A National Exhibit of Artists of Arab and Middle Eastern Heritage" on the campus of the University of Michigan–Dearborn in 2003 and "Near: Four Multinational Artists from the Middle East" a year later. In addition, the University of California–Berkeley brought together the works of eight contemporary artists of Arab and Iranian heritage in "Somewhere Else" at the Worth Ryder Gallery in late 2004. The stated goal of this show was to "bring[s] awareness of the impact of stereotypes in general and vilification of Arabs and Muslims in particular."[7] One of the better consequences of the events of 9/11 was to highlight the works of Arab American artists and bring their work together as social statements.

Arab American artists use diverse media and themes for their art. Sam Maloof is famous for the sculptural quality of his woodworking and for his combination of beauty and function in simple furniture designs. Maloof began his career in 1948, and one of his rocking chairs is in the White House's collection of American furniture. His creations are in the collections of the Smithsonian Institution, the Metropolitan Museum of Art, the Los Angeles County Museum, and at the Vatican. His house in California, which he built and filled with his specially crafted furniture, is considered a historic landmark.

Khalil Bendib is a well-known Arab American sculptor and ceramist who has a studio in Berkeley, California. His first major public monument (1994) was the "Alex Odeh Memorial Statue," honoring an Arab American community leader who was assassinated in 1985. Since that time, Bendib has completed many public artworks, including the "Deir Yassin Remembered Memorial Sculpture" at Hobart and Smith Colleges in New York State, a mural for the Arab Cultural Center in San Francisco, and a Venus and Mars bronze frieze as well as wall sculptures installed in California. Bendib's art includes paintings, sketches, and mosaics, in addition to ceramics and public art.

Zaha Hadid won the 2004 Pritzker Architecture Prize, the first woman to win this prestigious award. She was the first woman to design a major art museum, Cincinnati's Contemporary Art Center. Another famous Arab American female artist is Wasma' Chorbachi, who immigrated to the United States to pursue a doctorate degree in Islamic Design at Harvard University. Chorbachi began "molding clay and baking it along with the bread in her family's traditional Arab bread ovens at their home in Baghdad."[8] The influence of Islamic and Arab traditions is evident in her art and in the presence of Islamic calligraphy in her ceramic creations that use lusters and glazes. Mamoun Sakkal is known for his calligraphy, which is framed as complete works on paper. Islamic art does not generally contain representations of humans or animals, but Arab American Christians and some Muslims have chosen to go against this guideline. Leila Kubba, Lily Bandak, Doris Bitar, Etel Adnan, Rheim Alkadhi, Abdelali Dahrouch, Annemarie Jacir, and Samia Halabi are skilled and well-known Arab American visual artists and photographers.

Although Arab Americans artists are featured in some museums, most major art museums have objects from the Middle East, including Islamic art and calligraphy, in their own collections. The International Council for Women in the Arts is the only visual arts group organizing exhibits and shows in the United States that focus on the intersections between the Arab world and the United States. It runs educational programs, workshops, and programs that explore the visual arts and cultures of the Arab world.

Fashion is not strictly a type of visual art, but the achievements of Arab Americans in the industry are worth noting. A few of the top designers in the fashion industry, such as Joseph Abboud, Norma Kamali, Reem Acra, and Colette Malouf, are Arab Americans. Joseph Abboud and Norma Kamali design men's and women's clothes, as well as other items. Reem Acra is a specialist in high-end bridal fashions. Colette Malouf is an accessories and jewelry designer who uses exotic materials and caters to a celebrity clientele. A British-Egyptian industrial designer, Karim Rashid, is popular in the United States, and his line is carried in some major U.S. stores, such as Target.

THEATER, STORYTELLING, AND DOCUMENTARIES

Arab Americans have formed various theater groups across the country, particularly in California. The Arab American Children's Theater Company was founded in California in 1989 to encourage younger Arab Americans to be proud of their heritage. Additional Arab American theater groups exist in Chicago, Detroit, and San Francisco. In 1998, the Kanaaqeel Theater Group was established in Los Angeles to explore cultural issues of importance. Arab American theater developed as a form of entertainment for family and friends in private. The first Arab American productions were by amateurs who rehearsed at nights and on the weekends and performed in homes in the early 1900s. These plays were mostly in Arabic, and although some productions moved from homes to social clubs, they still catered to the members of the immediate community. When the community became more geographically dispersed through suburban flight in the 1930s and 1940s, Arab American theater ceased, and there are no records of its existence between the 1940s and 1980s.

In the 1980s and 1990s, there was an increase in theatrical performances as the third wavers enlarged the size of the community and yearned for plays that addressed their issues of concern in humorous ways. Today, the most important cities for Arab American theater are Detroit and Los Angeles. In Detroit, the performances are mostly in Arabic, whereas in Los Angeles, the plays are either bilingual or in English. In 1992, an Arab American anthropologist and filmmaker, Fadwa El Guindi, founded a bilingual theater group called *Al-Fanun Al-Arabiya* (Arab Arts) in California.

The rise of theater since 1980 mirrored a revival in the Arab tradition of storytelling in the United States. Two of the most famous Arab American storytellers are Elmaz Abinader and Emily Shihadeh. In this tradition, stories are told by the women in the family to the children to pass down fables with moral tales to the next generation. In the United States, these storytelling performances are usually done in English to both Arab and non-Arab audiences.

The storyteller reads a traditional Arabic story or crafts the performance with stories from his or her personal experiences or from the cultures and histories of Arabs and Arab Americans.

Since 9/11, there has been a rise in the number of Arab American comedic acts. In 2002, the New York Arab Comedy Fest was hosted by two Arab American comedians, Maysoon Zayid and Dean Obeidallah, and included Ray Hanania, Sherif Hedayat, Jim Asher, Omar Koury, and Nasry Malake. Arab American comedians have gone onstage in comedy clubs across the country, and two comedians—Zayid and Obeidallah—were the main entertainment at a the Arab American Institute's Kahlil Gibran "Spirit of Humanity" Awards gala event in 2005.

Arab Americans have made and assisted in the creation of three documentaries that focus on the Arab American community: *Tales from Arab Detroit, Benaat Chicago: Growing Up Arab and Female in Chicago,* and *In My Own Skin,* in which young Arab American women discuss what it means to be Arab and American in New York City in October 2001. Arab Americans have made numerous documentaries and films that deal with issues in the Middle East. One company, the Arab Film Distribution Company, based in Seattle, Washington, owns the distribution rights to many of these documentaries as well as other films.

Film festivals that bring movies, directors, and producers from the Arab world are organized in major U.S. cities. Although the initial impetus for showing Arabic films in the United States came from the Rashid Sales Company, today's film festivals are generally organized by Arab American film buffs or by institutions interested in showing a diversity of films within an international film festival. New York City probably boasts the most film festivals, including collaborations between *Alwan*, an arts nonprofit organization, and New York University. Washington, D.C., annually hosts the Arabian Sights Film Festival, San Francisco has the Cinemayaat Arab Film Festival, and Seattle holds the Arab and Iranian Film Festival, which was formerly known as the Arab Film Festival.

Some Arab Americans have also had substantial success in Hollywood and in radio. Famous Arab American actors are Danny Thomas and his daughter Marlo Thomas, Tony Shalhoub, Kathy Najimy, Selma Hayek, and Shannon Elisabeth. Radio presenters include Casey Kasem and Don Bustany, who hosted "America's Top 40," as well as other shows for 40 years, and Diane Rehm, who has her own program, the "Diane Rehm Show," on National Public Radio. Arab American singer-songwriters include Paul Anka, Frank Zappa, and Tiffany. Grammy-award winner, American Idol judge, singer, dancer, and choreographer Paula Abdul is also Arab American. Some of these personalities are included in Appendix B: Noted Arab Americans, but a fuller listing can be found on the Arab American Institute's Web site.[9]

THE ARAB AMERICAN NATIONAL MUSEUM AND OTHER COLLECTIONS

The Arab American National Museum is the first and only museum dedicated to Arab Americans. Opened in May 2005 in Dearborn, Michigan, it showcases "the rich cultural heritage of the Arab American community and the contributions it has made and will continue to make to this country." The museum acts as an educational facility, an institution of preservation, and a community center that focuses on Arab American immigration, employment, religion, history, arts, and culture.

Two other notable museum collections of Arab American historical documents and objects are the Naff Collection at the Smithsonian Institution and the Near Eastern collection at the Immigration History Research Center at the University of Minnesota in Minneapolis. The Naff Collection was donated by the notable Arab American historian, Alixa Naff, and includes photographs, books, manuscripts on the Arab American experience, as well as rare items, including wedding gowns, jewelry, peddler's wares, and embroidery. The collection is held in the permanent archives of the National Museum of American History in Washington, D.C.

POLITICAL ACTIVISM AND ORGANIZATIONS

Since the 1880s, Arab Americans have created and reformed community institutions. From that time until the 1960s, most Arab American institutions were either small-scale media organizations, churches, or mosques or purely social networks that mainly consisted of Syrians and Lebanese Christians— the majority of the Arabic-speaking population at the time. After the 1967 Six-Day War and the influx of new immigrants, some Arab American academics, professionals, and politicians formed organizations to galvanize the community and to reach out to non-Arab American audiences. From the late 1960s to the mid 1980s, four main national organizations were formed: the Arab-American University Graduates (AAUG), National Association of Arab-Americans (NAAA), American-Arab Anti-Discrimination Committee (ADC), and Arab American Institute (AAI). In the last two decades, a local organization, Arab Community Center for Economic and Social Services

(ACCESS), based in Dearborn, Michigan, has created a network of community organizations across the United States and is becoming a player at the national level. This new organization is called the National Network for Arab American Communities. Meanwhile, these organizations sometimes pool their resources and energies under the banner of the National Arab American Organizations (NADO).

The AAUG was founded in 1968 to present accurate information about the Arab world and to be a catalyst for Arab American activists, academics, and professionals. Throughout its history, the AAUG held democratic elections that ensured a rotating leadership and board of directors, often empowering women and younger members. Two women, Faith Zeadey and Elaine Hagopian, served as presidents of AAUG in the 1970s and 1980s. In the 1990s, Hala Maksoud, Nadia Hijab, and Afaf Mahfouz were AAUG presidents, and the executive director was also a woman in the late 1990s and early 2000s. AAUG published books and three publications, including its flagship, *Arab Studies Quarterly*, and held vibrant annual conventions. However, the many events in the Middle East caused rifts in the organization that undermined its financial base and forced it to downsize in 2001. Despite the slowdown in operations, *Arab Studies Quarterly* is still in production, and a few active board members are reviving the organization, which is now housed with the arts organization, *Diwan*, in New York City.

The ADC was founded in 1980 by Senator James Abourezk to counteract the use of stereotypes of Arabs that came to light with the exposure of an FBI sting operation called ABSCAM. In this operation, FBI agents dressed up as Arab sheikhs and bribed congressmen who were then put on trial for corruption. Senator Abourezk, who grew up on a Native American reservation, was inspired to establish an organization to defend Arab Americans from victimization by discrimination and stereotypes and to fight against misleading and incorrect information being disseminated by the media and schools. Today, the ADC is the largest Arab American grassroots organization, offering cultural, political, and civil rights activities, and maintaining two regional offices (one in Dearborn, Michigan, and the other in New York City), as well as 39 local chapters in the United States. It has had both women and men as presidents throughout its 25-year history. The current president is a former congresswoman, Mary Rose Oakar. A past ADC president, Hala Salaam Maksoud, established the Hala Foundation in her will to promote the training and development of leadership in the Arab American community. With such examples and precedence, it is likely that women will continue to hold leadership roles in ADC.

Founded in 1972, the NAAA was established to act as lobbyists for Arab issues and points of view in Washington, D.C. Its leadership consisted of

American businessmen and professionals of Arab background who wanted to monitor U.S. foreign policy and give relevant information to the U.S. government to improve U.S.-Arab relations. In the 1970s and 1980s, the organization often endorsed American-led initiatives in the Middle East, such as the Camp David Accords, but it shied away from seeking substantial change within U.S. foreign policy, unlike AAUG and ADC. On January 1, 2002, the NAAA officially merged with the ADC for financial reasons.

In 1985, James Zogby, founder and president of AAI, left the ADC to establish AAI, an organization that concentrates on mobilizing Arab Americans to respond to local, national, and international policy matters and developments through civic and political engagement. AAI focuses on campaigns, elections, policy formulation, and research by involving Arab Americans directly in U.S. politics through running for and serving in public office and working in campaigns. AAI runs its own get-out-the-vote campaign called "Yalla Vote," which registers Arab Americans with the goal of creating a strong Arab American turnout and voice on election days. AAI is based in Washington, D.C., and has a foundation that runs extensive educational and outreach programs.

ACCESS, established in 1972, is the most successful and enduring of the local Arab American organizations. Activists who had blocked the destruction of homes in the South End of Dearborn and the transformation of the working-class residential area into an industrial park, came together to form the Arab Community Center for Employment. They secured $1,000 from AAUG and opened a counseling center in a storefront location. From the outset, ACCESS, as it came to be known, had founders and board members from a variety of Arab backgrounds and so enjoyed wide acceptance by the community. During the 1973 war, ACCESS focused on foreign policy in the Middle East; groups such as the Arab Workers Caucus, the Arab Women's Auxiliary, and the Arab Media Committee were formed to meet community needs. ACCESS also appointed its first volunteer director, a Muslim Arab American woman, Hajjah Aliya Hassan. ACCESS today has continued in this tradition and includes many women in its top leadership positions.

ACCESS helps needy and low-income families and "provides a wide range of social mental health, educational, artistic, employment, legal and medical services." In 2002, ACCESS started the Arab-American Community Service Initiative, in which it works with existing local Arab American community-based organizations in nine U.S. cities to strengthen the services provided to the community by coordinating fundraising efforts and providing training, assistance, and volunteers through AmeriCorps. This national network meets annually in a conference format, aiming to improve and expand the local community infrastructure for Arab Americans. ACCESS also opened the Arab American National Museum in Dearborn in 2005.

In 1963, Islamic Society of North America (ISNA) was founded, and eight years later, a second, major Muslim American organization was founded, the Islamic Circle of North America (ICNA). In the 1980s and 1990s, the American Muslim Council (AMC), Council on American Islamic Relations (CAIR), the Muslim Public Affairs Council (MPAC), and other American Muslim organizations were founded. In March 2005, these national American Muslim organizations met in Chicago to form the National Council of American Muslim Non-Profits, a proactive community-initiated measure that sets out to develop a comprehensive oversight process to ensure transparency and protection of American Muslim institutions. These organizations do not solely represent the Arab American community in the United States, but rather focus on the broader Muslim community and so will not be examined here.

A few of the American Muslim organizations and most of the national Arab American organizations share a focus on U.S. foreign policy. The overriding concern now is the political situation in the Middle East, with particular care for the creation of a free and independent state for Palestine, as well as the situation in Iraq. Arab Americans' concern for the rights of Palestinians and support for Palestinian independence led to a great deal of opposition by pro-Israeli groups, which has strained the relations between Arab Americans and some Jewish Americans. The Christian Right has weighed in on the Arab-Israeli conflict, contributing to the recent anti-Islam rhetoric that coincides with its pro-Israeli position. The events of 9/11 served to strengthen the argument that posits East and West as inherently antagonistic, and their differences as a "clash of civilizations."[10] Many people in the United States have adopted this as a justification for excluding Arab and Muslim Americans from institutions and circles where multiculturalism is embraced. These attitudes indicate that many Americans believe that the United States is now at war with Islam and the Arab world, rather than with the radical extremists.

An equal shared concern for the Arab American national organizations is with the situation of Arab Americans in the United States. National issues that have taken priority are civil rights and liberties, the use of secret evidence, airport profiling, immigration laws, and religious tolerance. On the local level, other issues take priority, including Social Security, Medicare, crime, taxes, school vouchers, and abortion. There is community consensus that the most important issue facing Arab Americans today is the eroding civil liberties as embodied by the U.S. Patriot Act. Signed into law on October 26, 2001, the act gives broad new powers to law enforcement agencies and the Executive Branch that has allowed the FBI and security and immigration agencies to carry out surveillance and detain people whom they deem to be threats to national security. Under this act, noncitizens can be arrested and deported without being charged, without access to lawyers, and without a trial. If they are charged, they can be held indefinitely in prisons in the United States. If designated as "unlawful enemy combatants," even U.S. citizens can be stripped of their rights, held in jail in secret, indefinitely. The Patriot Act has also been used to target Arab and Islamic charities, some of which have been closed due to investigations and/or decreased contributions. For these and many other reasons, many civil rights groups have protested the Patriot Act. Under the act, phone, bank, library, and Internet records can be requested, and law enforcement agencies can search and share information with a variety of government entities. Title III of the act focuses on financial crimes that give the government the power to freeze assets of an organization and individuals and to defend its actions on the basis of evidence that is kept from the defense. Because of its enforcement to date, and focus on the Arab/Muslim community, this act is believed to target Muslims, particularly Arab Muslims, and infringe on their civil liberties.

Since 1967, American Muslims have been active in interfaith councils, parent-teacher associations, school boards, rotary clubs, and chambers of commerce on the local level, but until recently, they have been less active in political advocacy. Although American Muslim organizations are not ethnically based, Arab Americans are sometimes disproportionately represented among the leadership of organizations such as the American Muslim Council and the Muslim American Public Action Council. In mosques that are predominantly Arab, Arab American Muslims are usually the spiritual and community leaders, but there is a wide variety of Muslims in the United States. The largest ethnic group within the American Muslim community is African Americans. There are some significant divides in the community between Sunni and Shia branches, as well as congregations that are mainly South Asians (Pakistani, Indian, or Bangladeshi), as well as linguistic differences. The largest mosque in the Detroit area is the Islamic Center, which has 6,000 congregants and is headed by Imam Hassan Qazwini, an Iraqi Shia, even though 70 percent of the congregants are of Lebanese descent.[11] There are many calls by Muslims, particularly Muslim youth, to see the Muslim community, or *umma,* as one, and to downplay cultural, social, and national origin differences.

As a result of Imam Qazwini's leadership position and the importance of Michigan in the presidential elections, President George W. Bush consulted with him as part of his election outreach to religious communities. In 2000, the Muslim community in Michigan was supportive of his bid for presidency, but in 2004, Bush's support waned. This decrease of support stemmed from increasing Muslim and Arab concerns over the racial profiling sanctioned by the Patriot Act and the erosion of civil rights. At the national level, in some states, such as Michigan, it may be politically acceptable to actively court the Arab and Muslim vote; in other states and at other times, it is considered political suicide. In the past, some candidates have returned donations from Arab Americans because of attacks by pro-Israeli supporters insinuating that money from Arab Americans is necessarily connected to terrorism and therefore tainted. In the 2000 New York Senate race between Hillary Clinton and Rick Lazio, both candidates avoided all contact with the state's 340,000 Arab Americans. Hillary Clinton, responding to personal attacks levied by Lazio, returned $51,000 in donations from a number of Arab American and Muslim American donors. Many politicians see the balance between Arab American and Jewish American support as a zero-sum game. In states such as New York with its many Jewish donors and voters, Arab Americans are often excluded from campaign agendas and from having their issues at the forefront of a candidate's plans once elected. The return of campaign donations gives Arab Americans the impression that they are being excluded from politics and from the American political process because of their ethnicity.

As a result of vigorous "Yalla Vote" ("Come on, vote!") campaigns run by AAI, 88.5 percent of Arab Americans are registered to vote (which they do at a level consistent with the national average). Because Arab Americans live in key swing states, the two main political parties have become more aware of the community and its concerns, especially during presidential races. In 2004, eight out of nine presidential candidates spoke at the AAI Annual Leadership Conference in Michigan in person or by satellite feed. Arab Americans from 25 states attended both the Republican and Democratic Conventions. If the 2000 and 2004 election results are averaged, the Arab American community is evenly divided among Democrats, Republicans, and independents.[12] In 2000, Bush garnered much of the Arab American vote because he mentioned an important community issue, profiling, in a presidential debate. Pollsters assumed that because Muslims are often socially conservative that they were more likely to support the Republican candidate.[13] Polls carried out in the summer of 2004 found that Bush's support had slipped drastically among Arab Americans, particularly among Muslims. The reasons cited by a research group from the University of Chicago were the war in Iraq, the erosion of civil liberties under the Patriot Act, and the administration's heavy support of Ariel Sharon's policies in Israel. In a reversal of previous support for the Republican Party, 63 percent of Arab Americans voted for the Democratic candidate and 29 percent voted for President Bush in the 2004 presidential elections.[14]

Beyond voting and being active in political campaigns, few Arab Americans have been elected or appointed to high public offices. Most of the Arab

Americans in office are second-, third-, or fourth-generation Arab Americans, almost exclusively Christians of Lebanese descent. The first Arab American in a presidential cabinet was Donna Shalala, who served in President Bill Clinton's administration. The former governor of New Hampshire, John H. Sununu, became the White House Chief of Staff under George H. W. Bush (1989–91) and later was a commentator on CNN. His son, John E. Sununu, was recently elected to the U.S. Senate for the state of New Hampshire. Ralph Nader ran as a presidential candidate in the 1996, 2000, and 2004 elections. Ralph Nader has been active in politics since the 1960s, when the publication of his article in the *Nation,* "The Safe Car You Can't Buy," led to his lifelong work championing the cause of consumer protection. Arab Americans have served in the U.S. House of Representatives and the Senate as well as in state legislative bodies. More than 30 Arab Americans have been elected as mayors of U.S. cities. Although the vast majority of Arab American politicians are Christians of Lebanese descent, Arab American Muslims are taking an increasing role in public life. In 2003, the first Arab American Muslim mayor in the United States, Abdul Haidos of Wayne, Michigan, won 70 percent of the vote.

ACADEMIA

Arab American academics are engaged in a variety of disciplines and research a wide variety of topics, only a few of which are related to Arab Americans, the Middle East, or Islam. The Center for Arab American Studies (CAAS) is the first and only academic center to focus on Arab Americans. The center is based in the University of Michigan–Dearborn, and works with other academic institutions in the region, including the University of Michigan–Ann Arbor, University of Michigan–Flint, Eastern Michigan University, Wayne State University, and Henry Ford Community College. Among the ongoing projects of CAAS are the Arab American and Chaldean Archive Project, an oral history project, and a Detroit area study.

There are many Arab student organizations on university campuses across the United States that are occasionally chapters of national organizations or are often, independent student groups. In 2000, the Union of Arab Student Associations was formed and held its first national conference to bring together these organizations. The founders of this union later established the Network of Arab American Professionals, which currently has chapters in Baltimore, New York, Philadelphia, and Washington, D.C.

On campuses, certain university professors focusing on the Middle East have been the targets of a campaign by Campus Watch. Recently, this organization launched the Columbia Project to bring "attention to problems with Columbia University's Middle East Studies faculty" by listing each professor in alphabetical order with Campus Watch's critique. The targeted professors at Columbia and at other universities report being intimidated and even threatened by students, faculty, and administrators as a result of Campus Watch's pressure and media outreach. The academics that object to this pressure consider Campus Watch's actions to be extreme and motivated by anti-Arab and anti-Muslim political agendas.

INTERGROUP RELATIONS

Ironically, coalitions have been built around a common Arab American identity even while the singular label *Arab* has had derogatory connotations in the United States and is controversial within the community. The monolithic portrayal of Arabs as one category, instead of the diverse and heterogeneous group that it is, has harmed Arabs and led to frustrations by people from the Middle East who do not identify themselves as Arabs. Arabs and Muslims are presented through the media as inherently backward and inferior to mainstream white culture. These images rest on two constructed pillars: the Arab/Muslim culture as sexist and oppressive, and the Islamic religion as fanatical and violent. In the 1970s, the image of Arab men as rich oil sheikhs prevailed, juxtaposed with the Arab (Palestinian) terrorist. In today's climate, the dominant stereotype of the Arab man is as a bearded Islamic terrorist. Arab women continue to be stereotyped either as belly dancers or as an oppressed group that wears black dresses and veils with only their eyes showing. These images are often put in stark contrast to the peaceful, liberated American men and women, especially in times of war. Arab Americans suffer most from discrimination when the United States enters into a war that posits Arabs or Muslims as the enemy. The category of *Arab* is often erroneously conflated with Islam and portrayed with images of turbans, so that Persians, Turks, South Asians, and particularly (non-Muslim) Sikhs, experience discrimination and retaliatory attacks by people who wish to lash out against someone who seems to be "Arab-Middle Eastern-Muslim." Although each group continues to have its own issues, the common backlash effect during and after the Second Gulf War brought together the South Asian American and Arab American groups to fight for hate crimes legislation to protect their communities.

Further alliances with Asian Americans were fostered after 9/11, when Arab Americans were targeted by governmental authorities who singled them out on the basis of their ethnicity. Coalitions with South Asians, who were also targeted in the aftermath, deepened. The number of FBI interviews of Arab Americans and the submission of demographic breakdowns of Arab Americans from the Census Bureau to the Department of Homeland Security indicate that law enforcement officials are engaging in ethnic profiling. Asian Americans, especially sensitive to the dangers of ethnic profiling because of the release of census data that was used in the internment of Japanese Americans during World War II, have cooperated with Arab Americans, and their collaboration with Arab American organizations has increased greatly since 9/11. In 2004, the Japanese American Citizen League gave ACCESS executive director, Ismael Ahmed, the Edison Uno Civil Rights Award for his leadership in promoting tolerance and understanding after 9/11 and for his "exemplary commitment to the Japanese American community."[15]

Ethnic profiling has had the effect of creating a sense of fear and insecurity among Arab Americans. Non-Arab friends or colleagues may hesitate to discuss their image of Islam or Arabs with an Arab American, perhaps because the images are so negative, leading Arab Americans to ask themselves, "What should I do with an ethnicity that the very mention of which makes others uncomfortable?" The difficulties of even opening up discussions on Arab identity makes intergroup dialogue hard but not impossible. The events and impact of 9/11 forced some "closeted" Arabs to talk with their peers about the misrepresentation of Arabs and Muslims both by Al-Qaeda and by the media. However, many Arab Americans have reacted to the general negativity about their heritage with silence or denial. Some Arab Americans choose to say that their heritage or name is from somewhere else when asked directly. This is done by privileging their other non-Arab side if they are mixed, avoiding the question, or sometimes by outright lying. Educators have said that they think that hostility against Arabs and the absence of discussion about differences and stereotypes in the classroom has led to ambiguity over identity, and even depression, among Arab Americans.[16]

On a national level, Arab Americans have made coalitions and networks with other groups and organizations founded on issue-based work. The ADC and AAI have worked with civil rights and civil liberties groups as well as human rights and immigrant rights organizations and lawyers to wage a legal battle against the use of secret evidence in U.S. courts of law. The Rights Working Group was formed from these coalitions in June 2004 to urge Congress to pass the Civil Liberties Restoration Act, which redresses aspects of the Patriot Act and "troubling new policies such as arbitrary and indefinite detentions, secret hearings, severe restrictions on due process and violations of privacy and First Amendment rights."[17] AAI was part of the Network of Alliances to Bridge Race and Ethnicity, the National Coalition to Protect

Political Freedoms, the National Immigration Forum, and the Leadership Conference on Civil Rights.

In the political sphere, AAI has been active in party politics, participating in the National Democratic Ethnic Coordinating Council of the Democratic National Committee. AAI has also worked with the Census Information Center network consisting of 50 national nonprofit organizations that work with the Census Bureau on data issues for underserved communities. This working group brings together different ethnic groups to discuss the census and how to articulate race and ethnicity within the official census form.

The ADC has worked with the National Organization for Women (NOW) and other groups. The ADC, AAI, and ACCESS arrange discussions and educational presentations to student and civic groups. ACCESS has a National Outreach Department and Task Group to find common ground and prospects for collaboration. They have an Immigrant Rights documentation project that records how policies and procedures affect the lives and daily realities of all immigrants.

In terms of in-group coalitions, there is the Congress of Arab American Organizations that AAI restarted in 2001 from an older coalition; it now includes more than 130 groups. AAI also organizes a coalition of Arab Americans in public service and political life, called the Arab American Leadership Council.

Working-Class Relations

Arab Americans in the early years considered themselves part of the working class and so identified with people of other ethnicities who were in a similar situation in the United States. One of the most famous strikes in the early part of the twentieth century was the Bread and Roses Strike of 1912, which took place in the textile mills of Lawrence, Massachusetts. A half-Syrian organizer from the Industrial Workers of the World led this strike, in which 20,000 workers, including the women and children who worked in the mills, protested the working conditions and wages. Just before the strike, a new state law was passed that mandated a shorter workweek. The factories complied with the law but did not give hourly wage increases so that the law resulted in lower weekly wages for the workers. During the 63-day strike, their slogan was, "We want bread and roses too," reflecting that they were not against the new law but wanted to maintain their incomes. The Arab American women who worked in the mills participated in the strike and ran soup kitchens, serving the strikers at long tables. They cooked what they knew, food typical of Mount Lebanon and the surrounding area, "A typical menu was bread, lamb, crushed wheat (burghul), specially prepared cultured milk (laban), and coffee. Another meal consisted of bread, rice, lima bean stew (yakhnit fasoolya), and coffee."[18] Arab American women and children held meetings in the basement of the Arab American churches. The Bread and Roses strike led to pay raises that compensated for the decreased hours in the unionized factories as well as in other nearby industries.

Today, some Arab Americans are involved with union politics, especially in the auto industry in Detroit. Yemenis in particular have sided with the unions in disputes with the management. However, many others in the Arab American community have chosen to distance themselves from unions and being working class. Some political activists who may not be blue-collar workers themselves but who believe that the Palestinian struggle is part of the Third World revolutionary movement have allied with the antiglobalization movement that fights for worker's rights in the United States and overseas.

African American Relations

In court cases in the first few decades of the twentieth century, the first wavers fought against classification as Asians and strove to be classified as white. Through this process and others, Arab Americans began to gain an understanding of the construct of race in the United States with its hierarchical power structures. In the next few decades, as they saved their money and settled down in the United States permanently, those who were able to move to the suburbs aspired to the American middle-class lifestyle. Part of this lifestyle involved distancing from other races. Arab Americans, who had had good relations with different ethnicities and races in the United States, began to set themselves apart from African Americans to place themselves alongside Americans of Western and Northern European origins.

Today, on a national level, as well as sometimes on a local level, Arab Americans have good relations with African Americans. The Rev. Jesse Jackson was the first politician to speak of Arab Americans in sympathetic terms at a national party convention. At the 1984 Democratic National Convention, Rev. Jackson said, "Arab Americans, too, know the pain and hurt of racial and religious rejection. They must not continue to be made pariahs." Arab Americans, after African Americans, were the second-largest donor support group for the Jackson campaign that year. In the 1970s and 1980s, Arab Americans, who were considered people with an unpopular pro-Palestinian viewpoint, were often shunned by politicians and intimidated into silence. Arab Americans, who recognized their discrimination as being politically motivated, labeled their special genre of ethnic prejudice "political racism." Rev. Jackson's comments in such a public and important forum reflected the strong relations and communication between African American and Arab American leaders, notably James Zogby, the AAI president.

These cordial relations were somewhat helped by the composition of immigrants in the post-1965 era. The third wavers tended to be more Muslim than Christian and more diverse in national origin than the earlier immigrants. The Islamic concept of the *umma* stresses that all Muslims are equal before God and that religious conviction makes racial, ethnic, class, or any other differences inconsequential. There is a strong desire by Muslims across the world to show unity and interethnic harmony that results from belief in the same religion. On Fridays (during the noon prayers), on religious holidays, or during the annual pilgrimage, there are large multiethnic and multiracial crowds of Muslims praying together that reflect the transnational nature of Islam. In this way, mosques and Islamic activities have served to bring some Arab American, African American and other Muslims together.

Although Muslim leaders embrace in public and show their religious solidarity at a civic level, there are often more rifts in the Muslim community than the public sees. On the local and community level, there are strong interracial and interethnic tensions and even separate mosques defined by race, ethnicity, or language. The Muslim community is split over issues of national allegiance, ethnic identity, and religious orthodoxy. Even within the African American Muslim community there are divisions, and the two principal African American leaders, Imam Warith Din Muhammad (of the American Muslim Mission) and Louis Farrakhan (of the Nation of Islam), have different outlooks and stances on most issues. The leadership styles and approaches to other Muslims have led to better relationships between Arab American Muslims and the Sunnis of the American Muslim Mission than with the Muslims following the Nation of Islam. However, immigrant Muslims and African American Muslims tend to have different issues of concern and perspectives on U.S. culture and life. One of the criticisms leveled by African American Muslims at immigrant Muslims is that they are more concerned with "making it" in the United States and becoming Americanized than with the well-being of all Muslims. African Americans are more inclined to question the dominant culture because of past experiences with racism and tend to be more concerned with education and poverty in the inner cities, while Muslim immigrants increasingly move directly to the suburbs upon arrival in the United States and so have less understanding or concern with the conditions of inner cities. Even when an Arab Muslim family opens a store in an urban area that is predominantly African American, there are usually tensions between the ethnic grocery storeowner and the customers from the community. As with other ethnic groups, such as the Korean American storeowners in Los Angeles, these tensions can escalate into violence that results in fatalities.

THE IMPACT OF SEPTEMBER 11 ON ARAB AMERICANS

The first reaction of many Arab Americans to the 9/11 attacks was disbelief, followed by fear. Remembering the events of the Oklahoma City bombing in the mid-1990s, Arab Americans were concerned that they were being incorrectly "fingered" as the culprits, and that this would result, as it had in 1995, with violent hate crimes and attacks on Arab Americans. When it became clear that the hijackers were Muslims, there was an even greater fear for the safety of Arab and Muslim Americans. Whereas some Arab Americans have reacted to the post-9/11 atmosphere in the United States by distancing themselves from their heritage, most Arab Americans have felt a larger responsibility to educate others about their community and about the Arab world. As one young Arab American AmeriCorps volunteer said, "Being a young Arab-American living in the post 9/11 climate now comes with the responsibility to educate people about what our culture is really about, and not what the media portrays it to be.... It was our parents who brought Arab culture to this country, and now it is our responsibility to make it flourish."[19]

Many Muslim Americans thought that the terrorists had betrayed the ideals of Islam and had hijacked the religion itself. In the media frenzy following the events of 9/11, moderate American Muslims heard the real meaning of Islam being defined by non-Muslims who did not understand or agree with their religious tenets. The videotapes and messages from Al-Qaeda and anti-American zealots who used the Quran to justify mass murder were played over and over by U.S. news channels; then commentators, scholars, and politicians quoted back Al-Qaeda statements as "true" reflections of "the" Muslim viewpoint, as if there were no moderate Muslims who disagreed with the attacks or Al-Qaeda's version of Islam. American Muslims complained about the inaccuracy of the quotes from the Quran, citing bad translations and phrases taken out of context that left the viewers with no understanding that one of the core values of Islam is peace. Most American Muslims were nauseated by the media portrayals of Islam and the lack of moderate Muslim voices in the cacophony that followed 9/11.

Pleas and statements defending the Arab and Muslim communities by many prominent persons, including President George W. Bush and Secretary of State Colin Powell, and institutions including Congress, abated reprisals against local Muslim and Arab Americans. Nevertheless, in the nine weeks after 9/11, the ADC reported that there were more than 700 violent incidents targeting those perceived to be Arab Americans, Arabs, or Muslims. There were 80 cases of the removal of airline passengers after boarding, based on the passenger's perceived ethnicity. Once again, South Asians and Sikhs were the victims of hate crimes, in addition to Arab Americans. Hate crimes and discrimination continued into 2002 as the cases of employment and housing discrimination, violent incidents, threats, and instances of the denial of services were reported to the ADC. Even after the initial backlash in the months following 9/11, these statistics reflected higher levels of discrimination and hate crimes than in previous years, when U.S. military actions and incidents in the Middle East set off ethnically and religiously based reprisals. However, this backlash did not affect all Arab Americans equally. Two polls, taken in October 2001 and in May 2002, found that only one in three Arab Americans had personally experienced any discrimination but almost half of Arab American Muslims reported that they had personally experienced discrimination, with the bulk of these being foreign-born.[20] This indicates that religious affiliation in combination with a foreign accent, behavior, or dress may set off acts of discrimination and hate crimes.

Arab Americans responded to the attacks by emphasizing and outwardly displaying their patriotism for the United States. Immediately after the news, Arab and Muslim American organizations issued press releases condemning the terrorist attacks. These statements did not appear prominently in the media coverage even as the events and stories behind the attacks were unraveled in the 24-hour news cycles. Arab Americans and Muslim Americans shared in the mourning and horror of the day as news reached their families and friends that fellow Americans, some of them Arab and Muslim, had died in the Twin Towers. Arab American policemen, firefighters, and FBI agents worked at Ground Zero, and Arab American civilians in Virginia and New York helped with the recovery efforts alongside other Americans. More than 80 percent of Arab Americans showed solidarity with the victims of 9/11 by flying a U.S. flag, donating to the victims' funds, or giving blood.[21] The events of 9/11 had a positive impact for some Arab Americans as public demand for more information on the Arab world and Islam increased, and universities, schools, and educational boards requested materials from Arab and Muslim organizations and individuals. Directly after 9/11, two-fifths of Arab Americans reported that they were more likely to speak with their friends and acquaintances about events in the Middle East after 9/11 than in 2000.[22] In the process of educating others, some Arab and Muslim Americans became more informed on their history, cultures, and traditions and were recognized and valued by their peers as an Arab and/or Muslim American.

However, the long-term consequences of 9/11—the racial profiling and the Patriot Act—have tempered this enthusiasm for outward ethnic and religious expression. In a national poll taken after 9/11, the sample population was asked, "How likely do you think it is now that Arab Americans, Muslims, and immigrants from the Middle East will be singled out unfairly by people in this country?" Only 11 percent answered "not too likely" and "not at all likely," and 87 percent answered "very likely" and "somewhat likely" (2% answered "don't know/no answer").[23] As predicted by the general public, Arab and Muslim Americans were profiled at airports, schools, and universities, in the workplace, at border points, and by immigration officials in the selective enforcement of immigration laws. Many of the terrorists involved in the 9/11 attacks were both Muslim and Arabs, so the pursuit of the terrorists in the United States was focused on national origin, gender, and time of entry into the United States rather than on well-informed, specific intelligence. In the months after the terrorist attacks, the U.S. government detained 1,200 people, most of them men and Arab and/or Muslim. In the end, only three were held on material witness counts (of unknown value), and the rest were either released or deported without the Department of Justice suggesting that they had anything to do with terrorism or terrorist groups. In this roundup of "terrorists," the government refused to adhere to the Freedom of Information Act. It made arbitrary and extended detentions, denied suspects legal counsel, and did not let them contact anyone, including relatives. These people were held on "secret evidence" laws that were in place before 9/11, and the accused were not allowed to know the allegations against them, making formulating a defense difficult, if not impossible. Many in the Arab American community pointed out that these detentions were not effective law enforcement tools because they only netted three people and created great fear and suspicion in the broader public sphere. As predicted, the result of these detentions, as well as the Special Registration program at the U.S. Citizenship and Immigration Services (USCIS) and the Patriot Act, gave the impression that the U.S. government thought that Arabs and Muslims were a suspicious and dangerous group to whom constitutional rights and civil liberties did not apply. A movement by cities and communities across the country to pass resolutions calling the Patriot Act "a threat to the civil rights of the residents of their communities" is now acting to ameliorate that impression, but the laws still exist.[24]

Foreign students were also affected by the Patriot Act and the increased security in the post 9/11 environment. Despite a 65 percent increase of student and visitor exchanges from 1992 to 2002, foreign student admissions to the United States declined by 7 percent in 2002, a decline of more than 73,000 students between FY2001 and FY2002. After 9/11, security measures relating to the issuing of visas and U.S. embassies abroad (where visas are obtained) were heightened, creating more rejected and delayed visas. Students from Arab countries more concerned about discrimination on the part of immigration officials and faced long lines, closed visa offices in embassies, and tedious bureaucracy when applying for U.S. visas. In addition, under the Patriot Act, the Department of Homeland Security began a program in 2003 called the Student and Exchange Visitor Information System (SEVIS), which required all schools to enter information about foreign students into a central electronic database that had to be regularly updated to reflect information on each of the foreign students including visa status and type, biographical information, class registration, and address.[25] Although these regulations monitored all international students, Arab students (and potential students) feared more scrutiny. The net effect was chilling on the Arab student population and fewer Arab students have enrolled in U.S. universities as a result. This in turn, means that the students are less likely to choose to stay in the United States and eventually become U.S. citizens.

These increased security procedures and regulations did not have as drastic an impact on nonstudent and cultural exchange visitors. As Appendix C indicates, while immigration from Arab countries dipped by 30 percent between 2002 and 2003, in 2004 immigration bounced back and 36,814 individuals from Arab countries immigrated to the United States: a figure similar to the 2002 immigration numbers of 37,924. Between 2000 and 2004, Arab immigrants averaged 3.8 percent of total immigrants to the United States. Such a percentage, while less significant in the total immigrant population, means an annual 5 percent increase in the Arab American population.

THE FUTURE

Discrimination and scrutiny of Arab Americans occurred long before 9/11 but after the events of 9/11, the rights of immigrants were questioned again and Arab and Muslim immigrants in particular were targeted through selective immigration enforcement. As the war on terror escalates in foreign policy, it impacts those considered to be affiliated with terrorists at home. Through polls and past documentation, discrimination and hate crimes seem to disproportionately affect foreign-born Muslims. As the foreign-born segment constitute a significant proportion of Arab Americans, the impact of such occurrences affects the whole community, but it also indicates that there is an uneven brunt of discrimination and hate crimes against Arab Americans. In this environment, Arab Americans continue to struggle with the diversity of the community, and the needs of each group. As the national organizations endeavor to address their constituents, the question remains if there will be increasing divides between Muslims and Christians and between native- and foreign-born Arab Americans.

NOTES

1. Inea Bushnaq, "Arab Americans: Their Arts and New York City, 1970–2000," in *A Community of Many Worlds: Arab Americans in New York City,* ed. Kathleen Benson and Philip Kayal (New York: Museum of the City of New York, Syracuse University Press, 2002), 188.

2. Piney Kesting, "A Community of Arabic Music," *Saudi Aramco World*, 53, no. 5 (September/October 2002): 28–33.

3. Lisa Suhair Majaj, "The Hyphenated Author: Emerging Genre of Arab-American Literature Poses Questions of Definition, Ethnicity and Art," *Al-Jadid: A Review & Record of Arab Culture and Arts* 5, no. 26 (Winter 1999) available online at http://www.aljadid.com/features/0526majaj.html.

4. Gregory Orfalea and Sharif Elmusa, eds., *Grapeleaves: A Century of Arab-American Poetry* (Northampton, MA: Interlink, 2000), xiii.

5. Joanna Kadi, ed., *Food for Our Grandmothers: Writings by Arab-American and Arab-Canadian Feminists* (Boston: South End, 1994), xix.

6. Khaled Mattawa and Munir Akash, *Post-Gibran Anthology of New Arab American Writing* (Syracuse, NY: Syracuse University Press; Bethesda, MD: Jusoor, 1999), xii.

7. Birwaz, "Somewhere Else: A Premiere Contemporary AA Exhibition," October 19–November 5, 2004, http://www.birwaz.org/index.htm.

8. Anan Ameri and Dawn Ramey, eds., *Arab American Encyclopedia* (Detroit: UXL, 2000), 236.

9. Arab American Institute, "Arab Americans: Making a Difference," www.aaiusa.org/famous_arab_americans.htm (accessed September 6, 2005).

10. This argument was first put forward by Samuel Huntington in "A Clash of Civilizations," *Foreign Affairs,* 72, no. 3 (Summer 1993): 22–49.

11. Elizabeth Bernstein, "All the Candidates' Clergy," *Wall Street Journal,* 13 August 2004, W1.

12. In the 2000 elections, 45.5 percent of Arab Americans voted for George W. Bush, 38 percent for Al Gore, and 13.5 percent for Ralph Nader.

13. In 2000, 54 percent of Arab Muslim voters supported George W. Bush, 16 percent voted for Al Gore, and 19 percent for Ralph Nader. Nader is particularly popular among Arab Americans because he is of Lebanese heritage. See Bernstein 2004.

14. Ian Williams, "Arabs and Jews Together," *Middle East International,* 18, no. 738 (19 November 2004): 30.

15. Japanese American Citizens League, www.jacl.org/current_prs/040806.html.

16. Hajar, Paula. "Arab Families in New York Public Schools" in *A Community of Many Worlds: Arab Americans in New York city*, ed. Kathleen Benson and Philip Kayal (New York: Museum of the city of New York, Syracuse University Press, 2002), 154–55.

17. American-Arab Anti Discrimination Committee, "ADC Joins Introduction of Civil Liberties Restoration Act. New National Coalition Joins Community Groups Nationwide to Support Effort," press release, 16 June 2004.

18. As quoted by Loretta Hall, *Arab American Voices,* (Detroit: UXL, 2000), 23.

19. As quoted by George Selim, "Voices of ARC Members: Reflecting on a Year of Service," *Connections: News from the Arab-American Network,* 31 March 2004, 7.

20. Arab American Institute Foundation, *Profiling and Pride: Arab American Attitudes and Behavior since September 11* (Washington, DC: Arab American Institute Publication, 2002); also available online at http://www.aaiusa.org/resources.htm.

21. Ibid., 8.

22. Ibid., 2.

23. CBS/*New York Times* poll, 21 September 2001.

24. Dean Schabner, "Eight Cities in Patriot Act Revolt: Cities from Cambridge to Berkeley Reject Anti-Terror Measure," *ABC News,* 1 July 2002, http://abcnews.go.com/US/story?id=91497&page=1 (accessed September 6, 2005).

25. Maia Jachimowicz, "Foreign Students and Exchange Visitors" Migration Information Source, September 1, 2003. Migration Policy Institute. Available at http://www.migrationinformation.org/Feature/display.cfm?ID=154.

Appendix A: Census Statistics of Arab Americans, 1970–2000

Census Year	Arab American Population
1970	170,820
1980	596,306
1990	860,354
2000	1,189,731

All statistics derive from census tabulations taken by the Census Bureau that are believed to be represent one-third of the actual Arab American population.

Sources: 1990 and 2000 statistics: http://www.census.gov/prod/2003pubs/c2kbr_23.pdf; 1980 statistics: James Paul Allen and Eugene James Turner, *We The People: an Atlas of America's Ethnic Diversity* (New York: McMillan Publishing Co, 1988), 133; 1970 statistics: Beverlee Turner Mehdi, ed., *Arabs in America, 1492–1977* (Dobbs Ferry, New York: Oceana Publications, 1978), 137.

Appendix B: Noted Arab Americans

James George Abourezk (1931–)   Attorney, senator, and congressman. Abourezk was born in South Dakota to parents of Lebanese descent who were homesteaders and pack peddlers. His parents opened two general stores and settled on a Sioux reservation, where Abourezk grew up. He served in the Navy during the Korean War, later studying civil engineering and law. An attorney and a Democrat, Abourezk was elected to the House of Representatives in 1971; he became a senator for South Dakota two years later—the first Arab American to be elected senator. In 1980, Abourezk established the American-Arab Anti-Discrimination Committee (ADC) to combat stereotypes and prejudice against Arab Americans.

Khalil Gibran (1883–1931)   Artist and poet. Born in Lebanon, Gibran came to the United States in 1894 but attended college in Lebanon. Returning to the United States in 1902, he was active in the early Arab American community and worked to get Syrians and Lebanese to demand self-rule. Influenced by his life experiences in Lebanon and the United States, by the Bible, and by German philosopher Friedrich Nietzche, Gibran wrote prose, poetry, meditations, and essays about love, marriage, and the spiritual union of souls. He is best known for his book, *The Prophet* (1923), which has been translated into 20 languages.

Casey Kasem (1932–)   Radio personality and presenter. Kasem was born in Detroit as Kemal Amen Kasem to parents of Lebanese descent. Working as a radio DJ, Kasem pulled a *Who's Who in Pop Music* magazine out of the trash as he was beginning his shift one night and began to introduce the songs with stories about the artists and their songs. Thus, his formula for the "American Top 40 with Casey Kasem" and "American Top 20" was born. During his almost 50-year career, Kasem's voice became familiar to radio listeners across the United States. He has appeared in more than 24 movies and is also the voice actor of Shaggy from the *Scooby Doo* television series. Throughout his career, Casey has been an activist for vegetarianism, antismoking, and antidiscrimination campaigns.

Ralph Nader (1934–)   Presidential candidate, consumer advocate, author, and attorney. Nader was born in Connecticut to Lebanese immigrant parents who ran a restaurant and bakery in Winsted. He studied government and economics at Princeton University and law at Harvard University. After graduating from Harvard, he became concerned with car design and safety and wrote *Unsafe at Any Speed: The Designed-in Dangers of the American Automobile* (1965) and successfully lobbied Congress to pass the 1966 National Traffic and Motor Vehicle Safety Act. In 1971, Nader founded a consumer-rights organization, Public Citizen, which lobbies on Capitol Hill to protect public health and the environment, as well as safeguard citizen and consumer rights. He has also founded or helped start many advocacy groups, including the Public Interest Research Group (PIRG), Clean Water Action Project, and Democracy Rising. Nader ran as a write-in presidential candidate in the New Hampshire Democratic primary in 1992, as the Green Party candidate in 1996, and then as an Independent candidate in the 2000 and 2004 presidential elections.

Alixa Naff   Historian and scholar. Born in Spring Valley, Illinois, to Syrian-Lebanese parents, Naff attended the University of California–Los Angeles where she took classes on the social history of the United States. Naff earned a master's degree and a doctorate from Oxford University in England, studying social history of the modern Middle East. She later taught at universities in the United States and realized that there was a need for work on the Arab experience. After conducting research, she published a pioneering book, *Becoming American: The Early Arab Immigrant Experience* (1985). She also collected photographs, documents, and objects from Arab American history that she wanted to preserve for posterity. She donated them to the Smithsonian and archived the materials from 1984 to 1996. The Naff Collection, which focuses on the period 1880–1950, is located at the National Museum of American History in Washington, D.C.

Naomi Shihab Nye (1952–)   Poet and writer. Nye was born in St. Louis, Missouri, to a Palestinian father and a mother of Swiss-German ancestry.

When Nye was 14 years old, her father became the editor of the *Jerusalem Times,* and her family lived between Ramallah and Jerusalem. This experience inspired Nye's young adult novel, *Habibi* (1997). Now a long-time resident of San Antonio, Texas, and a self-described wandering poet, Nye travels, giving small talks and presentations on writing. She has published poetry, songs, and children's books as well as novels. She has gathered and published anthologies of poems and essays from writers around the world for children and young adults.

Edward Said (1935–2003)   Writer, scholar, literary theorist, critic, political commentator, and activist. Said, born in Jerusalem to Palestinian parents (although his mother was half-Lebanese), spent much of his childhood in Egypt before moving to the United States. After receiving his master's and doctorate degrees from Harvard University, he became an English and Comparative Literature professor at Columbia University in New York City, where he taught for almost 40 years, in addition to lecturing at Harvard, Yale, and other institutions. Said wrote more than 20 books, including *Orientalism* (1978), a book that argued that scholars and writers had transferred their imperialist views on the Middle East to their writings, creating an inaccurate and detrimental image of the region. The book, which was translated into more than 25 languages, influenced postcolonial studies and popular culture worldwide. Said wrote and lectured extensively about the politics of the Middle East and became a leading advocate of Palestinian causes. In this vein, he authored *The Question of Palestine* (1979), *The Politics of Dispossession* (1994), and *The End of the Peace Process* (2000). After the Oslo Accords in 1993, which he condemned, he broke with Palestinian Liberation Organization leader Yasser Arafat, eventually calling for one secular, democratic, Palestinian-Israeli state.

Zeinab Salbi (1970–)   Women's advocate and president of Women for Women International. Salbi was born in Iraq and was in the United States when the Second Gulf War began in 1991, and she could not return because of the sanctions. Sensitized to the plight of women in wartime during her childhood, she learned in 1993 that women in Bosnia were suffering from systematic rape and internment in concentration camps, and she was inspired to found an organization with her husband, Women for Women International. In 10 years, the Washington, D.C.–based organization has sent about $9 million to women on three continents and helped about 20,000 women who have survived war and other conflicts. She explained the logic behind her focus on the plight of refugee women around the world: "Women are barometers for how a society is going. Bad things in a society always start with women, and good things, too."[1]

Donna E. Shalala (1941–)   Educator, administrator, and public official. Born in Cleveland, Ohio, Shalala received her doctorate from the Maxwell School of Citizenship and Public Affairs at Syracuse University. Shalala taught political science, and in 1975, she became the director and treasurer of New York City's Municipal Assistance Corp. She was assistant secretary for policy research and development at the Department of Housing and Urban Development under President Jimmy Carter. She became the president of Hunter College in 1980 and the chancellor of the University of Wisconsin at Madison in 1988. In 1993, President Bill Clinton appointed her U.S. Secretary of Health and Human Services (HHS), where she served for eight years. In 2001, Shalala became professor of political science and president of the University of Miami.

Tony Shalhoub (1953–)   Actor. Born in Green Bay, Wisconsin, to parents who emigrated from Lebanon in 1920, Shalhoub was introduced to acting at a very young age and majored in theater at the University of Southern Maine and earned an MFA degree at Yale University. Playing the Italian cab driver in the television series, *Wings,* launched his career. Well known for his ability to infuse eccentric characters with comic genius and lovable personalities, Shalhoub has stared in 22 movies and two television series. He is now the executive producer and main character in the television series, *Monk.*

Michael W. Suleiman   Political scientist and writer. Suleiman received a master's and a doctorate from the University of Wisconsin and joined Kansas State University in 1965. From 1975 to 1982, Suleiman was the Chair of the Kansas State Political Science Department; he has written more than 70 publications on the comparative and international politics of the Middle East. He is a scholar on Arab politics, Arab Americans, and American attitudes toward the Middle East.

Danny Thomas (1912–1991)   Comedian and philanthropist. Born to Lebanese immigrant parents in Deerfield, Michigan, Thomas grew up hearing his mother, uncle, and neighbor telling stories for entertainment. After dropping out of high school, Thomas did occasional comedian gigs and stand-up stints in nightclubs, eventually making television appearances. His big break in entertainment came with the television series, *Make Room for Daddy,* later called *The Danny Thomas Show,* which was consistently in the top 10 programs of the week from 1957 to 1964. Thomas went on to produce popular television shows and appeared occasionally in some shows. Thomas, a Roman Catholic, honored Saint Jude Thaddeus, the patron saint of hopeless causes, by being the driving force behind the opening of St. Jude's Children's Research Hospital in Memphis, Tennessee, in 1962. St. Jude's fundraising arm is the American Lebanese Syrian Associated Charities (ALSAC), which was created after Thomas was able to secure donations from Lebanese and Syrian individuals and groups. St. Jude's has saved the lives of thousands of children with leukemia and other forms of cancer through its research and treatment programs.

Helen Thomas (1920–) White House correspondent. Born in Winchester, Kentucky, to Lebanese immigrant parents, Thomas grew up in Detroit and became interested in journalism after writing for the high school newspaper. After graduating from Wayne State University and moving to Washington, D.C., she was hired in 1943 by United Press International (UPI) to cover women's issues. Thomas worked hard and was promoted up the ladder at UPI, eventually becoming White House correspondent. She resigned in 2000 because UPI was sold to the Reverend Sun Myung Moon's Unification Church. For the last few years, Thomas has continued to cover White House briefings and presidential press conferences for Hearst newspapers, for which she writes a syndicated column. Under President George W. Bush's administration, her position as "dean of the press corps" and her seat front and center in the White House press room has been shaky after she asked the president pointed questions about the separation of church and state and about the Iraq war. She has written books on her experiences and memories including, *Thanks for the Memories, Mr. President: Wit and Wisdom from the Front Row at the White House* (Scribner, 2003) and *Front Row at the White House: My Life and Times* (Scribner, 2000).

James J. Zogby (1945–) Political commentator and president of the Arab American Institute (AAI). Born in New York State to Lebanese immigrant parents (though his mother was second generation), Zogby obtained his doctorate in religion from Temple University in 1975; he went on to become a cofounder and chairman of the Palestine Human Rights Campaign in the late 1970s. He later cofounded and served as executive director of the American-Arab Anti-Discrimination Committee. In 1985, he founded the AAI in Washington, D.C., which focuses on political empowerment of Arab Americans in the United States. As president of AAI, Zogby frequently appears on television and radio and writes a weekly column on U.S. politics for major Arab newspapers. A member of the Council on Foreign Relations, he currently serves on the Human Rights Watch Middle East Advisory Committee and on the national advisory boards of the American Civil Liberties Union and the National Immigration Forum. In January 2001, Zogby was selected by President Bush to be a member of the Central Asian-American Enterprise Fund, serving on its board of directors. In 2001 he was also elected to the Executive Committee of the U.S. Democratic National Party.

NOTE

1. Joan Ryan, "In Baghdad, Women Fear Everyone," *San Francisco Chronicle,* 27 January 2005, B1.

Appendix C: Immigrants Admitted by Region and Country of Birth: Fiscal Years 1989–2004

Region and country of birth	1989	1990	1991	1992	1993	1994	1995	1996
All countries	**1,090,924**	**1,536,483**	**1,827,167**	**973,975**	**904,292**	**804,416**	**720,459**	**915,900**
Asia								
Bahrain	47	58	58	81	93	87	78	76
Iraq	1,516	1,756	1,494	4,111	4,072	6,025	5,596	5,481
Jordan (1)	3,921	4,449	4,259	4,036	4,741	3,990	3,649	4,445
Kuwait	710	691	861	989	1,129	1,065	961	1,202
Lebanon	5,716	5,634	6,009	5,838	5,465	4,319	3,884	4,382
Oman	18	D	5	24	21	32	31	25
Qatar	49	33	56	59	88	51	60	79
Saudi Arabia	381	518	552	584	616	668	788	1,164
Syria	2,675	2,972	2,837	2,940	2,933	2,426	2,362	3,072
United Arab Emirates	114	192	164	172	196	286	317	343

(Continued)

(Continued)

Region and country of birth	1989	1990	1991	1992	1993	1994	1995	1996
All countries	1,090,924	1,536,483	1,827,167	973,975	904,292	804,416	720,459	915,900
Yemen	X	X	1,547	2,056	1,793	741	1,501	2,209
Yemen (Aden)	135	218	X	X	X	X	X	X
Yemen (Sanaa)	831	1,727	X	X	X	X	X	X
Africa								
Algeria	230	302	269	407	360	364	650	1,059
Comoros	—	—	—	D	D	D	D	D
Djibouti	8	22	21	14	14	10	25	19
Egypt	3,717	4,117	5,602	3,576	3,556	3,392	5,648	6,186
Eritrea	X	X	X	X	85	468	992	828
Libya	210	268	314	286	343	166	216	250
Mauritania	9	D	9	D	9	10	22	26
Morocco	984	1,200	1,601	1,316	1,176	1,074	1,726	1,783
Somalia	228	277	458	500	1,088	1,737	3,487	2,170
Sudan	272	306	679	675	714	651	1,645	2,172
Tunisia	125	226	275	216	167	149	189	228
Western Sahara	—	—	—	—	—	—	—	3
TOTALS	**21,896**	**24,966**	**27,070**	**27,880**	**28,659**	**27,711**	**33,827**	**37,202**
Percentage of Arab to total immigration	2.0	1.6	1.5	2.9	3.2	3.4	4.7	4.1
Unknown or not reported	34	49	70	18	5	4	D	5

(Continued)

(Continued)

Region and country of birth	1997	1998	1999	2000	2001	2002	2003	2004
All countries	**798,378**	**654,451**	**646,568**	**849,807**	**1,064,318**	**1,063,732**	**705,827**	**946,142**
Asia								
Bahrain	80	53	70	106	119	85	59	116
Iraq	3,244	2,220	3,372	5,134	4,985	5,196	2,460	3,494
Jordan (1)	4,171	3,255	3,274	3,909	4,593	3,980	2,935	3,431
Kuwait	837	749	803	1,018	1,270	1,063	710	1,091
Lebanon	3,568	3,290	3,040	3,674	4,601	3,966	2,964	3,811
Oman	36	25	40	51	55	61	76	122
Qatar	70	60	78	97	125	108	72	125
Saudi Arabia	815	703	763	1,063	1,185	1,018	737	906
Syria	2,269	2,840	2,056	2,374	3,368	2,567	1,944	2,256
United Arab Emirates	329	329	310	436	461	472	380	586
Yemen	1,663	1,859	1,161	1,789	1,615	1,228	1,386	1,760
Yemen (Aden)	X	X	X	X	X	X	X	X
Yemen (Sanaa)	X	X	X	X	X	X	X	X
Africa								
Algeria	717	804	789	907	878	1,031	760	804
Comoros	D	—	—	D	D	3	3	D
Djibouti	18	15	6	14	23	30	16	37
Egypt	5,031	4,831	4,429	4,461	5,182	4,875	3,355	5,522
Eritrea	948	641	326	383	544	561	556	673
Libya	171	166	156	181	224	159	140	185
Mauritania	51	78	24	88	117	124	131	170

(Continued)

(Continued)

Region and country of birth	1997	1998	1999	2000	2001	2002	2003	2004
All countries	**798,378**	**654,451**	**646,568**	**849,807**	**1,064,318**	**1,063,732**	**705,827**	**946,142**
Morocco	2,359	2,410	2,971	3,626	4,968	3,396	3,141	4,128
Somalia	4,005	2,629	1,710	2,465	3,026	4,537	2,448	3,929
Sudan	2,030	1,161	1,354	1,538	1,655	2,924	1,886	3,211
Tunisia	163	200	150	308	440	540	353	457
Western Sahara	—	D	—	D	3	—	—	—
TOTALS	**32,575**	**28,318**	**26,882**	**33,622**	**39,437**	**37,924**	**26,512**	**36,814**
Percentage of Arab to total immigration	4.1	4.3	4.2	4.0	3.7	3.6	3.8	3.9
Unknown or not reported	197	977	1,159	1,181	2,334	2,655	1,211	3,173

— = Zero.
D = Disclosure standards not met.
X = Not applicable.
[1] = Prior to 2003, includes Palestine; beginning in 2003, Palestine included in Unknown.
Source: Department of Homeland Security, Office of Immigration Statistics, "Yearbook of Immigration Statistics: 2004" Table 3. http://uscis.gov/graphics/shared/statistics/yearbook/YrBk04Im.htm.

Glossary

Abaya   A robe that covers the arms and legs of a woman

Aya   Verse in the Quran, the Muslim holy book

Caliph   See *Khalifa*

Debkeh   Line dance in which women and men clasp hands and dance rhythmically together

Durabakkeh   Goblet-shaped drum

Eid al-Adha   Lamb feast that commemorates Abraham's attempted sacrifice of his son, who Muslims believe was Ishmael rather than Isaac. It falls at the end of the *hajj* period of pilgrimage to Mecca

Eid al-Fitr   Weekend-long celebration at the end of Ramadan, the Muslim holy month

Fatiha   Opening verse of the Quran, the Muslim holy book, recited by practicing Muslims five times daily

Fiqh   Islamic law

Fusha   Classical Arabic or Modern Standard Arabic

Hadith   Collection of sayings and actions of the Prophet Mohammed

Hafla   Party or social gathering

Hajj   Pilgrimage journey to Mecca. As one of the pillars of Islam, all Muslims are required to make hajj once during their lifetime if they can

Halal   Code of morality set forth by Islam. Also refers to food, particularly meat that is prepared in an Islamically sanctioned manner

Hara   Arab American enclave in U.S. cities; literally translated as "neighborhood"

Henna   Brown or black dye made from the henna tree used to color hair or to decorate hands and feet with abstract patterns

Hijab   Head covering worn by Muslim women

Iftar Breaking the fast at sunset, usually during Ramadan, the Muslim holy month

Ijmaa Concensus of the Muslim community

Imam Muslim religious leader or chief

Intifada Palestinian uprising against Israel that began in 1987

Islam Religion founded in 610 C.E. The word *Islam* means submission to God, known in Arabic as *Allah;* literal translation is "submission to the will of God." It originates from the Arabic word, *salaam,* which means peace.

Islamist Extremist Muslim

Jihad Literally, "to Struggle." There is controversy concerning whether this refers to a war against unbelievers or a personal internal struggle

Kaaba Central shrine for Muslims located in Mecca. Originally a pagan shrine; in 630 C.E. Muslims entered and destroyed all idols contained in it, moving from polytheism to monotheism. It is believed to be built by Abraham and his son, Ishmael

Khalifa Leader of the Muslim community from 632 C.E. to 1918 C.E. Also known as *Caliph*

Khatib Muslim leader

Lingua franca Shared language

Mahrajan Festival, usually including music, dance, and art

Maronite The main sect of Lebanese Christians

Masjid Mosque in Arabic; a place of worship for Muslims

Muharram First month in the Islamic lunar calendar

Muslim Believer in Islam. The word *Muslim* means "someone who surrenders to the will of Allah"

Niqab Headscarf, one-piece robe, and a veil that covers the face and sometimes also the eyes of a woman

Oud Fretless stringed instrument that has a wooden face and a pear-shaped back. It is played by plucking the strings with a pick traditionally made out of an eagle's feather or a gazelle's horn

Quran Muslim holy book. Also spelled Koran

Ramadan Month in which Muslims fast from sunrise to sunset. The holiest month for all Muslims

Raqs Arabi (or Raqs Sharqi) One of the dance styles that became known as belly dancing in the United States

Sahra Informal evening gathering, usually including music as well as socializing

Salat Prayer; one of the pillars of Islam requires all Muslim to pray five times a day

Sawm Fasting during the month of Ramadan from sunrise to sunset. One of the pillars of Islam

Shahadah Profession of faith in one god and his prophet, Muhammad. One of the pillars of Islam required of all Muslims

Sharia Holy law of Islam that prescribes the way a Muslim fulfills the commandments of God and lives his or her life

Shaykh Muslim or tribal leader

Shia Followers of Shia Islam who contend that the descendents of the Prophet Muhammad (through Ali, Muhammad's cousin) should be the leaders of the Islamic world. Also known as Shiite

Sufi Muslim mystic

Sultanate Area ruled by a sultan, a community leader

Sunna Reported sayings and actions of the Prophet Muhammad that serve as a model of behavior for Muslims

Sunni Follower of Sunni Islam who contends that the leadership of the Muslim community should be based on merit. Also known as Sunnite

Sura Chapter of the Quran, the Muslim holy book

Tarboosh Red felt hat worn by men in the shape of a truncated cone with a black tassel. Originally from Turkey and also called a fez

Umma Arabic word for "nation," "civilization," "mother of." In the context of Islam, *umma* refers to the whole of the Muslim community

Zakat The act of giving money or goods to charity; one of the pillars of Islam required of all Muslims

Selected Bibliography

Abraham, Sameer. "Detroit's Arab-American Community: A Survey of Diversity and Commonality." In *Arabs in the New World: Studies on Arab-American Communities,* ed. Sameer Abraham and Nabeel Abraham. Detroit: Wayne State University Press, 1983.

Abraham, Sameer, Nabeel Abraham, and Barbara Aswad. "The Southend: An Arab Muslim Working-Class Community." In *Arabs in the New World: Studies on Arab-American Communities,* ed. Abraham and Abraham. Detroit: Wayne State University Press, 1983.

Abu-Laban, Baha, and Michael Suleiman. Introduction to *Arab Americans: Continuity and Change.* AAUG Monograph Series no. 24. Belmont, MA: Association of Arab-American University Graduates, 1989.

Ahdab-Yehia, May. "The Lebanese Maronites: Patterns of Continuity and Change." In *Arabs in the New World: Studies on Arab-American Communities,* ed. Sameer Abraham and Nabeel Abraham. Detroit: Wayne State University Press, 1983.

American-Arab Anti-Discrimination Committee. *Report on Hate Crimes and Discrimination against Arab-Americans: The Post-September 11 Backlash.* Washington, DC: ADCRI Publication, 2002. Also available online at http://www.adc.org.

Anderson, Jon. "Muslim Networks, Muslim Selves in Cyberspace: Islam in the Post-Modern Public Sphere." 2001. http://nmit.georgetown.edu/papers/jwanderson2.htm (accessed September 6, 2005).

Arab American Institute. "Arab Americans Win Re-Election in Mayoral, State and City Council Races." AAI Press Release, 7 November 2003.

———. *Healing the Nation: The Arab-American Experience after September 11.* Washington, DC: AAI Publication, 2002. Also available online at http://www.aaiusa.org/resources.htm.

Arab American Institute Foundation. "Facts on Arab American Voters." http://www.
      aaiusa.org/PDF/AAvoters.pdf (accessed September 6, 2005).
"Arab American Mirror: A Critical Look at Contemporary Arab American Issues."
      Volumes I–VIII, http://www.geocities.com/aamirror/ (accessed September 6,
      2005).
Arab Community Center for Economic and Social Services. http://www.
      accesscommunity.org (accessed September 6, 2005).
Aswad, Barbara. "Attitudes of Arab Immigrants toward Welfare." In *Arabs in
      America: Building a New Future,* ed. Michael W. Suleiman. Philadelphia:
      Temple University Press, 1999.
Barazangi, Nimat Hafez. "Parents and Youth: Perceiving and Practicing Islam."
      In *Family and Gender among American Muslims.* Philadelphia: Temple
      University Press, 1996.
Bendib. http://www.studiobendib.com.
Betts, Robert B. *Christians in the Arab East.* Rev. ed. Athens: Lycabettus, 1978.
Cainkar, Louise. "Immigrant Palestinian Women Evaluate Their Lives." In *Family and
      Gender among American Muslims.* Philadelphia: Temple University Press, 1996.
Catholic Information Network. http://www.cin.org/rite10.html (accessed
      September 6, 2005).
Daniels, Roger. *Guarding the Golden Door: American Immigration Policy and
      Immigrants since 1882.* New York: Hill and Wang, 2004.
Davidson, Lawrence. "Debating Palestine: Arab-American Challenges to Zionism,
      1917–1932." In *Arabs in America: Building a New Future,* ed. Michael W.
      Suleiman. Philadelphia: Temple University Press, 1999.
Einfoweb. http://www.einfoweb.com/mesopotamia/chaldeans/Eisenlohr,
      Charlene J. "Adolescent Arab Girls in an American High School." In *Family and
      Gender among American Muslims.* Philadelphia: Temple University Press, 1996.
Esposito, John. "Introduction: Muslims in America or American Muslims." In *Muslims
      on the Americanization Path?* New York: Oxford University Press, 1998.
Ferris, Mark. "Brooklyn's Musical Oasis." *ARAMCO World* 55, no. 4 (July/August
      2004): 16–19.
Friedlander, Jonathan. "Rare Sights: Images of Early Arab Immigration to New York
      City." In *A Community of Many Worlds: Arab Americans in New York City,* ed.
      Kathleen Benson and Philip Kayal. New York: Museum of the City of
      New York, Syracuse University Press, 2002.
Greek Orthodox Archdiocese of America. http://www.goarch.org/
Haddad, Yvonne. "The Dynamics of Islamic Identity in North America." In *Muslims
      on the Americanization Path?* New York: Oxford University Press, 1998.
Haiek, Jean-Michel. *Tare'kh al'elmy.* [Scientific History] Beirut, Lebanon: Maktabat
      Habib, 1996. Herbert, David, ed. *Religion and Social Transformations.*
      Burlington, VT: Ashgate, 2001.
Hitti, Philip K. *The Arabs: A Short History.* 2d ed., rev. Washington, DC: Regnery,
      1970.

Hourani, Albert. *A History of the Arab Peoples*. Cambridge: Harvard University Press, Belknap Press, 1991.

Ignatiev, Noel. *How the Irish Became White*. London: Routledge, 1995.

Jabara, Abdeen. "Being Arab American in New York: A Personal Story." In *A Community of Many Worlds: Arab Americans in New York City*, ed. Kathleen Benson and Philip Kayal. New York: Museum of the City of New York, Syracuse University Press, 2002.

———. "A Strategy for Political Effectiveness." In *Arab Americans: Continuity and Change*. AAUG Monograph Series no. 24. Belmont, MA: Association of Arab-American University Graduates, 1989.

Joseph, Suad. "Against the Grain of the Nation—The Arab." In *Arabs in America: Building a New Future*, ed. Michael W. Suleiman. Philadelphia: Temple University Press, 1999.

Kasem, Casey. "Arab Americans: Making a Difference. The Arab American Institute Foundation." 2004. http://www.aaiusa.org/famous_arab_americans.htm.

Kayal, Philip M. "Arab Christians in the United States." In *Arabs in the New World: Studies on Arab-American Communities*. Detroit: Wayne State University Press, 1983.

Khawly, Carol. "Impact of September 11 on Traditional Openness to Immigrants and Non-Immigrants: An Arab-American Community Perspective." *In Defense of the Alien: Proceedings of the Annual National Legal Conference on Immigration and Refugee Policy*. Vol. 25. New York: Center for Migration Studies, 2002, 41–46.

Kulwicki, Anahid. "Health Issues among Arab Muslim Families." In *Family & Gender among American Muslims*. Philadelphia: Temple University Press, 1996.

Lapidus, Ira M. *History of Islamic Societies*. Cambridge: Cambridge University Press, 1988.

Lee, Erika. *At America's Gates: Chinese Immigration during the Exclusion Era, 1882–1943*. Chapel Hill: University of North Carolina Press, 2003.

Lunde, Paul. *Islam: Faith, Culture, History*. New York: Dorling Kindersley, 2002.

Majaj, Lisa Suhair. "Arab American Ethnicity: Location, Coalitions, and Cultural Negotiations." In *Arabs in America: Building a New Future*, ed. Michael W. Suleiman. Philadelphia: Temple University Press, 1999.

———. "Boundaries: Arab/American." In *Food for Our Grandmothers: Writings by Arab-American and Arab-Canadian Feminists*, ed. Joanna Kadi. Boston: South End, 1994.

Marschner, Janice. *California's Arab Americans*. Sacramento, CA: Coleman Ranch, 2003.

Masalha, Nur. *Ard akthar wa-'ard aqal: siyasa "al-transfer" al-isra' iliyah fi al-tatbiq*. [More Land and Less Arabs: The Israeli "Transfer" Policy in Practice] Beirut, Lebanon: Institute for Palestine Studies, 1997.

Mattar, Mohamed. "Legal Perspectives on Arabs and Muslims in U.S. Courts." In *Arabs in America: Building a New Future*, ed. Michael W. Suleiman. Philadelphia: Temple University Press, 1999.

Muslim Student Association of the U.S. and Canada. http://www.msa-natl.org/

Naber, Nadine. "Ambiguous Insiders: An Investigation of Arab American Invisibility." *Ethnic and Racial Studies* 23, no. 1 (January 2000): 37–61.

Naff, Alixia. *The Arab Americans.* New York: Chelsea House, 1988.

Naseeb.com. http://www.naseeb.com/

National Geographic Society. *Peoples of the World.* Washington, DC: National Geographic Society, 2001.

"Newsmakers: Dr. James Zogby, President Arab American Institute. September 11 and the Arab American Community." *Philanthropy News Digest* 28 July 2003. http://fdncenter.org/pnd/newsmakers/nwsmkr.jhtml?id=40400036.

Orfalea, Gregory. "Sifting the Ashes: Arab American Activism during the 1982 Invasion of Lebanon." In *Arab Americans: Continuity and Change.* AAUG Monograph Series no. 24. Belmont, MA: Association of Arab-American University Graduates, 1989.

Ramussen, Anne. Insert for *The Music of Arab Americans: A Retrospective Collection.* Rounder Records, 1997. Also available online at http://www.rounder.com/index.php?id = album.php&catalog_id = 5512.

Rashid, Stanley. "Cultural Traditions of Early Arab Immigrants to New York." In *A Community of Many Worlds: Arab Americans in New York City,* ed. Kathleen Benson and Philip Kayal. New York: Museum of the City of New York, Syracuse University Press, 2002.

Rignall, Karen. "Building an Arab-American Community in Dearborn." *Journal of the International Institute* 5, no. 1 (Fall 1997).

———. Personal interview by author. 26 August 2004.

Saliba, Therese. "Resisting Invisibility: Arab Americans in Academia and Activism." In *Arabs in America: Building a New Future,* ed. Michael W. Suleiman. Philadelphia: Temple University Press, 1999.

Samhan, Helen. "Politics and Exclusion: The Arab American Experience." *Journal of Palestine Studies* 16, no. 2 (Winter 1987): 11–28.

———. "Arab Americans and the Elections of 1988: A Constituency Come of Age." In *Arab Americans: Continuity and Change.* AAUG Monograph Series no. 24. Belmont, MA: Association of Arab-American University Graduates, 1989.

———. "By the Numbers." 2004. http://www.allied-media.com/Arab-American/Arab_demographics.htm.

Schabner, Dean. "Eight Cities in Patriot Act Revolt: Cities from Cambridge to Berkeley Reject Anti-Terror Measure." *ABC News.* 1 July 2002. http://abcnews.go.com/US/story?id = 91497&page = 1.

Sengstock, Mary. "Care of the Elderly with Muslim Families." In *Family and Gender among American Muslims.* Philadelphia: Temple University Press, 1996.

———. "Detroit's Iraqi-Chaldeans: A Conflicting Conception of Identity." In *Arabs in the New World: Studies on Arab-American Communities,* ed. Sameer Abraham and Nabeel Abraham. Detroit: Wayne State University Press, 1983.

Shira. "Styles of Belly Dance in the United States, Part I". http://www.shira.net/styles.htm (accessed September 6, 2005). Shohat, Ella Habiba. "Reflections by an Arab Jew." http://www.bintjbeil.com/E/occupation/arab_jew.html (accessed September 6, 2005).

Simpson, Cam, Flynn McRoberts, and Liz Sly. "Profiling Illegal Immigrants in the U.S." *Chicago Tribune.* 18 November 2003: 1.

Sinno, John. "About Arab Film Distribution." http://www.arabfilm.com/aboutafd.html (accessed September 6, 2005).

Smith, Harvey, et al. *Area Handbook for Lebanon.* 2d ed. Washington, DC: American University, Foreign Area Studies, 1974.

Southern Federation of Syrian Lebanese American Clubs. "Conventions." http://www.sfslac.org/Conventions.htm (accessed September 6, 2005).

Suleiman, Michael. "Impressions of New York City by Early Arab Immigrants." In *A Community of Many Worlds: Arab Americans in New York City,* ed. Kathleen Benson and Philip Kayal. New York: Museum of the City of New York, Syracuse University Press, 2002.

Swanson, Jon C. "Ethnicity, Marriage and Role Conflict: The Dilemma of a Second-Generation Arab-American." In *Family & Gender among American Muslims.* Philadelphia: Temple University Press, 1996.

Temple, Bob. *The Arab Americans.* Philadelphia: Mason Crest, 2003.

Terry, Janice. "Community and Political Activism among Arab Americans in Detroit." In *Arabs in America: Building a New Future,* ed. Michael W. Suleiman. Philadelphia: Temple University Press, 1999.

Turner, Richard Brent. *Islam in the African-American Experience.* Bloomington: Indiana University Press, 1997.

U.S. Citizenship and Immigration Services. http://uscis.gov/graphics/othergov/roadmap.htm.

U.S. Department of Justice. Civil Rights Division. "Enforcement and Outreach Following the September 11 Terrorist Attacks." http://www.usdoj.gov/crt/legalinfo/discrimupdate.htm (accessed September 6, 2005).

Walbridge, Linda. "Five Immigrants." In *Family & Gender among American Muslims.* Philadelphia: Temple University Press, 1996.

Wolfe, Michael. *Taking Back Islam: American Muslims Reclaim Their Faith.* Emmaus, PA: Rodale, 2002.

Zogby, James. "A Tale of Two States." *Washington Watch.* 6 November 2000. http://www.aaiusa.org/wwatch/110600.htm (accessed September 6, 2005).

Index

Al-Qaeda, 140, 144

Alawis, 16, 18

American-Arab Anti-Discrimination Committee (ADC), 26, 60, 82, 106–7, 110, 113, 132–34, 145; in coalitions, 140–41

Arab: and border officials, 35, 61; meaning and definition of, 1–2

Arab American Institute (AAI), 60, 132, 137, 143; AAI Foundation, 66, 107–8; in coalitions, 140–41; and the "Yalla Vote" campaign, 134–35, 137

Arab Community Center for Economic and Social Services (ACCESS), 67, 104, 106, 133–34, 140; Arab American National Museum, 132, 135; in coalitions, 114, 125, 128, 141

Arabic food, 71, 84–85, 104, 119, 115–17, 123–25; *halal*, 85, 118; and language, 109; and literature, 84, 127; and strikes, 141–42

Arabic language, 1, 22; bookshops, 66; in Christian liturgies, 19–21, 89–91; dialects in the United States, 84; and generational changes, 41–42, 53, 83–84, 109–11; instruction of, 70, 72, 83–84, 92; and Islam, 1, 3–4, 13, 92, 136; and Jews, 22, 91; in literature, 126–27; in media, 42, 77, 86; Modern Standard Arabic or

classical Arabic, 1, 83, 90; in music, 71, 113–14, 116, 122–24; names 35, 53; in performances, 130–31; signage and 61, 104; spoken before 1965 in the United States, 24, 28, 35, 122–23; spoken in the United States after 1965, 70, 83–84, 86, 109–12

Armenians, 1, 5, 20, 22, 38, 46–47, 62

Asian and South Asian Americans, 70, 94, 136, 139–40, 145

Asians, classification as, 47, 52, 56–57, 59, 142

Association of Arab American University Graduates (AAUG), 62, 82, 106, 132–34

Assyrians: history of, 1, 3, 89; and identity, 62, 99, 107–8; and language, 83, 90; religion and 20, 46, 89–90, 119; statistics on, 46

Balfour Declaration, 6

Brain drain, 9–10, 34, 101–2

Campus Watch, 138–39

Catholics, 16, 19, 54, 76, 88, 90, 95; and the Roman Catholic Church, 19, 42, 53, 88

Caucasian, 45, 48–49, 52

Census, U.S., 24–25, 39, 46, 48, 66, 83, 106, 108; categories of, 56–61; and the

About the Author

RANDA A. KAYYALI is a Ph.D. candidate at George Mason University and has written on Arab American issues.